On Money and *Mettā*

Economy and Morality in Urban Buddhist Myanmar

Money and *Mettā* symbolize the interconnectedness of economic processes and moral ideas – *mettā*, 'loving kindness', constitutes a core concept of Buddhism. Political and economic changes in Myanmar have caused inequality to increase sharply in the past decades. A large part of the country's population relies on self-employment for its livelihood. While some capitalized on the opportunities of the early 1990s to build up successful businesses, others live increasingly precarious lives, marked by poverty, displacement and indebtedness. This book, based on eighteen months of ethnographic research in the town of Pathein, investigates the owners of small businesses, their family members and workers. It portrays proprietors who have managed to accumulate capital through their enterprises and investments, but also vulnerable individuals who survive by combining small-scale activities with low-paid wage-labour and are constantly threatened by indebtedness or even social exclusion.

Focusing in turn on the family, the workplace, and the wider neighbourhood community, Laura Hornig documents processes related to the formation and inheritance of businesses, recruitment and management of the labour force (including child workers), as well as participation in charity projects and credit arrangements. In doing so, she pays special attention to moral considerations and the specific values that shape how the inhabitants of Pathein pursue their livelihoods and how they interact with each other, both with equals and with those of different social and economic standing. The book illuminates the reasons why self-employment might be considered better than working for others and why inter-generational family businesses are more common among Pathein's ethnic Chinese than among Burmans. It also addresses how a 'good' employer should act, the responsibilities that come with wealth, and moral assessments of child labour and money lending. Kinship and Buddhism are identified as prime sources of ethical concepts and obligations. Laura Hornig offers an innovative analysis of the interplay of ethical factors with socio-economic conditions, both past and present. She argues that contemporary transformations of this under-studied country cannot be adequately grasped without attending to the historical evolution of moral considerations.

D1668533

Halle Studies in the Anthropology of Eurasia

General Editors:

Christoph Brumann, Kirsten W. Endres, Chris Hann, Burkhard Schnepel,
Lale Yalçın-Heckmann

Volume 43

LIT

Laura Hornig

On Money and *Mettā*

Economy and Morality
in Urban Buddhist Myanmar

LIT

Cover Photo: A woman is holding 100-kyat bills and candy during the annual *kahtein* festival (Photo: Laura Hornig, 2015).

This book is a revised version of a dissertation manuscript, submitted to the Faculty of Philosophy I at Martin Luther University Halle-Wittenberg in 2019.

This book is printed on acid-free paper.

Bibliografische Information der Deutschen Nationalbibliothek
Die Deutsche Nationalbibliothek verzeichnet diese Publikation in der Deutschen Nationalbibliografie; detaillierte bibliografische Daten sind im Internet über http://dnb.d-nb.de abrufbar.

ISBN 978-3-643-91340-1 (pb)
ISBN 978-3-643-96340-6 (PDF)

A catalogue record for this book is available from the British Library.

©LIT VERLAG Dr. W. Hopf
Berlin 2020
Fresnostr. 2
D-48159 Münster
Tel. +49 (0) 2 51-62 03 20
Fax +49 (0) 2 51-23 19 72
E-Mail: lit@lit-verlag.de
http://www.lit-verlag.de

LIT VERLAG GmbH & Co. KG Wien,
Zweigniederlassung Zürich 2020
Flössergasse 10
CH-8001 Zürich
Tel. +41 (0) 76-632 84 35
Fax
E-Mail: zuerich@lit-verlag.ch
http://www.lit-verlag.ch

Distribution:
In the UK: Global Book Marketing, e-mail: mo@centralbooks.com
In North America: Independent Publishers Group, e-mail: orders@ipgbook.com
In Germany: LIT Verlag Fresnostr. 2, D-48159 Münster
Tel. +49 (0) 2 51-620 32 22, Fax +49 (0) 2 51-922 60 99, e-mail: vertrieb@lit-verlag.de

Contents

List of Illustrations

Figures

Maps

Plates

(all photographs were taken by the author [2015-2018])

Acknowledgements

I could not have written this book without the support of many people in different parts of the world. First and foremost, I have to thank the people in Pathein who talked to me and invited me to observe and take part in their work and leisure-time activities. Among them were business owners, workers, and students, many of whom became my friends. As much as I wish things were different, I will follow the tradition of other Myanmar researchers and leave your names unmentioned for your protection. I owe you all a lot, not only for enabling me to 'gather data', but also for your help in practical and emotional matters, for your hospitality, and for your friendship. At Pathein University, Professor Nyunt Phay helped in several ways to make my research stay a possibility. Besides offering bureaucratic assistance, he welcomed me to make myself at home in a house within the university compound. The staff of Pathein University were always approachable when I needed help, for which I am grateful. I would also like to thank especially my friends Thura Aung, Cho Thet Aung, Thet Naing Oo, and Aung Kyaw Moe for all their help. I have also benefited a great deal from discussing my materials and thoughts in Myanmar with Aung Khine, Thiha Lay, Dr Khin Mar Cho, Wai Phyo Maung, Dr Myat Thu, and Sophia Huang.

At the Max Planck Institute for Social Anthropology I received crucial support from a great many people. I want to thank in particular Chris Hann, the head of our department and principal investigator of the ERC-funded REALEURASIA project of which my research formed a part, and Lale Yalçın-Heckmann, our project coordinator. I was fortunate to work alongside great colleagues. Special thanks go to Ceren Deniz, Sudeshna Chaki, Annabell Körner, Anne-Erita Berta, Sylvia Terpe, Luca Szücs, Matthijs Krul, Ivan Rajković, Kristina Jonutyte, Hannah Klepeis, Daria Tereshina, Kirsten Endres, Christoph Brumann, and Saskia Abrahms-Kavunenko. I am especially grateful to the fellow members of my research group: it meant a lot to me that we were able to offer each other companionship and support. During the writing process I received valuable support from Beata Świtek, Deborah Jones, and Robert Parkin who provided detailed feedback on considerable parts of the manuscript and helped with editing. I am also grateful to Jutta Turner for designing the maps and to Bettina Mann, who offered me valuable advice in the final phase. Berit Eckert played a crucial role in turning the text into an actual book. Moreover, I must also say a big thank you to the administrative staff and the IT and library team at the Max Planck Institute for all their help throughout the past years.

A lot of external guests have provided helpful comments over the course of the project. In particular I benefited from conversations with Patrice Ladwig, Chris Gregory, and Erik Bähre. I also want to extend my gratitude to Roland Mischung and Laila Prager, my professors at the University of Hamburg who supervised my earlier Myanmar-related research which, in a way, laid the foundations for the present project.

In past years I have enjoyed a number of opportunities to discuss my work with other scholars specializing in Myanmar. I received helpful advice from Matthew Walton and also from Ward Keeler, who later kindly agreed to become an examiner for my thesis. Moreover, I benefited greatly from a graduate student workshop at the University of Oxford where Hiroko Kawanami in particular provided extensive feedback and helped me to sharpen some of my arguments. At home, I was lucky to be part of a Myanmar-interested community in the German-speaking world, the 'Myanmar-Institut e.V.', with whom I enjoyed sharing parts of the journey. I would like to thank in particular Johanna Neumann, Esther Tenberg, Jella Fink, Mandy Fox, Felix Hessler, Georg Winterberger, Andy Buschmann, and Cordula Meyer-Mahnkopf, all of whom have at one point or another provided important company and ideas. Judith Beyer and Felix Girke have known me since my first encounters with anthropology, and throughout this PhD project they have been a great source of support and encouragement. Uta Gärtner has patiently offered her invaluable advice on language-related questions which often inspired vital more general discussions.

Ultimately I owe a lot to my family and close friends who have supported me throughout the past years, regardless of the fact that at times I was too busy to give them much in return. I had the great privilege to do my PhD in a place where part of my family is at home, and where I could enjoy their regular company and the great comfort and food that my grandparents provided. I thank them as well as my parents, who have instilled in me a curiosity and empathy toward the culturally unfamiliar from a young age on. The fact that they acquired their own experiences in Myanmar made it easier for me to share my impressions and memories at home. Finally, I want to thank Lammert for going through the ups and downs of this journey with me and being incredibly supportive, for our wonderful travels, and for so many moments of joy and laughter.

A Note on the Text

I refer to a number of Burmese and Pāli terms in this book. In some contexts I use Pāli words instead of their Burmese versions, since the former are more usual in scholarly discourse. This is the case for many Buddhist terms, such as *mettā*, *dāna*, and *kamma*.

There is no single standard transcription of Burmese. Instead, there are several different methods, and it is still common to find variants of a word in different scholarly works on Myanmar. In the present work I have followed the 'standard conventional transcription' method suggested by John Okell (1972: 66–67), diverging from this method only where specific transcriptions have been widely used for certain terms (e.g. the names of places, but also some frequently discussed concepts). In these cases I have written the terms as they are usually transcribed. Hopefully this should provide convenience in reading and enable readers with a knowledge of English to recognize and pronounce the Burmese words I refer to.

When speaking of the country, I use its current official name, 'Myanmar', except when referring to events that took place before the country was renamed in 1989, in which case I use 'Burma'. Concerning the population, I use 'Burmese' for citizens of the country in general, regardless of their ethnicity, and 'Burmans' when referring to the majority ethnic group, to which most of my informants belong.

Throughout the book I use an average conversion rate calculated from the daily conversion rates during my main period of research from August 2015 to August 2016. This average rate is 1,377 Kyat for 1 EUR.

All names of persons, with the exception of public figures, have been changed to maintain confidentiality.

Map 1. Map of Myanmar.

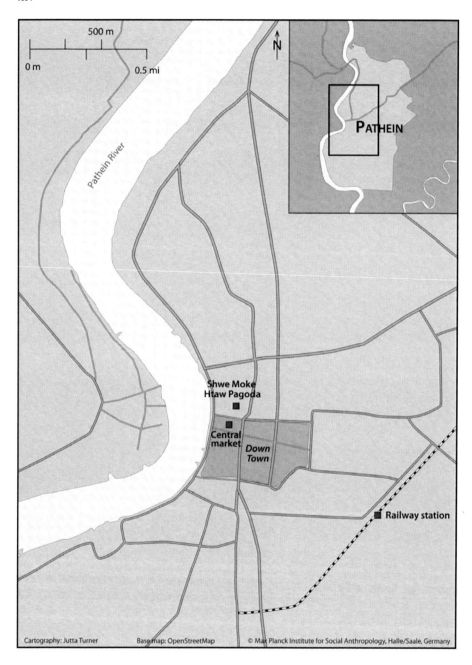

Map 2. Map of Pathein.

Chapter 1
Introduction

Myanmar is changing, and change has many layers. This book focuses on people's economic activities on the micro-level. It is based on fourteen months of research in the medium-size town of Pathein, the capital of Ayeyarwady Region. In one of the first in-depth ethnographic studies of urban economic processes in contemporary Myanmar, I take both employed and self-employed people as my interlocutors and unveil the manifold and complex social and moral dimensions of their economic actions.[1] In doing so, I pay special attention to the role of religious ideas. While Myanmar is a multi-ethnic and multi-religious country, my research has a special focus on Theravāda Buddhism, to which the majority of the population, including most of my informants, adheres (87.9 percent according to the 2014 census). A main argument of this book is that Buddhist ideas stand in a dialectical relationship with economic ideas, judgments, and actions among Buddhists in Myanmar. The title *On Money and Mettā* stands symbolically for this interconnectedness of moral ideas and economic activities, with *mettā*, the teaching of 'loving kindness', being a main concept of Buddhism.

Since the military government in Myanmar was replaced by a semi-civilian[2] government in 2011, much has been written about the country's apparent 'transition' to a democracy. The 2015 general elections marked a milestone, leading to a new democratically elected leadership under the former opposition party, the NLD (National League for Democracy). These steps towards democratization, as well as their overshadowing by violent conflicts in several parts of the country, are at the heart of most analyses of

---

[1] This research was conducted for my doctoral dissertation. It was part of a project at the Max Planck Institute for Social Anthropology in Halle, funded by the European Research Council (ERC Grant Agreement No. 340854), which explored the links between morality and economic activities in several countries in Europe and Asia. See Hann (2016) on the theoretical argument that lies behind the project, which sees the opposing of strongly liberal-individualist values for the sake of society's more general collective interests as generally characterizing for the societies that emerged in Eurasia during the Axial Age.

[2] Twenty-five percent of the seats in parliament remained reserved for the military.

Myanmar currently. Apart from a number of publications dealing with land-related issues, relatively little attention has been paid explicitly to the economy in this process (exceptions include Woods 2014, 2018; Odaka 2016; Crouch 2017a), especially on the micro-level. In particular, more often than not anthropologists and scholars of related disciplines seem to leave the study of the economy to political and development-related institutions, which usually results in quite large-scale quantitative analyses rather than in-depth studies on lived economic realities (for example, World Bank 2018). While the initial scholarly emphasis on politics and identity is under-standable, it goes without saying that political developments can never be fully understood without taking into consideration economic concerns and processes on the ground. Some recent analyses have addressed more specifically the entanglement of economic developments with other aspects, including political ones (see Thant Myint-U. Forthcoming; Chachavalpongpun et al. Forthcoming). People's struggles to earn a liveli-hood are of immediate importance to them and shape their choices. This applies to the ethnic majority as well as to all ethnic minorities, whether in moments of concrete political activism and elections or when it comes to decision-making in everyday life. This book is an attempt to shed more light on economic realities in Myanmar.

I shall begin with a quick look at what has happened in the past decades. The more recent political changes have attracted much attention among outside observers. However, in terms of livelihood, the introduction of a market-led economy in the early 1990s had a more significant impact on many of those who will appear in this book. Although it enabled some to open profitable businesses and build up considerable wealth, for others the challenge of making ends meet grew greater. In order to understand political developments better and perhaps even to predict, or influence, future perspectives on Myanmar, one might be tempted to undertake comparisons with other cases. Such comparisons can be made with reference to various aspects. For instance, numerous publications deal with transformations toward a market-led economy elsewhere. There are both overarching analyses and country-specific ethnographies of examples from both Eastern Europe and Asia (e.g. Verdery 1996; Hann 2002; Luong 2003). Myanmar's change to a market-oriented economy within a one-party political system typically prompts comparisons with Vietnam and China rather than with the former Soviet Union. However, in Myanmar more than in China and Vietnam, internal policies, structural hindrances, and Western sanctions continued to constrain the market considerably in the first years after the shift.

Shifting the gaze to other aspects, one noticeable difference from many other postsocialist countries was the strong public presence and the government's promotion of the majority population's religion throughout much of the period of the dictatorship. Also nowadays, despite the increasing pace of economic and political changes since 2011, nothing indicates a decline of Buddhism, but rather the opposite: more radical and politicized interpretations of Buddhism have spread and gained adherents. The predominance of the Theravāda Buddhist tradition is something Myanmar shares with other countries in the region, namely Laos, Thailand, Cambodia, and Sri Lanka. A rise in Buddhist nationalist sentiments and Islamophobia is particularly reminiscent of a rhetoric known from radical groups in contemporary Sri Lanka, where a combination of Buddhist and nationalist attitudes had also already emerged as a reaction to British colonial rule in earlier periods, as was the case in Myanmar. British colonial rule was an experience that both countries shared with India, but Myanmar's recent political course from military rule to a democratic system in some ways resembles rather the case of Indonesia after the downfall of the New Order regime.

Needless to say, despite a number of parallels, there have also been a range of important contrasts between Myanmar and the cases I have just mentioned. While other ethnographies of economic and political transformations especially can certainly be inspiring, each case will be different, which is one of the reasons why the widely used term 'transition' remains problematic, as has already been pointed out for the post-Soviet context (Verdery 1996: 15). Here, the term had rightly been problematized because it assumes a clearly defined development, often implicitly portrayed as desirable, from a specific state 'a' to a specific state 'b' (Verdery 1996: 15; Hann 2012), for example, from authoritarianism to democracy, or from socialism to market capitalism. Such approaches rarely leave enough room for the many complexities and particularities of specific cases. Thus, I prefer to think of current developments in Myanmar as a 'transformation', a period of vast changes, however, none with a clearly foreseeable outcome in sight.

So far Myanmar's economic growth has been heavily based on natural-resource extraction. It involves what Harvey terms 'accumulation by dispossession' (Harvey 2003, 2004) and has not generated many jobs. These developments led to newly emerging or intensifying livelihood challenges, especially for the landless – both those who never owned land, and those who have lost theirs (according to 2017 estimates, up to 50 percent of the rural population are landless; see USAID 2017). These people are among the most vulnerable in Myanmar economically. Even though the 'Burmese Way to Socialism' had left the overall economy in dire straits by the late 1980s, many of my informants who were young in socialist times reported that, in their childhoods, their fathers could support the whole family with their incomes. Now, they said, it had become difficult even for two earners to feed their children (similar remarks were documented as early as the 1990s; see Kumada 2001: 17). The 1990s brought with them rising prices for rice, while the socialist system of rations for the general population was abandoned. This, in combination with a number of other factors, such as inflation, dramatically increasing land prices, and a decline in wages for agricultural labourers, led to growing overall poverty among the landless rural population, and to growing wealth stratification in general (Fujita 2009: 257). The socialist system was certainly not able to sustain itself, but was kept alive by a large black market and was forced to undertake adjustments from time to time (e.g. the acceptance of foreign aid or the slight relaxation of private investment in the 1970s; see Tin Maung Maung Than 2007: 260). Nevertheless, in areas not affected by conflicts, feelings of livelihood security and stability within the population may have exceeded what many experience today. Indeed, socialist Myanmar was a largely agrarian country, and while the state and military apparatus employed many as civil servants, there were no massive industrial undertakings comparable to other socialist regions, in which the industrial workforce would experience a depletion of their industries, mass unemployment, the dismantling of public institutions and the loss of welfare through a transition towards market economy. And yet, such a shift has brought challenges also in Myanmar. While the socialist economy was marked by scarcity in many regards, especially when it came to consumer goods, and the accumulation of wealth was near to impossible for most, the widely shared attitudes that earning a livelihood was not as challenging a task as it is today is noteworthy.

Nowadays, those who make just enough money to get by are under the constant threat of unforeseeable expenses suddenly becoming necessary. Indebtedness has become a serious problem for the urban poor, as well as among farmers, who have struggled with inflation, falling prices for paddy, and instable exchange rates since the end of socialism, but especially in the past couple of years (see also Dapice et al. 2011). Health-care costs, from small expenses for vitamins to large problems like surgery, often cost more than people have available. In some cases, addictions such as alcoholism or gambling, can pose serious problems and lead to debt spirals. Members of older generations tended to blame changes in individual consumer patterns and a decline in morals rather than socio-economic structures for poverty-related problems. According to them, a rise in materialism and greed on the part of individuals, a concern with money rather than with the family, was to blame. Notably, it was not uncommon that interlocutors remembered the old as a time in which only a very few goods were available, as opposed to now, when children 'want to have everything'. They also reported that illegal lotteries were not common, and there was always enough food, if not as varied as today. Basic health care was available for free in state-run hospitals. Medicines had to be purchased from private funds, but prices were not as high as they are today. Nowadays it is widely regarded as compulsory to send children to costly afternoon tuition classes. Moreover, in the past families formed bigger and more stable support groups. It was customary for elderly parents to live with their children, and fewer people left home to find work elsewhere. It happens increasingly now that old people live alone, since their children have moved elsewhere. Informants found it astonishing that nowadays it was not uncommon to see people above the age of seventy working in the fields because no children are there to do the work. People instead noticed the growing number of working children in the cities, who joined migrant labour in search of an income in the industrial world. People with low and fluctuating incomes repeatedly made statements to the effect that life seemed to be getting more and more difficult year by year.

Political developments since 2011 considerably increased the pace and extent of economic changes. They brought about the liberalization of the rice trade, the unification of the exchange rate system, and new laws and regulations that paved the way for more foreign investment, leading to a growing manufacturing and service sector. Even though the number of people in Myanmar who have bank accounts remains extremely low (estimated between 5 and 10 percent in recent years, see Turnell 2017: 125; Förch 2018: 202–205), the banking sector is rapidly expanding, with the two biggest banks opening new branches by the week. New land regulations have fuelled a commodification of farmland, which, as elsewhere, has led to a new wave of land speculation. There has also been a growing number of conflicts over land and cases of land dispossession by the government or by private companies after 2011 (Woods 2014). Further urbanization has occurred, especially in Yangon, and development and aid projects have also mushroomed in various parts of the country.

Assertions that Myanmar's development is 'highly uneven, exploitative, rapacious and often violent, generating a narrow economic elite, widespread corruption and deep social conflicts' (Jones 2018: 189) are not wrong and draw attention to important challenges. However, there is a group of people whose success stories date back to the onset of market liberalization: those who used the new opportunities to build up successful businesses. The number of registered 'Private Industrial Enterprises' increased dramatically in the first half of the 1990s (Kudo 2009: 70). While some of these enterprises had already been active in the shadow economy under socialism, they were now legalized and encouraged to expand. In addition, many people started new ventures. The existence of such enterprises complicates Melissa Crouch's assertion that the attempts to shift to a market economy after 1988 were 'largely stillborn' (Crouch 2017b: 8). Crouch is not the only one to focus on the constraints of the macro-economic developments. Often, discussions of this period fail to mention the new owners of small businesses, and when speaking of economic beneficiaries, they only account for the elite that emerged consisting mainly of tycoons with close links to the military (e.g. Jones 2018: 181). By tracing business histories in Pathein, I demonstrate how small businesses that were established in these first years of the economic liberalization led to considerable wealth accumulation and upward mobility for the families of their founders, many of which had started from scratch. In some cases, the children of these small business owners were the first members of their families to receive a university education. These families often successfully enhanced their profits through investments in land, thus benefitting from exploding land prices as another consequence of capitalist expansion.[3] Such developments therefore did not benefit only the absolutely wealthy elite, but also a number of smaller business people, even though the vast majority of the population remains excluded. Thus, while my examples of business owners[4] who managed to accumulate wealth should not detract from the fact that for many others the struggle for a decent livelihood intensified, these people are an interesting group to look at.

Even though many of the business owners I worked with had only just reached adult age by the end of socialism when they took on the newly

---

[3] Myanmar's 2008 constitution states that the state is the ultimate owner of all land. However, a range of additional laws and regulations have established a system that comes close to the ownership of private property. In urban areas, long-term use rights (from ten to ninety years, with the possibility of extension) for 'Grant Land' (which is what most urban land is classified as) can be acquired, sold, mortgaged, rented out, and inherited. When I say that people 'own', 'bought' or 'sold' land, I am referring to these usage rights.

[4] When I speak of business owners, I do not use the term 'entrepreneur' because it carries certain implications and, as a result, it does not characterize my informants very well. While the term 'entrepreneur' is often used broadly among anthropologists – and could cover 'both, a flower vendor in a street market and Bill Gates' (Smart and Smart 2005: 3) – such broad usage obscures important differences in attitudes, strategies, and values. In economics, Schumpeter, for example, saw it as defining for 'entrepreneurs' that they seek to distinguish themselves through excellence, innovation, and ambition, and that they measure success in profit (Schumpeter 1934). Following this perspective, the mere condition of being self-employed does not make an entrepreneur. Most of my informants saw their economic activities first and foremost as a means of livelihood, rather than as an innovative entity they strongly identify with, take pride in, and plan to expand. Thus, I primarily speak of 'self-employed' or 'business owner' and, if applicable, 'employer'.

emerging opportunities, they would nevertheless notice that economic pressures had increased with the expansion of capitalism. This was not necessarily the case for themselves if they had built up successful ventures, but rather for others, mostly those without land and those who make a living as day labourers. Regarding their own situation, their assessment of the economic shift and developments since the 1990s, varied considerably, for instance, according to their area of trade. Rice-traders and rice mill-owners were among those who greatly welcomed these developments and appreciated not having to work and trade according to fixed regulations any more or being forced to operate in the black market. Liberalization had enabled them to accumulate wealth. In contrast, the owner of a pottery business that produced larger pottery items such as water-collecting jars or cooking pots explained that his situation had worsened. Under socialism he had a degree of protection against competition from imported goods made form plastic, aluminium, and steel, as well as a guaranteed quota of sales set by the government. Now he has to stand his ground in the free market, facing competition from imported goods and competition for skilled workers (see Chapter 5). Regardless of their different experiences in the changing economy, the vast majority of people I met (exceptions were a small number of people among my informants who run ventures on military compounds) decisively expressed their support for the political changes and appreciated the election of a new government and the lessening of political oppression. A certain nostalgia for economic stability and less competition among people should definitely not be mistaken for moral or political backing for the former military dictators.

Analysts have voiced concerns that current challenges, including rural displacement, a lack of good jobs to reabsorb displaced workers, and inadequate state-organized social protection, could lead to the erosion of social bonds between members of high- and low-income groups, which traditionally have often resembled patron-client links (Prasse-Freeman and Phyo Win Latt 2018: 404). Elites might orient themselves towards an exclusionary upper-class consumption culture, instead of acting as patrons for the poor, which had been their expected role in the past (ibid.: 412). Indeed, especially in the metropolitan areas of Yangon and Mandalay, those at the very top of the economic ladder now appear to constitute an exclusive club, which, it seems, more and more people aspire to join. However, the ethnographic evidence in this book suggests that, despite considerable differences in wealth, people in different economic strata remain linked through manifold ties (Chapter 6). Local support for charitable causes from Patheinians who have become wealthy (although remaining far from oligarch-level wealth) remained strong, and their activities often still seemed to be anchored in Buddhist ideas of generosity and responsibility for others, rather than in the newly emerging self-help and business literature (the rising popularity of which has been observed by Prasse-Freeman and Phyo Win Latt, 2018: 412). Furthermore, at least among Burman small business owners, self-identification rarely resembled the proto-capitalist 'entrepreneurial self'. In fact, many of my informants emphasized their role as 'good' Buddhists and 'good' family or community members, while downplaying their business achievements (Chapter 4).

Nevertheless, newly introduced economic and political developments certainly produce tensions with pre-existing patterns on the ground. For example, Myanmar had been advertised as a promising location for industrial investors, partly because of its young and growing labour force, but in fact the new garment factories, just like long-established local small businesses, find themselves struggling heavily with a high labour turnover (Deval 2015; Bernhardt et al. 2017: vii). Likewise, while international investors opening businesses in Myanmar must promise not to employ under-age workers, children have become an increasingly attractive work force for urban small businesses, as big new garment factories now absorb a large part of the adult labour force. Furthermore, while microfinance programs launched in the past five years were quickly taken up by locals, they did not replace pre-existing neighbourhood-initiated credit groups or local moneylenders with high interest rates. Instead, previously existing financial mechanisms will continue to co-exist with newly emerging initiatives. How do we make sense of examples like these? A good start would be to acknowledge that many existing economic arrangements, including those outside the formal sector, are more than just the best possible stopgap in a dysfunctional economy but are actually grounded in networks of social relations and values that go beyond mere financial benefits. It is these social relations and values that I uncover in this book.

Embedded Economies

What I explore might be called the social 'embeddedness' (Polanyi 2001 [1944]; Gudeman 2008), 'moral dimension', or 'ethical context' (Hann 2018: 247) of economic thought and action among my interlocutors. Karl Polanyi, in his classical contribution to the subject, has famously argued that a person does not engage in economic actions predominantly to possess material goods, but to 'safeguard his social standing, his social claims, his social assets. He values material goods only in so far as they serve this end' (Polanyi 2001 [1944]: 48). While Polanyi saw embeddedness as specific to pre-industrial societies and associated capitalist developments with a process of 'disembedding', I follow Stephen Gudeman (2001, 2008, 2009), who argued that the economy remains embedded, including in market-dominated contexts: it never becomes fully detached from social and moral factors, which conventional economic models too often regard as 'trivial, marginal, and often counterproductive' (Narotzky and Besnier 2014: S4). The urban economic landscape of Pathein, and elsewhere for that matter, is shaped by such social interactions to a crucial degree and is thus much more than simply a result of market logics.

As for the term 'value', this is multilayered. Values not only matter in monetary terms in the stock market, as there are also entanglements of material, social, and moral values in people's lives that they navigate over time and in different social spheres in order to construct a life worth living (Narotzky 2017: 213). Ethnographies of small businesses, whose owners might be suspected of being particularly strongly driven by a concern to maximize profits, reveal instead that running a business is shaped by 'complex relations of love and profit, accumulation and distribution, communal solidarity and individual achievement' (Yanagisako 2002: 6).

This means that while this book looks at economic processes, it is inevitably also concerned with matters of family, gender, community, and religion. In real life, domains such as the family and the economy cannot be regarded as separate 'spheres' in the sense of Max Weber, who argued that they are governed by different values, which pose constant value conflicts for individuals (Weber 2004: 215, 219). Instead, we must study how these different domains are interconnected. If we take the examples of the family and the economy, we must explore how business activities are organized with due consideration being given to family needs and vice versa. After all, one of the most important objectives of economic practices is to sustain life across generations (Narotzky and Besnier 2014: S6), thus making kinship inherently important for economic activities. This is true also of capitalist societies, as is already evident through the immense importance of property and inheritance for wealth accumulation (Yanagisako 2015). However, in what ways family negotiations shape a business landscape, for instance, can vary considerably. The case of 'family firms' in Sylvia Yanagisako's well-known ethnography from Italy (2002), for instance, differs from what I have observed among Burmans in Pathein (see Chapter 4). Thus, all this must be studied with reference to values but also to the socio-economic context in which people act, since taking into account social conditions is crucial to understand lived experiences (Bourdieu 1977). Economic activities, like all activities, must be understood from a non-essentializing standpoint as resulting from dialectical relationships between certain values, personal attitudes, and current as well as historical socio-economic circumstances. A mutual construction takes place between such circumstances and the human actors within them. People are not only influenced by, but can also either reproduce or alter societal conditions, relations, and meanings through their daily practices.

Pathein, like other urban areas of Myanmar, displays a preponderance of small and medium-sized businesses and one-person ventures. The activities happening here are collective processes in the sense that each individual is embedded in his or her social surroundings. The people portrayed in this study are no exception to this. For many self-employed, self-employment is in many cases an economic necessity rather than an occupational dream, as attractive employment options are scarce and access to them limited. In making an argument for studying the informal economy, Kathleen Millar has criticized David Harvey (2003) for only addressing how capitalism produces a large group of unemployed persons – people 'outside' capitalism – without considering how these people act and how their practices in turn influence capitalist relations (Millar 2008). While not studying the separation of informal and formal practices as such, I build on her approach by not only engaging with business owners themselves, but also taking into account the perspectives of their family members and workers, as well as of people who could potentially be workers but prefer small-scale self-employment. This enables me to explore how the attitudes and actions of those 'outside' the actual business are both affected by and affect the business.

As a consequence of this broad approach, this book cannot be understood as an ethnography of one specific, relatively homogenous group. Instead it will explore the lives of people with considerably different economic backgrounds and the relationships between them. While some parts of the book will look at relatively wealthy business owners who enjoy regular holidays abroad, other parts will describe the lives of landless daily paid workers struggling heavily with indebtedness, addiction, and social conflicts. Such a diversity of informants occurs naturally when one follows economic relations, flows, and developments, making it necessary to take it into account in order to present a realistic picture of socio-economic conditions. Although not as stark as in Yangon, for instance, considerable differences in wealth also exist in medium-size towns. It goes without saying that a business owner employing around twenty workers is usually in a better economic position than a street vendor, although the street vendor might well have a higher income than a teacher. Furthermore, like all social relations, economic relations too are not free from tensions and conflicts. These might arise within a family, between employers and workers, or within the wider neighbourhood. These aspects will be addressed in the following chapters that explore various activities, such as founding, running, and passing on a business, accepting or refusing a job, hiring or firing certain workers, and donating or lending money to friends or strangers.

Morality-inspired Economies

I have so far outlined the theme of the social embeddedness of economies as a main approach taken in this book. Connected to this is the role of morality in economic processes. Economies, like other social processes, are based on assumptions of what is 'good, desirable, worthy, ethical, and just' (Fischer 2014: 17). For values, recent anthropological contributions like that of Joel Robbins (2012: 117) have taken up a conventional definition which sees values as things that people, whether as individuals or collectively, not only desire but that are also seen as *desirable* (following Kluckhohn 1962: 395). In fact, seeing something as desirable means acknowledging its general desirability even when one does not directly desire that thing constantly or at a given moment oneself (Robbins speaks of a 'second-order way' of acknowledging that these things are generally worth desiring; 2016: 774). For instance, even though a man might personally not wish to spend time as a monk because he would find it tiring or is not willing to give up his worldly pleasures, he can still acknowledge the general desirability of devoting one's time fully to the study of religion, as monks do, and admire them for that. However, values are only one aspect of morality. Morality also entails norms, which have a more restrictive and obligatory character compared to more positively motivating values (Joas 2000: 184; see also Terpe 2018). Put differently, morality is not only related to desires but also to duties (Robbins 2017: 155). Neither values nor norms are timeless, unchangeable entities specific to a certain group of people: instead, they are subject to ongoing processes of negotiation. That means that people have to balance different (and perhaps competing) values, and the desires these entail, as well as react to the obligations and expectations of themselves and of others.

In respect of these moral considerations, religion has been identified as being particularly important (Robbins 2013: 112; 2016). It offers people criteria for what is a morally good way of being. In the realm of transcendence, values are seen as realized in their clearest form and fullest force. People encounter these values, for instance, through participation in rituals or specific exemplary persons, such as monks. In ordinary everyday life it is impossible for people to fully realize any one value, since they usually have to navigate between conflicting value-pulls. Nevertheless, in these ordinary situations as well, people will recognize a value's general desirability, familiar to them from the context of religion (Robbins 2016: 775–780). In the case of Myanmar, visitors easily observe that religious rituals are of great importance in the life of many Buddhists there.

Buddhism shaped understandings and the organization of kingship and statehood prior to colonialism, and while its role was greatly changed during colonialism, it was never fully erased. After independence, Buddhism and politics were openly reconnected by the government. Under military rule, the sangha (the Buddhist monastic order) was closely monitored. However, unlike the ways in which many other socialist countries dealt with religion, Buddhism was often publicly practised and supported. At times it was even used as a basis for legitimizing political rule as much as political resistance by both supporters and opponents of the regime (Schober 2011). Buddhism has been shown to influence ideas on politics (Houtman 1999; Walton 2017a), gender (Ikeya 2011; Harriden 2012; Tharapi Than 2014), and social hierarchies (Schober 2011; Keeler 2017). For many believers, Buddhism, while certainly not being the only source of moral ideas and values, constitutes a set of guidelines, or 'a repertoire of raw materials' (Walton 2017a: 4) with which to make sense of the world and develop moral ideas. Matthew J. Walton has argued that 'a (not the) Burmese Buddhist worldview [...] has been the primary influence on Burmese political thinking and political discourse throughout most of the twentieth century' (Walton 2017a: 3).

A crucial aspect here is the Buddhist framework of cause and effect. This is 'moral' because it concerns itself with what people see as the correct or incorrect conduct of individuals, and it sees this conduct as crucial for the individuals' future experiences (Walton 2017a: 8). Walton stresses that this 'moral universe' is neither static nor totalizing, nor is it universally shared among all Burmese Buddhists in the same way. Instead, there is significant variation in how they interpret and use key Buddhist concepts and combine them with other sources of morality (Walton 2017a: 8). I argue that the role that Walton prescribes to the Buddhist 'moral universe' for the under-standing of politics among Burman Buddhists applies in a similar way to the economy. However, unlike Walton I am less concerned here with over-arching discourses, for example, analyses of how Buddhists in Myanmar understand concepts like 'the economy' or 'capitalism'. Rather, I am inter-ested in how concrete economic ideas and practices on the ground are influenced by moral considerations.

Links between morality and the economy have been framed through the concept of the 'moral economy' (Thompson 1971; Scott 1976), which originally referred to notions of justice and fairness among certain groups in their reactions to changing economic situations. Charles Keyes com-plemented this approach by underlining the importance of locally particular circumstances for shaping moral attitudes, activities, and reactions. By that he meant not only socio-political conditions but also specific values and word views. With reference to Scott (1976), Keyes stated that his informants in north-eastern Thailand 'have a distinctive economic ethic and, thus, a distinctive moral economy not because they are peasants, but because they are Buddhists who are also peasants' (Keyes 1983a: 865). Max Weber, in his *Protestant Ethic and the Spirit of Capitalism,* linked religion to economic action not only for Protestants but for other major religions as well. The adherents of Buddhism, he argued, were not able to develop a spirit of capitalism, partly because of Buddhism's 'other-worldly' nature (Weber 1958: 217–222). However, Weber had drawn his insights mainly from doctrine, not from research among actually practising Buddhists.

This brings us to Edmund Leach, whose studies of the Kachin are not of direct relevance here, but whose distinction between what he called traditional and practical religion certainly is. The latter is religion as it is 'lived' and practised. In contrast to theology, which is often greatly preoccupied with the life hereafter, practical religion is concerned with life in the here and now. Referring to a study of Thailand, Leach stated that Buddhism as practised by the people is 'a cult for the living, not a theology for the dead and dying' (Leach 1968: 3). Empirical studies among Theravāda Buddhists in Burma, Thailand, and Sri Lanka (Pfanner and Ingersoll 1962; Spiro 1966; Keyes 1983a) have shown that Buddhist ideas indeed play a role in economic practice, albeit in different ways than Weber had imagined. I situate my book in the tradition of such studies, that is, at the crossroads of economic anthropology and the anthropology of lived Buddhism. I have studied the ordinary focused on everyday activities of lay people rather than on lay-sangha relations and religious rituals in order to understand the more subtle and underlying ways in which fragments of religious morality influence people's actions and social relations.

It is not particularly difficult to detect a number of links between Buddhism and economic activities in Myanmar. The economy of merit, in which merit-making promises a better rebirth and enhances one's social standing, leads many people to donate considerable amounts of their incomes to Buddhist institutions and, usually to a lesser extent, to charitable causes. In the realm of business more specifically, most business owners invite monks to perform a blessing ceremony, for instance, when they open a business, or annually at around the time of Thingyan, the Buddhist New Year. Apart from rituals with members of the sangha, business owners also perform rituals alone. Most shops have a small Buddhist altar where business owners put fresh water and small amounts of food twice a day as offerings, in the early morning and at noon. In addition, business owners report reciting certain teachings (*sutta*) daily, such as the *Mettā Sutta*. Other acts are performed specifically with the aim of preventing harm and increasing merit, and perhaps profit. Many business owners consult astrologers[5] before starting their businesses to determine a suitable name for the enterprise. Astrologers might also identify a certain family member whom they deem particularly suitable to have the business named after, preferably someone born on a Tuesday or a Thursday.[6] Sometimes the location of a business needs to be assessed. The chosen place might be inhabited by spirits (*nat*s) that need to be pacified, or a business could run into problems if trees are cut down, or if it has unknowingly been built on an old pagoda ground. In contrast, business owners considered it beneficial to be able to see the top of a pagoda from the shop's location. Such religious aspects were regularly mentioned alongside the worldly aspects relevant for business success, like proximity to a busy road, which would guarantee customers. However, in this book I aim to move beyond such publicly observable activities to outline how values and moral ideas shape activities and social relations in more hidden ways.

Research has shown that lay followers who have never spent time in the sangha, who claim to not know much about Buddhist teachings, and who regularly emphasize the distinction between religious 'experts' and themselves, nevertheless also deploy religious ideas to explain life circumstances and justify, or condemn, their own and other people's actions (Gombrich 1991; Kumada 2001; Cassaniti 2015). People's religious practice and interpretations can differ quite considerably from the doctrinal sources – which is not to say that my informants were 'wrong' in the way they interpreted Buddhist ideas. Moreover, Buddhist practice undergoes changes in the light of changing societal, political, and economic circumstances (see Gombrich and Obeyesekere 1988, on Sri Lanka; Foxeus 2013 and Jordt 2007, on Myanmar). This proves that values are in a constant interplay with changing socio-economic circumstances, which might lead to changing priorities or give rise to new value conflicts, as has been described for Myanmar's neighbour Thailand. When villagers in northeast Thailand who had previously lived largely from a subsistence economy increasingly became part of the global capitalist order and migrated to the cities for work, they felt a tension between their ideas of what 'good' Buddhist action should look like and the actual actions of themselves and others around them. The responses to this tension constituted 'a new practical morality, albeit one that is still recognizably Buddhist' (Keyes 1990: 171).

---

[5] Phenomena like the belief in *nat*s (spirits) and astrology are an important dimension of religious practice for many Buddhists (Brac De La Perrière 2009; see also Chapter 3).

[6] In Myanmar, the weekday of one's birth is of crucial importance for one's local horoscope.

While earlier long-term ethnographic studies that dealt with Buddhism as practised in Burma focused on village societies in Upper Myanmar (Nash 1965; Spiro 1982; Kumada 2001), I studied people residing in an urban area in Lower Myanmar. Nevertheless, I found many older observations concerning Theravāda influences to be valid in my field-site as well. This shows that many core ideas of the Theravāda framework have a certain resilience, still clearly recognizable and yet adaptable amidst changing circumstances in an urban and ethnically much more diverse environment than was described in earlier studies. While Myanmar has experienced vast changes of different kinds in recent years, including increasing liberalization of the economy and a change of government, there are no signs of a religious decline. Streets are plastered with posters advertising upcoming *dhamma* talks by monks, and while various new bank branches opened during my time in Pathein, several Buddhist monasteries were being renovated as well. Buddhist practice also integrated newly available technologies, like smartphones, which have flooded the market within only a few years. They are not only used to keep in touch with people via messages, to transfer money or to buy and sell products on Facebook, but also to read and share religious messages and broadcast one's donation activities. Teachings like the *lokanîti*, a traditional collection of old life maxims, can now also be downloaded as an app, to receive regular reminders of good moral practice on the phone display.

Access to Field Site and Methodology

When in April 2008 Cyclone 'Nargis' hit Myanmar's coast and took the lives of around 140,000 people, I was working as an intern at a radio news station in Berlin. After finishing high school the previous year, I was eager to gain some experience of the world of journalists and politicians. To cover the developments after 'Nargis' I interviewed aid workers and country experts over the phone discussing what could be done to help. The government's own reaction to the disaster, namely to hinder access to international aid for its own citizens, left a deep impression on me as an eighteen-year-old. Three years later, and with a BA in Social Anthropology, I went to Thailand to volunteer in the refugee camps along the Thai–Myanmar border, which back then accommodated a total of around 120,000 refugees from Myanmar, mostly ethnic Karen. Like many other outsiders, I initially learned much about Myanmar from refugees, migrants, and activists in exile. Only the political changes of 2011 made it possible for me to carry out long-term research in the country for this book a couple of years later.

My data were gathered mainly in a period of twelve months from August 2015 to August 2016, most of which I spent in Pathein. Only in the first few weeks did I stay in Mandalay in order to explore the nearby area of Sagaing, a centre of Buddhism in Upper Myanmar clustered with pagodas and monasteries. Here I conducted interviews with religious specialists, including monks, nuns, astrologers, and spirit mediums, before settling in Pathein, my main research site, where I concentrated more on lay followers. I returned to Myanmar in February 2018 for an additional two months of follow-up research. My main research units were small businesses, in some of which I only interviewed the owner once, while in others I spent time regularly. I looked at businesses in different sectors, including crafts, as well as food- and beverage-processing, retail shops, service providers, and restaurants. None of the businesses I regularly visited had more than thirty employees, and many had fewer than ten. I also included people in my research pursuing one-person ventures such as vending or trishaw-driving. While for many of my informants their business activities were their only source of income, some combined it with employment, for example, running a shop besides having a public-sector job. Others had started their businesses only after retiring from employment, while yet others had changed frequently between employment by others and small-scale self-employment.

My research took place in an ethnically and religiously diverse town. While in most of the book I focus on ethnic Burman Buddhists, ethnic Chinese business families are taken into account in Chapter 4 since their situation highlights a relevant contrast in business matters and historical experiences. Not limiting myself to only one business or to a certain sector allowed me to explore the economic landscape of the town as a whole. I discovered patterns of entrenchment between different ethnic groups, for instance, the fact that a lot of businesses in downtown Pathein, including those in prime locations, are owned by people of Chinese and to a lesser extent Indian descent, many of whose ancestors have been involved in business activities in Myanmar for two generations or more, which often resulted in them becoming successful intergenerational family businesses.

The extended presence of a foreigner was seen as unusual by many Patheinians, and initial surprise was fortified by the fact that I was an unmarried woman, since these do not typically live or travel unattended in Myanmar. However, my friendship with university students (some of whose parents ran small businesses) helped me to establish important contacts and gain their trust. As foreigners were not permitted to stay in local people's homes, I lived on the university compound. I was able to set up rounds of English-language conversation with students and occasionally attended workshops or conferences. In retrospect it seems that I was lucky to conduct my initial research during a period of relative political openness. With the help of the local university I had no problems in obtaining permission to stay for a full year. More recently, since the country's human rights image has deteriorated, the authorities seem to have become more reluctant again to grant long-term access and support to researchers. This may be why I had many more difficulties in obtaining the necessary documents for my visa in 2018 than in 2015, even though the planned duration of research was much shorter. However, during both stays I felt unrestricted while collecting the data that was of interest for me in Pathein, but of course I was nevertheless concerned and careful not to endanger any of my interlocutors.

My methodology centred on the classical combination of participant observation, semi-structured interviews, and informal conversations. I had prepared myself with two short-term language courses prior to the research that equipped me with the ability to read the Burmese script and a basic knowledge of grammar and vocabulary. In the field I was able to use these skills, but I also had the privilege of working together with two people who regularly provided me with research assistance, mostly for interpreting, whether in interview situations or in retrospect, when we went through recorded materials or collected questionnaires together. In addition to interviews, conversations, and participant observation, I conducted a quantitative survey of forty business people. This survey was prepared prior to fieldwork with colleagues from the Max Planck Institute for Social Anthropology in order to gather comparable data sets. The majority of the questionnaires were filled out between December 2015 and April 2016. The people I surveyed ran businesses that were mostly very small in size, many even one-person ventures, justifiable in so far as small entities dominate the overall business landscape in the country. Respondents were active in different sectors, such as trading, the food industry, wholesale, and crafts. I conducted surveys in different wards of the town to ensure local variety. The survey helped shed light on values and business-related matters. It underlined the importance of religion and Buddhist ideas for ordinary people, but it also helped me to understand the economic aspects, for instance, the provision of starting capital for businesses, the role of the business owner's family in work organization, and common obstacles business owners face. Moreover, the survey helped to introduce certain topics, which I then explored further through qualitative methods and observation. While the concrete survey results will not be published in this book, they have certainly informed the qualitative analysis I present in the following chapters. Combining quantitative and qualitative methods turned out to be a fruitful research strategy in my ethnographic endeavours.

Studying people's business activities is inherently challenging for the anthropologist because she will very often encounter people at moments when they are busy. However, a long-term stay allowed enough time to have conversations, observe, and participate. Typically I would have breakfast with students at the university compound and then set out on my motorbike to visit businesses in different locations in Pathein. While in some businesses, such as retail shops, I mainly assumed the role of a customer, there were other instances in which I helped to set up a new business, for instance, by designing the menu of a new coffee shop. In restaurants I could sometimes help prepare food, which allowed me some time with the work force.[7] Talking to workers turned out to be more difficult than talking to business owners. Differences of wealth and power between the two groups were often considerable. In some instances I had the impression that business owners were eager to present their businesses in a good light, while workers were rather reluctant to talk when the business owner was present as well. Perhaps they feared being seen as lazy or did not want to get under the impression of being disloyal by criticizing their bosses. To overcome this problem I began meeting with workers outside of working hours. This was not always possible though, for instance with child workers, who lived and slept at their workplace (see Chapter 5). Here, I managed to make conversations in the quiet afternoon hours, and with the permission of the owner we did some drawing and writing together. In other cases, I did not even enter the workplace, such as the large garment factories in Pathein's industrial zone. While focusing on smaller businesses, I was nevertheless interested in the perspective of the garment workers in order to compare their situations with what I had seen in small businesses. Several times I visited garment workers in the evening in their shelters outside the factory compound, and sometimes I met them on Sundays, their only day off.

Apart from looking at activities within businesses, I also spent a lot of time with people outside their working hours, accompanying them to family events and Buddhist ceremonies in Pathein or on pilgrimages to pagodas in the town's surroundings. Beyond the businesses, I tried to make contacts all over the city. I spent time with students, trishaw-drivers, and public-sector employees. Quite regularly, I spent afternoons with some older women, who, thanks to having been educated in mission schools, had an excellent knowledge of English. They told me a lot about how Pathein has changed, their own family affairs, and their relations with their neighbours. Such contacts greatly inform the sixth chapter of this book, in which I show how

---

[7] Research among child workers (Chapter 5) demanded extra careful methodological and ethical considerations. During the whole process I prepared my steps well, consulting specific methodological literature (Christensen and James 2008), obtaining consent from caregivers and children, and ensuring that the children would not encounter any problems because of my presence. My research was completely in conformity with the ethics guidelines for researchers issued by the European Commission (European Commission 2013).

people have built a social support system in the absence of state support. It displays a preponderance of small and medium-sized businesses became clear that, to understand livelihood matters, it is necessary to look beyond business units. After all, what mattered to people were not only the threads of commerce but also the threads of social support.

Pathein

I selected Pathein, the capital of Ayeyarwady Region, as a research site in order to collect data in an urban setting while avoiding the particularities of the large and more rapidly changing areas of Yangon and Mandalay. Pathein, located 152 kilometres west of Yangon, is a medium-size port town with 287,071 inhabitants according to the 2014 census. Its inner town is located around the Pathein river, a tributary of the large Ayeyarwady river which crosses the whole country from north to south. The town's long river front and the streets surrounding the market and the main pagoda consist of concrete buildings with on average three storeys. Only occasionally do higher buildings occur, for instance, a few newly built hotels. Usually the ground floors of houses have open gates during the day where businesses activities take place, while house owners or tenants reside in the upper floors. Many houses date back to colonial days or to the years after independence in 1948. Street names also remind one of colonial days ('Merchant Street'), as do other landmarks, such as the clock tower or the prison. The town has been inhabited by Theravāda Buddhists presumably since its emergence many centuries ago and the population remains predominately Buddhist. Nevertheless, Pathein has also long displayed great religious and ethnic diversity, similar to other urban areas of Myanmar. One can find not only countless Buddhist pagodas and monasteries of all sizes, but also churches of different denominations (Catholic, Baptist, Adventist), various Hindu temples, several mosques, a Sikh temple, and a number of Chinese temples, all of them located within short distance of one another.

Under its Pāli name of *Kusima*, Pathein is mentioned in Sri Lankan rock inscriptions from 1165 (Paranavitana 1928–1933: 312–325, as cited in Aung-Thwin 2002: 42). In Old Burmese it was mentioned in AD 1265, and it was probably already known before that (Luce 1969–70: 2, attachment; as cited in Aung Thwin 2002: 42). Pathein's history has not been researched extensively, except for a few sources, including a Burmese-language book by U Magha (1967). The area in which it is located, Lower Burma[8], is often

---

[8] The distinction of the areas that later became known as Lower Burma and Upper Burma is a local one and presumably as old as the Pagan period. It emerged mainly due to differences in

mentioned as having been part of Buddhist Mon Kingdoms, before the Burman Pagan Kingdom expanded its influence to the area in the eleventh century. While the presence of Buddhist Mons in the area is likely, the hypothesis that an early Mon polity existed there has been challenged (Aung-Thwin 2002, 2005). There is no doubt, however, that from the eleventh century onwards the power centres controlling the area were mostly located far away, in Upper Burma. It was also here where most of the population resided. Lower Burma, in contrast, was then largely jungle and swamp land, apart from a few coastal towns (Aung-Thwin 2002: 32). It remained a periphery of the kingdoms in Upper Burma, with local authorities bridging the gap with the rulers further north (Frasch 2002: 62). An exception to this was a period in the fourteenth, fifteenth, and sixteenth centuries when Lower Burma was controlled by a Mon kingdom with a strong (Sinhalese) Buddhist tradition and its capital at Pegu (now Bago). This was also a time in which commerce had started to grow in importance (Aung-Thwin 2002: 26). With Lower Burma not playing a very important role in rice cultivation, the advantages of its towns rather lay in their access to the Bay of Bengal.

Long-distance and especially international trade had only marginal economic importance for the Burmese kingdoms, which were heavily based on agriculture (Frasch 2002: 59). Nevertheless, Burmese ports, including Pathein, have been known to the international trading community for a long time (as evidenced by 10th and 11th century reports, see Frasch 2002: 65). The presence of Armenian, Portuguese, Arab, Jewish, Chinese, and Indian traders in Burma during the Pagan period has been proved or is strongly suspected (Frasch 2002: 65). It could be that the presence of Arab traders was what gave Pathein (or rather, its older version, 'Patkain') its Burmese name (from the Burmese word for Muslim, *pathi*; see Lothian 1955, as cited in Yegar 1972: 7). Many Arab traders later settled in Burma's coastal towns, where European visitors reported considerable Muslim communities in the sixteenth century (Yegar 1972: 3–4). In 1826, Pathein's population was estimated to be only around three thousand people, albeit very diverse, including Burmans, Karens, Mons, Chinese, and Indians (Crawfurd 1829: 462). Apart from imports, mostly of textiles, port towns were also important for networks of religious exchange with Sri Lanka and India, as Buddhist monks came and went through these ports (Frasch 1998; 2002: 65–66).

Pathein fell to the British in 1852, in the second of three Anglo-Burmese Wars (1852–1853), and the occupiers changed its name to Bassein. The Ayeyarwady Region was turned into the most important rice-cultivating

---

environment between the two regions, with Upper Burma referring to the Dry Zone, roughly north of what is now Pyay (Aung-Thwin 1985: 105).

area of the country under British rule, with the help of hundreds of thousands of migrants from Upper Burma and India. Pathein became a major trading hub for rice. Still today, many of Pathein's bigger businesses focus on rice-processing and trade, but other sectors such as salt-processing and fisheries are of importance too. While it has no considerable role in international trade today, Pathein remains a lively port town, with regular transport of goods to the surrounding villages and to the north via the river networks. Increasingly, road networks are replacing waterways for the transportation of goods and people: the overnight ferry from Yangon to Pathein, for example, ceased in 2015. Today Pathein enjoys national fame for its handmade bamboo parasols (Burmese *Pathein hti:*), as well as a sweet snack called *halawa*, both popular souvenirs for Burmese who pass through the town. The town itself of no immediate relevance for tourists, whether local or foreign. However, visitors would often stop for a lunch break on their way from Yangon to the nearby beaches of Chaung Tha and Ngwe Saung.

Plate 1. Pathein street corner in the evening.

Myanmar's economy remains largely agriculture-based, but especially in urban areas the sheer scale of one-person ventures and the high number of small and medium-sized businesses indicate the relevance of these entities. In downtown Pathein, countless stores sell all kinds of items – groceries, clothes, plastic goods – and provide manifold services such as tailoring, hair-dressing, printing, repairing, and more. While many people work from a store on the ground floor of a building, others are mobile and carry their goods through the streets, or transport people and materials on bicycles, motorbikes or trishaws. Boats are loaded at the jetty, from where traders bring products to the villages of the Ayeyarwady Delta. Near the river, rice- and salt-mills and warehouses employ a larger number of workers. Apart from the so-called 'Industrial Zones', which now consist mostly of garment production, there has been no real systematic attempt to strengthen medium-size towns such as Pathein economically, even though this could help Yangon in its struggle to cope with the pace and intensity of change, which has led to burgeoning housing prices and congestion. The Pathein area has seen nothing comparable to Yangon in terms of change. Apart from the factories, it has not developed many new employment opportunities in recent years. No large private companies have appeared that could bring innovation to the region and attractive jobs to the educated. Many of the local bigger businesses that employ larger numbers of people date back to the early 1990s. While small-scale self-employment is thriving, setting up larger ventures that could offer employment has become increasingly difficult. Land prices have risen considerably, as elsewhere in the country. Businesses that have started recently were usually financed either through money earned abroad, or through capital that had already been in the founder's family, for example, from former business activities and often from investments in land.

According to the censuses of 1983 and 2014 respectively, the population of Pathein increased from 144,096 to 287,071 between those years. However, while there has been population growth in the Ayeyarwady Region[9] as a whole, a trend paralleled across the entire country, strong urbanization has not taken roots in the Region's towns, including Pathein. In fact, the proportion of the urban population in the Region even decreased by almost one percent from 14.9 in 1983 to 14.1 in 2014. In contrast, the country's overall rate of urban population rose from 24.8 percent in 1983 to 29.6 percent in 2014, with Yangon experiencing the strongest growth (Myanmar Department of Population 2016: 106–107). The lack of growth of

---

[9] In the Ayeyarwady Region, the population grew from 4,994,061 in 1983 to 6,184,829 in 2014 according to the respective census reports. The whole population of the country grew from approximately 35,315,623 in 1983 to 51,486,253 in 2014 (Myanmar Department of Population 2015: 17). Ayeyarwady Region ranks second in population size when compared to the other administrative units of states and regions, surpassed only by the Yangon Region. Despite the overall growth of the population in the region, its share of the country's total population shrunk from 14 percent to 12 percent between 1983 and 2014 (Myanmar Department of Population 2015: 11). One should note that in 1983 quite large parts of the country's border areas were controlled by ethnic armed groups and were inaccessible to the government, which distorted the census data for 1983. Regarding the 2014 census, the government has been criticized for excluding the Rohingya (Ferguson 2015; Heijmans 2015).

Ayeyarwady Region's towns has to do with internal migration. Of all regions, Ayeyarwady Region has experienced the largest amount of out-migration in recent years. Yangon is the major destination for people from this area. Explanations for these migration flows lie in a fluctuating rice price, as the region is heavily dependent on rice cultivation, and in the relatively close proximity and easily accessibility of Yangon (Myanmar Department of Population 2016: 27, 38, 108). As a consequence, many people from the Delta region migrate directly to Yangon for work instead of going to one of the regional towns. Certainly Pathein has experienced some in-migration from rural areas, especially in the early 1990s, and again with the opening of big garment factories in the last few years, but the extent of this increase is very far from what Yangon has seen (Kraas et al. 2017: 74–78).

Plate 2. Shwe Moke Taw Pagoda in Pathein.

Overview of Chapters

The book is divided into seven chapters, including an introduction and conclusion. The following two chapters at the beginning of the book provide background information taken from the relevant literature. Chapter 2 deals with Myanmar's political economy, from early Buddhist kingdoms to recent changes in the country and their consequences for the economic realities on the ground. Chapter 3 introduces the role of values and morality, focusing specifically on Myanmar's Theravāda Buddhist tradition. The subsequent three chapters are based on my own data. They are divided according to the different spheres of embeddedness, or domains of social interaction, in which business owners are active: family relations (Chapter 4), relations with non-kin workers (Chapter 5), and relations within the 'community', that is, the wider social landscape outside the business (Chapter 6). While such a segmentation, just like the separation of domains such as 'economy' and 'family', is also fundamentally artificial, as social realms overlap in reality, it helps structure the analysis effectively. Chapter 4 presents two case studies of small businesses, one owned by ethnic Burmans, the other by ethnic Chinese. I look at the family situation of their respective founders over three generations, thus also taking into account their parents and children. The chapter compares kinship moralities, attitudes toward business ownership, and ideas of prestige and status, putting all these aspects into the context of different historical developments and the opportunities and constraints they entailed. Contrasting these two cases allows me to address emic under-standings of social reproduction and social mobility, as well as to show how inner-family negotiations contribute to the prevalence and prosperity of some businesses and to the disappearance of others. Chapter 5 addresses relations between workers and employers in small businesses. It starts from the observation of a high labour turnover among workers (which has been noted, but has remained largely unexplained in quantitative studies; see Bernhardt et al. 2017) and the fact that many people in the low-income sectors prefer small-scale self-employment over working for others. Employers, in their struggle to find and bind workers to their businesses, use a range of strategies beyond the payment of wages. The chapter devotes a special section to child workers, who are becoming an increasingly common labour force in urban areas, one that is particularly vulnerable. Chapter 6 retains self-employed people as its main subjects, but the economic activities described here happen outside the actual businesses. I describe a non-state social-support system consisting of neighbourhood assistance, charity projects, and access to informal credit and savings options. Engaging with different monetary flows, such as donations and loans, I discuss ideas of inequality, responsibility and redistribution.

Chapter 2
Myanmar's History and Political Economy

Buddhist Kingship and British Imperialism

This chapter addresses crucial historical developments and recent changes to Myanmar's political economy with reference to the business landscape and the labour market, in order to provide a meaningful context for my own data, to be presented in Chapters 4, 5, and 6. Much of the area that later became known as Burma/Myanmar[10] had for centuries been ruled by the kings of Pagan, a kingdom that emerged in AD 849 and ended in 1287. Following more than two centuries of political fragmentation in the region, the Taungoo (1587–1752) and later the Konbaung (1752–1885) dynasties emerged as Pagan's successor realms. The Konbaung dynasty ultimately fell when the British took power over Upper Burma in 1885. The history of these dynasties was by no means a period of smooth rule, but one marked rather by shifting state centres, power struggles, and changing relations with neighbouring kingdoms, like those of the Shan, the Mon, and the Arakanese, as well as with China and Siam (now Thailand). What was remarkably stable amidst the considerable political changes within the different kingdoms was the influence of Buddhist teachings and institutions (Taylor 2009: 16).

In all succeeding kingdoms, the rule of the king was understood and legitimized within a Theravāda Buddhist framework.[11] The main functions of the sangha, the community of monks, were to preserve and spread the Buddha's teachings and to provide formal education (at least for boys) in monastic schools. This ideological connection between religion and state power, with merit and *kamma* (Burmese *kan*) as its main ideological pillars (Foxeus 2017a), remained largely unchallenged in its fundamentals over the

---

[10] 'Burma' will be used in those parts of the chapter that deal with events before 1989, when the country was renamed 'Myanmar'.

[11] This synthesis of state power and Buddhism was inspired by the model of King Ashoka, who had ruled the large Maurya dynasty in India in 268-232 BCE and contributed significantly to the spread of Buddhism itself and of the model of Buddhist kingship to other Asian regions (Foxeus 2017a: 215).

centuries, its institutional manifestation only being destroyed with the arrival of the British. Administratively, the pre-colonial kingdoms were ruled through village (*ywa*) and township (*myo.*) authorities, a patrimonial structure with patron – client dyadic relationships from the monarchy down to the village level (Taylor 2009: 17). The state collected some taxes on land and population, and later increasingly on trade and commerce, which, together with economic surpluses, allowed the financing of the state apparatus and the sangha (Taylor 2009: 43). Overall the economy functioned largely on a subsistence level. Rulers were as careful to prevent people from acquiring private power through wealth accumulation as to prevent peasant opposition, one of the reasons for their reluctance to raise taxes. The population for its part generally avoided the state rather than seeking to rely on it (Taylor 2009: 39). Like the sangha, over the centuries these organizational structures were able to survive the political turmoil at higher levels, where the rulers had to face the constant threat of rivalries from sangha members, lower-level authorities, and power centres on the state's margins, where non-Burman ethnic groups resided. Concerning the latter, the state's control over many areas further from the centre remained limited (Adas 2011: 218). Here, rulers of the respective ethnic groups asserted direct authority over the people, but were obliged to pay tribute. They remained relatively undisturbed by the state for the sake of overall political stability and security (Taylor 2009: 23).

Lower Burma, for most of the time, existed largely as a periphery of Upper Burma, where the power centres were located. The existence of a Mon polity in the area before the rulers of the Bagan kingdom absorbed it in the eleventh century had long been assumed, but its existence has more recently been challenged by scholars (Aung-Thwin 2002, 2005). Only in the fourteenth, fifteenth, and sixteenth centuries was Lower Burma undoubtedly controlled by a Mon kingdom with a strong (Sinhalese) Buddhist tradition and its capital in Pegu (now Bago). Commerce had started to grow in importance in that period (Aung-Thwin 2002: 26), but it never became close to the importance of agriculture. Sparsely populated, the value of the area lay in its access to the Indian Ocean. Under the Taungoo and Konbaung dynasties, political and administrative skills, a strengthened military, and growing domestic agriculture had led to an increase in central power and influence over the tributary areas, as well as to longer periods of overall peace, stability, and rising productivity (Taylor 2009: 19). Surplus from growing Indian Ocean trade allowed King Mindon, who ruled from 1853 to 1878, to introduce reforms, including a new tax system and the initial countrywide monetization. However, Mindon's attempt to strengthen his power could not avert the threat from the colonizers (Taylor 2009: 46). The short reign of his son, Thibaw Min, ended after the British finally defeated the Dynasty in the three Anglo-Burmese Wars (1824–26, 1852–52, 1885).

The fate of Lower Burma was to change massively under the British. The new rulers derived the name 'Burma' for the newly annexed territory from the main inhabitants of the central areas, the *Bamar*. They also largely replaced existing administrative structures, commissioning members of the Indian Civil Service (ICS) to govern Burma. A new secular school system, complemented by Christian mission schools, gradually replaced the Buddhist monastic schools (Tin Maung Maung Than 2007: 7; Schober 2011: 56–59). Government support for religious institutions was greatly reduced (Adas 2011: 191). Villages were reorganized into new territorial units, and village headmen were appointed to administer them. These were often individuals who were willing to cooperate with the new rulers, for instance, rich landowners or members of minority ethnic groups (Taylor 2007: 74). Thus, tasks and the legitimation of village and township authorities now rested on impersonal and territorial factors, rather than on personal patron–client ties, as had been the case in the past. These new policies thus altered the existing social order in the central areas of the country.[12] Since there was no longer a king, it was now the laity's responsibility to preserve and protect Buddhism. The rise of print technology contributed to the spread of doctrinal Buddhism among the laity, and practising *vipassanā* meditation became more popular during that time (Jordt 2005, 2007). Many of the reactions to colonial rule, like militant uprisings, the formation of urban Buddhist associations, a newly emerging urban meditation movement, and nationalist rebellions, were implicitly or explicitly linked to anger over the devaluation and suppression of Buddhism (Turner 2014).

When the British arrived, many areas of the fertile river delta in Lower Burma, including the region surrounding Pathein, were still jungle and swamp where property rights over land were not an issue, as land 'was so abundant that it was of little more value to the cultivator than the air he breathed' (Furnivall 1957: 42). With the opening of the Suez Canal a promising market for rice had emerged, and the British saw in the Irrawaddy

---

[12] However, for reasons of convenience the British did not replace the existing social structures with their system in more remote areas inhabited by minorities, such as the Chin and Kachin. Instead they implemented a form of indirect rule through existing headmen, chieftains, and local lords (Taylor 2007: 75). In the administration and the army (but also in educational materials) the British categorized and organized ethnic groups roughly according to languages. In the later periods of colonial rule, the British preferably recruited members of ethnic minorities into the police and army, often through pastors who had started their missionary activities mainly with the non-Buddhist groups. Multiple nationalisms fuelled by these policies would erupt into violent conflicts after independence, with some of these conflicts lasting until today (Taylor 2007).

delta much unused potential. They created a system of industrial agriculture with production based on a large-scale division of labour and financial arrangements involving borrowed capital, more characteristic of industrial settings than of agriculture. These specific features in such an extreme development were 'perhaps unparalleled in economic history' (Furnivall 1957: 44).

For this massive undertaking, the British encouraged immigration to the delta region from Upper Burma as well as from India. Indians came in their thousands, in some years more than 300,000 (Furnivall 1957: 73), and many stayed to work after the harvest season, for example, as coolies in the rice mills. While land was plentiful no major tensions occurred, and the country experienced substantial economic growth. As a trading hub Pathein grew in importance, being located on the margins of rural areas and on the main water trade routes. However, in the second half of the colonial period the situation became more competitive. To cultivate more land people took out loans, often from Indian Chettiars, a community heavily involved in trading, banking, and money-lending (Adas 2011: 112–119). More and more often, borrowers were unable to repay their loans and had to dispose of their land to satisfy the debt. Soon, much of the land was in the hands of businessmen rather than cultivators (Adas 2011: 223). While under domestic agriculture inner-family hierarchies had been paramount, there was now a new hierarchy of social differentiation between landlords, cultivators, and labourers. Many agriculturalists were heavily indebted to moneylenders, making them the 'effective owners' of the land (Furnivall 1957: 61–62). Short tenancy periods led to high mobility among cultivators and labourers, which disrupted village units and their annual cycles of religious rituals and festivals (Furnivall 1957: xiii; Adas 2011: 30).

Through these intense economic measures, Burma became the 'rice bowl of Asia', exporting more rice than any other nation in the world. In 1856–7 around 662,000 acres of land were under cultivation in Lower Burma, just a few years after the British had annexed the area in the Second Anglo-Burmese War (1852–1853). In the 1930s this had risen to over eight million acres (Adas 2011: 22, 127). Besides rice, oil and timber were also exported, and export surpluses were used to develop infrastructure, as well as the processing and mining industries (Tin Maung Maung Than 2007: 9). This capitalist endeavour came with vast social consequences, and Burmese were certainly not the first in line to benefit. Furnivall spoke of a 'plural society', whose different groups lived side by side but did not mix (Furnivall 1957: 304). He saw the root of this development in the almost total exclusion of Burmans from the state apparatus, as well as from most of the newly emerging economic activities, except for agriculture. The situation was

especially obvious in urban areas. Rangoon (now Yangon) had developed
into an advanced port city, but in 1941, 56 percent of the whole population
was Indian (Tin Maung Maung Than 1992: 586). Indians and Chinese[13] also
dominated trade, banking, and land-owning (Taylor 2009: 101). Burmese
entrepreneurial activities were few and small in scale and did not thrive.
Traditional crafts had lost their importance, and locally produced goods had
been replaced by imports. None of the large-scale enterprises emerging
under the British had been run by Burmese, and Burmese were rarely
employed in these ventures, not even in subordinate positions (Brown 2011:
739).

To make things worse, the Great Depression hit the rice sector hard.
Here, the Burmese were the most vulnerable (Adas 2011: xviii). Thus, in the
few endeavours 'where the Burmese did engage with the modern world – in
the cultivation of rice for export – by the final complete decade of British
rule, they were left impoverished, debt-ridden, and landless' (Brown 2011:
139). Competition for jobs and land fostered tensions in the 1920s and
1930s, which led to violent race riots and pogroms targeting Indians and
Chinese and which contributed to the emergence of anti-British and
independence movements. The major peasant rebellion led by the Buddhist
monk Hsaya San and its suppression resulted in the deaths of thousands
(Adas 2011: 200–4). James Scott (1967) drew on this event to develop his
arguments about how peasant rebellions result from a subjective feeling of
economic injustice and loss of autonomy and control as a consequence of the
disruptive nature that colonial politics and the market economy posed to
socio-economic structures.[14]

Furnivall summarized the complications as follows:
> Everywhere there is rivalry and some degree of conflict between
> Town and Country, Industry and Agriculture, Capital and Labour:
> but when rural interests are Burman and urban interests mainly
> European, with Burman Agriculture and European Industry, Burman
> Labour and European Capital the elements of conflict are so deep-
> seated and so explosive that even the best good will on both sides
> can hardly avert disaster (1957: xvii).

However, Adas cautioned that we should acknowledge the complexity of the
reasons for the disruption of social harmony, instead of applying 'simplistic
condemnations of imperialist exploitation, Chettiar ruthlessness, or Burmese
ineptitude' (Adas 2011: 216). His study of the colonial period suggested that

---

[13] See Mya Than (1997) on ethnic Chinese communities in Myanmar and their histories.
[14] Scott developed his arguments further and analysed everyday-forms of peasant resistance
(1985), as well as avoidance of state control among the Southeast Asian highland populations
(2009).

Burmans often apparently opted for a relatively poor life in the countryside close to their families, rather than working as coolies in urban areas. They may deliberately have left many better paid positions in construction and industry to the Indians, who were desperate to send some money home. According to Adas's sources, typical industrial, manual tasks were seen as boring and monotonous and as less prestigious for the Burmans, whereas as agriculturalists, at least when they could obtain their own land, they remained their own masters (Adas 2011: 120, 219). Taylor's analysis (2009: 124–139) also complicates the notion that ethnic lines and class lines were largely coherent and warns us not to overstate Burmese powerlessness. Although perhaps lower in numbers than Indians, Burmese too acted as traders, moneylenders, lawyers, and landowners. Especially in the early twentieth century, a predominantly urban 'white-collar' Burmese middle class emerged. The share of Burmese employees also grew in some other sectors, like films and the printing industry, both of which relied on Burmese speakers (Furnivall 1957: 164). When the Second World War was drawing to a close, thousands of Indians fled via Assam under horrendous conditions, leaving many important positions unoccupied, for instance, in the military, the state apparatus, and the medical sector, as well as in industry. While Burmese generally now had more access to some jobs, the British favoured ethnic Karens over Burmans in important government and military positions (Taylor 2007), which fostered further divisions along ethnic lines and contributed to the emergence of violent conflicts after independence.[15] In urban entrepreneurship, the descendants of migrants from India and China continued to play an important role and still do so today, although they faced serious discrimination under military rule, which confined many to small-scale undertakings on the black market.

After the Second World War had taken many people's lives and destroyed large parts of its cities, Burma eventually gained independence in 1948. The Burmese, who had been denied any considerable access to policy-making or higher economic positions for a century, were left with a destroyed infrastructure, an economy in dire straits, a weak state, and an unstable social order. The colonial experience was at least in part responsible for the later policies of the military junta, in particular their emphasis on self-reliance and 'Burmanization', which resulted, for instance, in the nationalization of land and of all the industries that had largely been under

---

[15] Armed conflicts mainly broke out after independence. Considerable parts of Myanmar's border areas have been under the control of ethnic minority groups ever since, some of which have established state-like structures, but they remain under constant threat from the Burmese army (see Smith 2007). These conflicts are highly complex and cannot be explained further here. They constitute a major challenge in the country's current attempt to democratize.

foreign ownership in colonial days (Brown 2011). Colonial policies had not only fostered ethnic tensions within the country, but to at least some extent most Burmese had also experienced foreign power and its economic modernity mainly 'as the key to the means of their exploitation' (Taylor 1995: 53). Moreover, no considerable Burmese entrepreneurial class had developed under colonialism that could have pitted their experiences and interests against the policy of socialist autarky (Brown 2011: 744).[16]

Independence and the Burmese Way to Socialism

Only months before independence, some of the leaders of Burma's independence movements were assassinated. Among them was thirty-two-year-old General Aung San, father of Aung San Suu Kyi, who is the leader of today's officially governing party, the National League for Democracy. Aung San had a major role in the negotiations for independence. Aung San had been part of a younger generation of Burman leaders who had organized nationalist resistance against the British in the last phase of colonial rule. Several organizations had been founded, and intellectual discourses on freedom and leadership were ignited; Marxist literature now found its way to Burma as well. Aung San had not only negotiated with the British but had also made efforts to reach out to representatives of ethnic minorities in order to find peaceful solutions for coexistence. Today he is still regarded a national hero in Myanmar. Although the case was never fully resolved, a man named U Saw, former prime minister under the colonial government, was arrested and executed for instigating the murders. After Aung San's death, U Nu became the leading political figure and the first Prime Minister of independent Burma. A democratic system was established, and several parliamentary elections were held over the years. U Nu aimed to establish an industrial welfare state through the so-called Pyidawtha Plan. He was a devout Buddhist and promoted Buddhism as the moral basis of the nation-building process (Jordt 2006: 198). The new leaders introduced a kind of mixed policy containing elements of socialism, Buddhism, nationalism, and market mechanisms (Myat Thein 2004: 16–21). In U Nu's visions, the socialist ideology combined fruitfully with Buddhist ideas in so far as it would reduce attachment to material possessions and thus help individuals to achieve a more moral state of existence (Walton 2017a: 118–120). The

---

[16] Brown argues that, if foreign entrepreneurs with their capital and knowledge had stayed after the end of colonial rule, as for example in Malaysia, the economy might have taken a very different turn, e.g. through policies that encourage joint ventures between Indians and Burmese, or similar moves in that direction. Paradoxically, now the withdrawal of Indians and Chinese became a factor that contributed to economic problems and that fostered autarky (Brown 2011: 747).

economic situation after independence remained difficult mainly due to the destruction of infrastructure and industries in the war and a severe shortage of foreign capital. Moreover, the government had many additional challenges to address, such as factions within the leading party, ideological struggles, and external armed groups seeking power. Finally, in 1962, the military took power through a coup (Tin Maung Maung Than 2007: 19, 49–60).

What followed was a period of nearly fifty years of military rule under a regime that would become notorious for the oppression of its people. The military junta under General Ne Win introduced an economic program called 'The Burmese Way to Socialism'. The rulers nationalized all major industries, schools, and hospitals. Private exports and imports were forbidden. The mixed economy and shrinking state sector of the post-independent period was replaced with a state-controlled economy, with the military aiming to keep complete control and reduce foreign influence as much as possible. After the coup, another 300,000 Indians and 100,000 Chinese left the country (Brown 2013: 135–136).[17] Civil servants were replaced or had to rotate, to discourage loyalties towards other groups than the military. Thus, administration and political decision-making became highly centralized and ineffective (Myat Thein 2004: 63). The country became known for various human rights violations, including high numbers of political prisoners and child soldiers, large-scale forced labour, and war crimes against minorities. Very few foreign governments maintained diplomatic relationships with Burma. Unlike in many other socialist states, the major religion of the country remained strongly visible. Initially, General Ne Win had withdrawn support for Buddhist institutions and disrobed monks opposing the system. However, when the rulers noticed a growing closeness between the sangha and the laity (e.g. a rise in lay people joining monasteries to meditate), they increasingly promoted and supported a conservative scriptural Buddhism again, while nevertheless keeping strong control over the sangha to prevent charismatic religious leaders from asserting political influence (Jordt 2003: 68; Schober 2011: 82–84). Orthodoxy came to be emphasized, while esoteric congregations and spirit worship were depicted as inferior to scriptural Buddhism, or even as a threat (Foxeus 2017a: 224).

Economically, the regime's new policies led to the stagnation of the formal economy soon after their implementation. Agriculture continued to

---

[17] Those who remained lost their businesses and were often forced to start from scratch, facing further discrimination through citizenship laws that prevented them (and their children) from entering certain institutions of higher education or taking jobs in the public sector (Mya Than 1997: 119; Brown 2013: 135–136).

be the most important sector in terms of employment and exports. It now consisted mainly of small family farms, in which cultivators were forced to grow a certain type of crop and to sell fixed amounts of rice to the government for much less than the open-market rate (Myat Myat Thein 2004: 91). The state procurement and rationing system and the strict regulations regarding cultivation, combined with the state's isolationist policies, constrained the agricultural sector and led to a decline in official rice exports. However, the rationing system ensured a relatively sufficient supply of rice for large parts of the population (Okamoto 2009: 225). Besides the country's influential elite, the majority of the population was not affected by large economic disparities. Reportedly, landless agricultural labourers had almost the same income as small and medium farmers (Fujita 2009: 264).

On the macro-level, Burma had to rely on the increased production of metallic minerals and gemstones to supplement export earnings because it had begun to import oil (Myat Thein 2004: 102). State-owned enterprises were run inefficiently, suffered from underutilization, and did not create enough employment opportunities. The industrial sector remained under-developed (Tin Maung Maung Than 2007: 253). New industries were barely established and existing ones not maintained, so there was little revenue with which the state could compensate for the lack of foreign exchange. The electricity and communications sector had been nationalized, neither being properly maintained or further developed, while the nationalized mono-bank sector failed to reach the majority of the population (Myat Thein 2004: 63, 102–108). To compensate for budget deficits the government printed money, which increased inflation.

A period of public unrest in the mid-1970s prompted the government to make some changes (Tin Maung Maung Than 2004: 162). The newly formed Burma Socialist Programme Party, still dominated by the military under General Ne Win, raised procurement prices for crops and allowed private investment in several industries. The most influential change, however, was that the regime started to accept official development assistance from foreign nations, a lot of which came from Japan. With these foreign loans and aid new businesses were set up, most of them small in size. However, these new small enterprises had to compete with illegal imports from neighbouring countries (Tin Maung Maung Than 2007: 260, 265). These illegal imports were part of the massive informal trade that had emerged and that, according to some estimates, was sometimes two to three times the official trade. This informal trade benefited not only ordinary people but also insurgents in the border areas[18] (Myat Thein 2004: 77). The black market was largely tolerated since it compensated crucially for the shortage of consumer goods, in fact becoming 'the economic lifeline for the military élite and simple folk alike' (Myat Thein 2004: 80).[19] At the end of the Ne Win era, the black market price was twenty-two and twenty-eight times the official price in Yangon and Mandalay respectively (IMF 1988: 14, as cited in Tin Maung Maung Than 2007: 280).

While the infusion of foreign aid and loans brought about a brief relaxation of the economic situation, it did not solve its core problems. Foreign assistance had resulted in growing debts for the state, and GDP fell again. From the mid-1980s Myanmar's economy ultimately fell apart, and by 1987 the country was almost bankrupt (Brown 2013: 154). This forced the government to seek 'least developed country' status from the UN lending agencies (Turnell 2009: 223). While the elite enjoyed access to scarce resources and privileges, the ordinary population, suffering from economic hardship and political oppression, became increasingly dissatisfied and desperate. Many thousands had left the country to seek work elsewhere, mostly in Thailand or Malaysia (Tin Maung Maung Than 2007: 236). The government tried to regain control of the situation by cutting down on imports and public spending and by printing money. Exploding inflation led the leaders to demonetize the *kyat* in 1985 and again in 1987 as another attempt finally to target the informal sector. The informal trade was indeed hit hard by these measures, but so were ordinary people. The year 1988 brought with it a political uprising that eventually put an end to the Ne Win regime (Turnell 2009: 252–255). Protesters were met with harsh violence, with thousands losing their lives and even more being sent to long years of imprisonment and torture (Fink 2009: 52). After the protests, elections were announced and carried out in 1990, which the opposition party (the National League for Democracy, the party of Aung San Suu Kyi) won. However, the army, now under new leadership, refused to hand over power. Opposition leaders were arrested, and General Than Shwe took control.

---

[18] Tannenbaum and Durrenberger give a rare account of the activities in the infamous golden triangle region, which they interpret as a consequence of the 'Burmese way to Socialism' (Tannenbaum and Durrenberger 1990: 283).

[19] It has been widely assumed that state officials kept close ties to illegal businesses involved in gem stones, and perhaps also opium- and drug-smuggling. They provided remuneration, and even financed official events and activities, leading to the emergence of a rent-seeking economic regime that served the interests of the influential actors (Tin Maung Maung Than 2007: 225–226). Many authors suspected that huge amounts of money raised through illegal activities such as drug-smuggling were being channelled into the formal economy through money-laundering (see, for example, Lintner 2000; Chin 2009: 225–228; Turnell 2009).

1990 until Today: From Early Market Liberalization to Recent Attempts at Democratization

In the aftermath of the 1988 uprising, the military renamed its party the 'State Law and Order Restoration Council' (SLORC)[20] and the country became 'Myanmar'.[21] While remaining politically oppressive, the rulers abolished the 'Burmese Way to Socialism' and turned towards a market-led economy. The agricultural sector was reformed and the private sector expanded. A new law encouraged foreign investment, and private banks reopened (Turnell 2009: 258). Imports and exports were largely privatized, with the exception of rice exports, which the government continued to control tightly, together with the price of rice (which was kept stable at about half of the free market rate), out of a fear that an increase would hit the population dramatically, especially landless labourers in rural areas. In 2017 this group was still estimated to account for up to fifty percent of the rural population (USAID 2017). The high number of landless rural households constituted a major difference between Myanmar and China or Vietnam, where liberalized rice exports and the development of rural industries propelled economic growth (Fujita et al. 2009: 6–10).

The illegal border trade was partly regulated, and official import and export activities increased greatly, bringing new goods into the country, as did the number of registered small businesses. In contrast to most existing small and medium enterprises, which were resource-based and often linked to food production and processing, many of the new enterprises concentrated on plastic products, electrical products, and construction materials (Myat Thein 2004: 203). The new business owners had accumulated their capital either domestically or while working abroad, and some were eligible for loans from the newly opened private banks. Among these business people were also many ethnic Chinese who had either remained in the country throughout the socialist period or who had come after 1988 to set up businesses of all sizes. In addition, more and more state-owned enterprises were privatized, and by 1999 the private sector's share of GDP was already 76 percent. As a result of economic growth, Myanmar's physical appearance changed especially in the big urban centres, where supermarkets, high-rise hotels, and apartment blocks appeared.

---

[20] In 1997, the SLORC changed its name to State Peace and Development Council (SPDC).

[21] There is no real difference in meaning. In the country's language, 'Myanmar' is the written, literary name of the country, while 'Bama' used to be the spoken name of the country. Nowadays, 'Myanmar' is also used a great deal in the spoken language. Both names refer to the majority group of people, the *Bamar* (Burmans).

However, the economy remained largely based on the primary sector (agriculture and forestry), which contributed most to GDP and employed most of the labour force. Economic growth was also hindered by a failure to modernize state-owned enterprises, (which in 1998 employed 1.5 percent of the total working population, but were responsible for 20 percent of GPD; see Fujita et al. 2009: 12), a lack of foreign exchange, and heavy Western sanctions that strongly affected the garment sector (Fujita et al. 2009: 4). Therefore, Myanmar's economy has remained far behind that of most other countries in the region. Trade and investment ties remained or were strengthened with China, Thailand, India, Singapore, and South Korea. In the financial sphere, the US dollar became a widely used currency, mainly because of inflation and the unrealistic official exchange rate. The currency was floated only in 2012, which ended the double exchange rate system. The banking sector had been hit hard by a crisis in 2003, and even since its recovery it has not managed to cover a large proportion of the population (Turnell 2009: 218). Most small enterprises relied on self-financing or loans from family, friends or moneylenders, and for many this is still the case today.[22]

All the reforms introduced after 1988 were a necessary tool for the government to ensure their control over the country. They often tied business opportunities to political loyalty, which resulted in the emergence of a business elite (parts of which had gained wealth through the gemstone, drugs, opium, and weapons trades), with close ties to the generals. A large part of the country's economy, including banks, airlines, hotels, and big companies, were, and partly still are, in the hands of a few government-allied families. Myanmar was said to be suffering from a 'resource curse', that is, resource revenues foster corruption and undermined democratic developments, thus allowing the government to neglect the needs of its citizens (Turnell 2014: 210). In 2005, the government introduced Nay Pyi Taw in central Myanmar as the new capital of the country, replacing Yangon.

---

[22] In 2015 it was estimated that no more than about ten percent of the population had a bank account, and very few have access to formal lending. In addition, it was estimated that less than three percent of Myanmar's population had access to any type of formal insurance (Turnell 2017: 125). Even those who have bank accounts often use banks only for storing money, not for investments or other financial services. In many areas of the country, banks are simply difficult to reach for people. Other reasons are that the bureaucratic procedures appear complicated or that people simply do not see the need for bank accounts. Banks also demand collateral (e.g. land) for loans, which most people cannot provide. Moreover, there seems to be a profound mistrust of banks, perhaps partly due to the issuing of several different denominations in the country's history and periods of large inflation (USAID 2014).

While the overall economy grew, the new economic course had considerably increased the stratification of wealth in both rural and urban areas. Despite the government's control over rice prices and exports, which was only eased from 2003 onwards, rice prices went up in the 1990s. This, in combination with the abandonment of the rice-rationing system for the general population, inflation, shorter hiring periods for rural labourers, and a change from in-kind (rice) to cash payments during the harvest season, led to the expansion of overall poverty among the landless rural population in the 1990s. Workers experienced falling wages, accompanied by other problems such as rising indebtedness (Fujita 2009: 257, 263). At the same time, prices for paddy land had gone up roughly a hundred-fold during the first ten years after the change alone, making it more difficult for landless people to purchase land, while those who owned land benefited disproportionally. As a result, economic disparities increased considerably between landless labourers and farmers (Fujita 2009: 256, 264). However, farmers too, especially smallholders, struggled increasingly with indebtedness due to fluctuating rice prices, inflation, unstable exchange rates, and their vulnerability to weather and climate-related difficulties, putting many at risk of losing their land (Dapice et al. 2011).

These challenges recall other 'transition' contexts, even though Myanmar has not experienced a 'transition shock' in the same way as countries in the post-Soviet region did. The economic changes in the early 1990s were far-reaching in some regards, but they remained constrained by certain policies of the government (such as control over rice exports) and other factors, like internal structural weaknesses and Western sanctions. Like the cases of Vietnam and China, the economic changes were not accompanied by a fundamental policy change. Moreover, while policies like the general rice-rationing system were abandoned after 1990 and general economic disparities grew, there was no systematic dismantling of structural social safety nets as in postsocialist contexts of eastern Europe and Central Asia – such benefits had not been available to most of the Burmese population in the first place. A social security board established in 1954 was technically meant to include all employees of public and private firms with more than five workers. This contributory scheme was supposed to provide medical care and support in cases of sickness, maternity/paternity, death (funeral grants), and work injury, but not pensions. In reality, the scheme only covered a tiny fraction of the population (for instance, 365,000 persons in 1975; see Tin Maung Maung Than 2007: 282). In 2015 only an estimated three percent of the whole population, including both public- and private-sector employees, were covered by a state social security system, and this coverage was often rather insufficient (Dutta et al. 2015: 31–32).

Politically, the military continued to suppress all attempts at political opposition. The National League for Democracy was banned and its leader Aung San Suu Kyi put under house arrest, where she would remain for sixteen years. The educational curriculum was marked by the regime's propaganda, and the war against ethnic minorities continued. With regard to religion, the new military junta established an 'autocratic state Buddhism and the promotion of Buddhism as a source of authority and legitimacy' (Foxeus 2017a: 216). By taking part in public Buddhist ceremonies, the military leaders presented their own rule as being in the tradition of the Burmese kings. Succession ceremonies in leadership within the military were performed with symbolic references to Buddhist coronation ceremonies (Jordt 2003: 68). Buddhist pagodas were renovated or newly constructed, courses on Buddhism were given throughout the country, and the extent of lay devotion increased. However, parts of the sangha became active in the political resistance movement, for example, by supporting opposition leader Aung San Suu Kyi and her party from the late 1980s onwards. Monks also played an important role in the protests of 2007 that later came to be called the 'Saffron Revolution'.

Political events after 2011 propelled the speed of change enormously. In March the military government was replaced by a new civilian government, and the country's new president, Thein Sein, implemented a range of reforms pointing toward democratization. Changes included the relaxation of press restrictions and the release of child soldiers and political prisoners. In response, the EU and the USA lifted economic sanctions, and many countries have re-established diplomatic ties with Myanmar.

Recent years have made certain dividing lines visible in the sangha, namely those between groups of monks such as the MaBaTha ('Organization for the Protection of Race and Religion'), whose members have openly spread nationalist and anti-Muslim sentiments, those who oppose them, and those who maintain that monks should not become involved in politics at all. Myanmar has seen a number of violent attacks against Muslims in different parts of the country, first and foremost in Rakhine state, on the border with Bangladesh, where clashes were followed by a military campaign against the Muslim Rohingya in 2017, prompting hundreds of thousands to flee over the border. The hate speech associated with anti-Muslim sentiment was partly propagated by monks through public talks and social media. It was phrased with reference to Buddhism and the preservation of the *sāsana*[23] (Walton and Hayward 2014). Even though only 2.3 percent of the population identify

---

[23] *Sāsana* refers to the entirety of the Buddha's teachings and instructions, practices and practitioners, 'that is "Buddhism" as a social fact' (Foxeus 2017a: 213).

as Muslims according to the 2014 census[24], fears were spread of the impending Islamization of the country. While these radical monks do not represent the majority of the sangha, their attitudes resonate with quite considerable parts of the Burmese population. Laidlaw (2017) remarked that ethical reflection intensifies in some moments, not only in the individual but also within society (p. 184). While Islamophobia is certainly not a new phenomenon in Myanmar, its increasing spread (or growing public propagation) seems to be partly linked to the massive political and economic changes of recent years. Within these changes, minorities such as Muslims and Chinese have become scapegoats, for example, in media discourses, for new or intensifying problems of poverty or inequality (Prasse-Freeman and Phyo Win Latt 2018: 412). The new government has been a target of strong criticism from the outside world, primarily due to the conflict in Rakhine state and the persecution of the Rohingya. Many other border areas too are seeing ongoing conflicts, with the emergence of nationalism afresh and, in some areas, communal violence in different regions of the country.[25] Moreover, journalists, students, and activists have been detained for protesting on several occasions.

Economically, the reforms after 2011 constituted a new wave of liberalization. Several new laws were implemented addressing core issues like land rights and foreign investment. The rice trade was fully liberalized, and farmers were granted a free choice of what crops to grow. The exchange rate system was unified, the state monopoly on insurance was ended, and microfinance organizations were given official status. Several such organizations have since started to hand out loans in rural and urban areas. The country has also seen a range of new business initiatives, an increase in foreign direct investment (FDI), mostly from China, especially in the fields of gas and oil, mining, and hydropower, and manufacturing. Other consequences were a growing service sector, urbanization, especially in Yangon, an increase in foreign aid, and the mushrooming of development projects. Many factories and smaller firms have been privatized since 2011. VISA, Master Card and Western Union came in 2012, and various new private banks have been established and are continually opening new branches in the country's cities.

The land and real estate sector, as well as the technology sector, present perhaps the clearest indications of change. Smartphones have flooded the market, with some sources reporting that the nation's mobile-phone usage rate has gone up from 10 percent to above 80 percent in just

---

[24] However, the government had excluded several hundreds of thousands Muslim Rohingya from the census as it does not recognize them as citizens (Heijmans 2014; Ferguson 2015).
[25] See Walton and Hayward (2014).

two years, from 2014 to 2016 (Matsui 2016). Low mobile use prior to 2014 was due to government-set SIM-card prices, which in 2009 still amounted to 2000 USD. Prices have fallen since then, with cheap SIM cards at around 1,500 kyat (ca. 1.08 EUR)[26] now being available for almost everyone. Inflation was still a problem, and the cost of living went up. The explosion of real-estate prices in downtown Yangon has resulted in rents at times higher than in Manhattan or the city centre of Singapore, though they have fallen again since then. With new farmland regulations in 2012, tillage rights to farmland became closer to property rights in the sense that they could now be legally sold, mortgaged, leased, exchanged, donated or inherited. Polanyi has called land a 'fictitious commodity' (2001: 71–80), and as elsewhere, the commodification of farmland in Myanmar has led to a dramatic increase in land prices and large-scale speculation in farmland, as well as in urban land (Franco et al. 2015, see also Polanyi 2001 [1944]; Okamoto 2018: 195, 198). Various protests over land-grabbing by the government or private companies erupted after 2012 (Okamoto 2018: 197). In contrast to the developments that Polanyi observed, however, in the case of Myanmar there are very few industrial jobs capable of absorbing the dispossessed (Prasse-Freeman and Phyo Win Latt 2018: 411).

While during socialism those who were not in the political elite were rather 'equal in their poverty' (Prasse-Freeman and Phyo Win Latt 2018: 404), Myanmar has become a country of significantly growing wealth stratification and economic disparities since the 1990s, the pace increasing with the changes after 2011.

The 2014 census offered some important insights into the working population, revealing that 4.8 percent of respondents among the total working population defined themselves as employers, while 32.9 percent said they were private-sector employees, 6.0 percent were government employees, and 38.8 percent replied that they were 'own account workers', making this the largest group. The latter category covers people pursuing their own one-person business ventures, for instance, market traders and street vendors, and small shops and stalls that do not have employees (Myanmar Department of Population 2017a: 40). What is particularly relevant for this book is the role of small businesses. According to a large survey from 2015, businesses with fewer than ten workers made up around 86 percent in the services and manufacturing sectors, while businesses with 10–19 workers accounted for 10 percent and 8 percent in these sectors respectively. Businesses with 20–49 workers made up only 3 percent and 4

---

[26] I use an average conversion rate calculated from the daily conversion rates during my main research period from August 2015 to August 2016. This average rate is 1,377 Kyat for 1 EUR.

percent respectively, and those with 50 or more workers made up only 2 percent in both sectors. In the resale/trade sector, 92 percent of businesses had fewer than 10 workers, 6 percent had 10–19 workers and 2 percent had 20–49 workers (UNDP and CSO 2015: 12). Such data show that larger businesses with fifty or more workers constituted only a tiny fraction of the country's overall economy and underline the importance of studying small businesses upon which many people rely for their livelihoods.

Also in 2015, in August, the German Institute for Development Evaluation (DEval) published the results of a large 'small and medium enterprise survey' (2015). Around 2,500 businesses were surveyed in eleven cities, including Pathein. The survey sheds some light on the importance of informal networks as well as on challenges business owners encounter. Main findings show that most of the businesses were micro-sized (67 percent) or small (31 percent). Twenty-one percent of the firms were unregistered, thus defining them as belonging to the informal sector. Most of the firms surveyed have been operating for ten years or more. Most were not located in specific Industrial Zones (IZs), and their main revenue came from the local market. Further interesting findings are that around half of the business owners regularly interact with banks, but only for day-to-day tasks, like current accounts and money transfers. The majority of respondents stated that they do not really see a need for banks. Around 20 percent of the surveyed firms had an outstanding loan, for which friends, relatives, and customers were listed as the main sources. Personal acquaintances were also the main way to recruit employees (DEval 2015). The surveyed business owners listed a number of major obstacles: a lack of skilled labour, high labour turnover, political instability, and the prices of raw materials. Many business owners also complained about the unsatisfactory electricity supply, as blackouts are common in Myanmar, even in the cities.

The survey indicates how important informal financial and employment strategies are for small businesses. A large number of people in Myanmar have never had any contact with written work contracts, bank accounts or a formally institutionalized social support system. The findings presented by DEval show similarities to a number of other large-scale enterprise studies in Myanmar (for example, Abe and Molnar 2014; UNDP and CSO 2015; World Bank 2016). Such results point to a range of key features in Myanmar's current business landscape, including the overall dominance of micro and small businesses, the importance of informal procedures in business matters, and the challenge of a high labour turnover. While surveys can detect the magnitude of such factors, they are not able to explain the underlying social and moral aspects that contribute to them. Anthropological inquiries can help fill this gap.

On Informal Economies and Civil Societies

Many of the activities explored in this book happen in what can be called the 'informal economy'. Moreover, those patterns described in Chapter 6 could also count as a part of 'civil society'. Both concepts are complex and problematic in themselves. I will take a closer look at them, beginning with the informal economy. It was the anthropologist Keith Hart (1973, 1985) who crucially contributed to the development of this concept. Initially, he meant all economic practices that are invisible to the bureaucratic gaze, with particular reference to the labour of city-dwellers in Ghana, pointing out that those of them who do not appear in government statistics were not necessarily unemployed. In fact, most were not. The informal economy was later used to refer to all those activities that are not supervised by the state and not regulated by official laws. However, it is important to point out that informality is not the same as illegality. While many practices that happen within the informal sector may be illegal under the laws of the country where they take place, this is not necessarily the case. The differentiation between the formal and the informal sectors, which constitute each other, is greatly based on the understanding of the nation state in the Weberian sense – there can only be informality where formality has been constructed. What is 'in' and 'out' of the formal economy depends on what governments choose to or are able to measure (Tannenbaum and Durrenberger 1990: 282).

The informal sector became large and crucial, especially in cases when formalized, regulated and planned systems were unable to satisfy social requirements (Lomnitz 1988: 42–55). This was the case in Myanmar as well, where '(…) to ignore the "informal" because it is not recognized by government ideology and rhetoric, is to ignore most of the economic system' (Tannenbaum and Durrenberger 1990: 296). However, in Myanmar informal practices are just as widespread today, almost thirty years after a market-led course was introduced. It can be expected that both sectors will continue to coexist, with the boundaries between them remaining blurred (on Vietnam, see Lainez 2014). For instance, we have seen in other postsocialist contexts, as elsewhere, that interpersonal relationships and the 'informal' arrangements that can come with them, continued to play a key role in economic processes. Simplified labels such as 'corruption' or 'nepotism' do not grasp the complexities of such relations, but disregard the role of values, ethics, and morality (see Humphrey 2002; Mandel and Humphrey 2002; Morris and Polese 2014; Henig and Makovicky 2016).

The informal economy should be situated in relation not just to the nation state, but also to the market. Since the 1970s, when the term 'informal economy' was coined for activities that are unregulated by the government, the market gained ever more influence, while the role of nation states in controlling it has weakened. The informal sector did not disappear: on the contrary, in many contexts it expanded and became more competitive. Those who migrated from rural to urban areas in development contexts often relied on an urban informal sector to make a living, and formally employed people also supplemented their incomes increasingly from informal activities. The informal economy must thus be acknowledged as an inherent part of all market economies (Hart 2005). Nevertheless, economic analyses, while they may acknowledging its importance, often continue to treat the informal sector as a sort of 'black box' whose internal workings cannot be grasped. Practices in the informal sector are socio-culturally embedded, quite possibly functioning in a logic that is different from economic rationality or state ideology. To understand them, as to understand the entire economy, one needs to grasp the functioning of social bonds, hierarchies, and values. More than that, in practice the formal and informal sectors are interlinked and cannot be understood as separate spheres (Hart 2005). For instance, government officials may participate in informal economic activities. Similarly, a business owner might have a license to run the shop but nevertheless recruits and employs most of his workers on an informal basis. Thus, when studying processes on the ground, the distinction between informal and formal economic activities might matter in some regards while in others appearing rather artificial, with no real relevance for people's actual activities.

In both the formal and informal sectors, economic processes remain embedded in social relations and moral frameworks. Periods of intensifying economic change will not simply bring about the replacement of existing patterns in Myanmar. Rather, these will be negotiated, adapted, and altered with regard to newly emerging patterns. Dialectical tensions will remain, between community and market, the formal and informal, the old and the new (Gudeman 2001, 2008, 2009). Communities can (but do not necessarily have to) take the shape of small on-the-ground associations, solidarity groups that share specific interests and functions through trust, mutuality, and interpersonal relations. Mutuality within communities may be constructed through shared language, rituals, speech codes, and practices, as well as norms, laws, and other social agreements (Gudeman 2008: 27). Such communities offer a degree of security, certainty, and predictability. They can overlap or be embedded within one another. Markets, in contrast, are shaped by short-term exchanges. Both realms are present in people's lives side by side, and even though they may function internally in different ways, they are interlinked (Gudeman 2008: 95–123). All economic practices are situated in value contexts, and no market system works without relationships, mutual understanding, and communication. Conversely, within communities there are also markets. Market expansion can change community values, but community values can also influence market dynamics, such as innovations. Understanding the economy in this way is a suitable approach to studying both formal and informal activities as overlapping processes, as well as the role that the market and the state play in both.

As far as the state is concerned, the reader might notice that it does not feature prominently in the following chapters. Often, however, it is present in the background. For instance, it matters to business owners in Myanmar not only because they have to interact with the state for licenses and taxes, but also as a potential alternative employer for themselves or their children. With attractive and respected private-sector employment still rare in Pathein, state jobs remain the goal in many people's aspirations. State employment might provide only a relatively low income, but it comes with stability and benefits and sometimes (in the higher levels) useful connections, as well as some degree of prestige. Moreover, the state is also a concern insofar, as many business owners have an underlying fear of unfavourable policy changes, or even that their businesses or land could be confiscated. Furthermore, the state plays an indirect role precisely because of its absence. Community-based social protection mechanisms, moneylenders, saving groups, and wealth redistribution through donations are crucial social support arrangements for many people where the state fails to provide any sort of protection or support.

Scholars who adopt a state-centred approach may define such activities as part of 'civil society' (on Myanmar see Lorch 2006, 2007; South 2008; Prasse-Freeman 2012). The international community took notice of Myanmar in 2007, when thousands of students and monks marched through the streets of Yangon in what was called the 'Saffron Revolution', a powerful public outburst of political opposition which the government responded to with brutal oppression. The year after, in May 2008, Cyclone 'Nargis' hit the country, leaving more than 140,000 people dead, not least because the government prevented all international aid from entering the country for more than a month (Fink 2009: 108). However, people on the ground organized a quite impressive response in providing food, shelter, and medical aid to the survivors, despite their limited resources (Jaquet and Walton 2013). This sheds light on the fact that the people of Myanmar had developed patterns and strategies of mutual help outside the sphere of the state, proving that such activities can occur despite, or even perhaps because of, an oppressive regime. However, there are indications that organized social support has increased since the 1990s, when earning a livelihood became a more challenging task for parts of the population, and when at the same time non-state organizations began to experience less oppression from the government (McCarthy 2016: 315–16). Such support activities can include livelihood-related groups, like savings- and credit groups, free-funeral groups, different charities, educational initiatives, and political activism. Support groups are often linked to religious institutions, and in areas controlled by ethnic minorities they are often connected to the political organizations that are active in these regions (South 2008). The government had tolerated many instances of welfare provision by non-government actors, as the state itself was not able, or not willing, to provide even minimal welfare to most of its population, preferring instead to spend large shares of its budget on the military.

The usefulness of the concept of 'civil society' for anthropological analysis has been questioned (Hann and Dunn 1996). Analyses of 'civil society' often focus on its political role, on a realm that gives room to an 'emerging politics of the daily' (Prasse-Freeman 2012: 387). Are all such activities inherently political, though? Some observers might answer yes, but I am primarily concerned here with livelihood management, and thus with 'the economics of the daily'. While the political aspects certainly matter, because political decisions influence people's livelihoods a great deal, I look mainly at the concrete social organization of livelihood and welfare on the ground. While political influences and implications surely feature in the background, they are not always reflected as such by the people themselves. In many cases economic support relations are no different from ordinary social relations, like those circling around kinship, friendship, or work connections. A 'civil society' concept may indeed be suitable for studying macro-level processes, outlining, for example, the role of non-state actors in promoting developments in democracy. On the ground, however, the state is not necessarily needed as 'the other' in order to analyse patterns of social organization, including mutual support and cooperation among people. Like all social relations, such patterns are never fully free of conflicts and tensions. Thus, we must neither idealize mutuality and solidarity, nor under-estimate people's agency, but rather understand social processes as inherently ambivalent and under constant negotiation.

The strength of economic anthropology is its ability to shed light on the many 'black boxes' of most approaches in economics – 'culture', 'informality', 'social relations', 'civil society'. If we stick to these macro-categories, we simply reproduce these black boxes as concepts, and a range of questions will remain unanswered. As we have seen, the business surveys mentioned earlier have shown that most business owners obtained their starting capital from friends and family – but how do the negotiations happen here? Likewise, if most employers recruit people through personal relations and do not use formal contracts, how do they ensure loyalty, and how do they act when conflicts arise? Moreover, we can see that the extent of child labour has increased, but what relationships exist between the families, the children, and the employers? What social obligations, restrictions, and responsibilities are at play? And also, if the state does not provide social protection to most people, how do communities manage situations of adversity? How is indebtedness dealt with, and how is it morally judged?

The following chapters will address these questions, among others. In doing so, I will pay specific attention to values and moral considerations. In the introduction I suggested that, like all human action, economic activities and ideas are influenced by values, ethics, and norms. I further stated that, in this context, Buddhism provides a moral framework for many people, which is deployed to make sense of the world and of activities, one's own and those of others. Before moving on to the ethnographic part of this work, therefore, I will outline key Theravāda concepts and their economic implications in the following chapter.

Chapter 3
A Moral Framework: Key Concepts of Theravāda Buddhism

Morality is 'intrinsic to social life' (Lambek 2017: 138). The approaches immediately relevant here are those that explore why certain aspects and experiences in life are seen as ethically important and how they shape social processes (see Fassin 2012; Mattingly et al. 2017). When speaking of morality, we need to consider both values and norms (Joas 2000; Durkheim 2010; Terpe 2018). I follow a definition of values as things that are not only desired but also generally seen as *desirable* (Kluckhohn 1962: 395). That is, not only things people want, but ideas about what people *ought* to want. Norms, on the other hand, are rather restrictive, being linked more to duties and obligations.[27]

A number of core components appear frequently in ethnographic (and philosophical) discussions of morality and ethics: virtue, possibility, the ordinary (or immanence), and freedom (Dyring et al. 2017: 11). More precisely, this includes, for instance, individual efforts to be recognized as a person of virtue according to shared assumptions of what such a person should be like. In debates on morality, two general lines of thought have been differentiated. One sees ethics and morality in Durkheimian fashion, mainly in the ordinary or in the everyday, while the other sees morality and ethics precisely in moments of choice and rupture, when conventions cannot easily be followed anymore and instead reflection and conscious decisions are needed (Laidlaw 2002; Zigon 2007). It is possible to take a middle ground here by acknowledging that everyday negotiations in the social world always entail both conventional expectations stemming from collective norms and values, and possibilities for freedom and choice. Every situation comes with its own specifics and challenges that demand moral judgements. While the ethics of the ordinary (for example, conventions and practices

---

[27] See Graeber (2001) for an overview on how anthropologists have studied values, and 'value', starting from the value of objects and the meaning of exchange for social relations.

linked to kinship) give life foundation, continuity, and direction, people everywhere nevertheless negotiate a tension between obligation and freedom or between the expectations of others and one's own individual desires (Lambek 2017). After all, life is not an experience in which everyone subscribes to the same shared values all the time. Rather, individuals may subscribe to different (and sometimes contradictory) values simultaneously (Robbins 2013), and the same goes for norms. People might encounter internal value conflicts, and conflicts over what good moral conduct entails can also occur between groups, or, for example, between generations. Thus, in everyday life, one has to juggle not only one's own different (sometimes competing or even incommensurable) desires, but also the obligations and expectations of others that might or might not contradict one's own wants (Lambek 2017: 139–140). Furthermore, neither values nor norms are static: instead they are subject to change and negotiation, always standing in a dialectical relationship with socio-economic conditions.

The Role of Religion

Religion has been identified as playing a crucial role in matters of morality. It offers criteria with which to judge actions as morally good or bad (Lambek 2017: 149). The realm of the transcendent also comes into play in processes of moral inspiration and value transfer. For instance, the shared values of a group are established and maintained through (religious) rituals, in which people encounter these values in their clearest form. Besides that, key values are often encountered first through exemplary persons who are regarded as successful in fully realizing these values. Values encountered in the sphere of religion, even though people may not realize them fully in their normal activities, still influence their ordinary actions because they remain aware of the general desirability of such values (Humphrey 1997; Robbins 2017: 161).

For Myanmar's Buddhists, the role of providing moral examples often falls to Buddhist monks, the most highly admired members of society, and in particular to monks who are seen as extraordinarily spiritually powerful.[28]

---

[28] In the Pathein region, for instance, one of the most famous monks is *hsayadaw* U Nya Naw, the head monk of the '108-cubit' pagoda. He attracts large crowds of people who worship him and donate considerable sums of money. Many people believe that he is an *arahant*, a Buddhist saint who has reached *nibbāna*[28] (Kawanami 2009). People also say the *hsayadaw* is able to foresee the future and had, for example, predicted 'Nargis', the cyclone of 2008. Some visitors hope that the monk will give hints as to the correct lottery numbers. During the time of my research he had reached old age and was barely able to speak or move on his own. Still, the line of people who came to see him was considerable, day after day. His

Such monks have the ability to draw massive crowds at public *dhamma* talks and regularly receive large financial donations from lay admirers. Monks share moral messages through Buddhist teachings in public sermons or private conversations. The admiration monks receive results from the assumption that they successfully realize specific values such as spiritual purity, wisdom, and detachment to a greater extent than lay people do. The 'example' of the monks reminds the lay person of those values that he himself fails to realize fully in everyday life but nevertheless holds in high regard. Lay followers may aspire to political power and material wealth while at the same time highly admiring and worshipping the Buddhist monk precisely because he disdains and renounces these things, thus displaying morally (in the religious logic) superior behaviour, something that Melford Spiro identified as a tension between worldly and other-worldly values (Spiro 1982: 475).

Concerning economic behaviour in particular, the concept of 'moral economy' did not originally put religion in the foreground and instead focused on class (Thompson 1971; Scott 1976). While class consciousness is without doubt influential in the formation of moral ideas, anthropologists have emphasized the role of Buddhism in constructing a 'moral economy' in Buddhist communities (Keyes 1983a: 865). In Myanmar too, Theravāda Buddhism offers a 'relatively consistent set of beliefs and concepts within which many Buddhists in Myanmar cognitively organize and engage with their social and political worlds' (Walton 2017a: 36). There are certain core ideas, concepts, and practices that are known, shared, and reproduced among most of these believers. These ideas provide a framework for moral considerations, although one that exists alongside several others in people's lives, one that is not exactly the same for everyone, and it is neither static nor totalizing (Walton 2017a: 8). This framework does not suppress individual agency, but if it is a world view which gives meaning to action, then action happens from within this world view (Walton 2017a: 37).

In Myanmar the sheer number of pagodas, monasteries, and monks indicates the importance of Buddhism in those parts of the country that are mainly inhabited by Buddhists. The transfer of knowledge about key Buddhist concepts and moral implications happens through public sermons given by monks, but also through other rituals, through leaflets, popular stories, and maxims like the *jātaka*, the Buddha's birth stories, often also referred to as *nga: ya nga: hse* (which simply means 'five-hundred-fifty', even though the actual number of stories is 547), or the *lokanīti*, a popular

---

power lies in the realm of the supramundane, and his physical weakness does nothing to diminish that.

treatise of old teachings.[29] Myths and stories are also pictured on temple walls and in popular books, and since the arrival of the internet, people share religious content on social media. I am concerned with Buddhism as interpreted and practised by lay people rather than with purely doctrinal Buddhism. Like all value systems, Buddhism is not static but adaptable to changing socio-economic conditions. Understandings of core ideas such as *dāna* (generosity) may broaden or shift in emphasis in the light of changing socio-economic circumstances. Thus, the focus on charitable donations as acts of *dāna* can intensify in times when such donations are urgently needed (see Jaquet and Walton 2013, on Cyclone 'Nargis'). We have to account for the tensions between culturally reproduced world views, with their underlying ontological assumptions, and the social conditions that constrain people's lives, as 'one is not the reflection of the other' (Keyes 1983a: 855). While this book explores how lay Buddhists interpret Buddhism and deploy these interpretations in their daily activities, it seems appropriate to outline here a few core concepts of Theravāda Buddhism, with a specific focus on their possible implications for economic values and action.

Theravāda Cosmology and Key Concepts

Sangha–lay Relationships

Buddhism emerged in India around five centuries BCE, and it came to what is now Myanmar probably at the beginning of the Common Era. To this day, Buddhism has existed under very different political and economic circumstances, including the end of the monarchy, the rise and end of the colonial system, military rule, processes of nation-building and modernization, and recently the expansion of capitalism and first attempts toward democracy. Major political changes clearly had an impact on the way religion was organized, promoted, experienced, and performed within the country (Foxeus 2017a: 212; see also Chapter 2).

The current developments and growing influences from the outside that Myanmar has seen since the political changes of 2011, especially in the big cities, have so far not led to a visible decline of Buddhism. A look at Myanmar's Buddhist neighbour indicates that this should not be surprising: Buddhism flourished in the market-oriented environment of Bangkok a few decades ago, during a phase of growing urbanization and business development. Firms of all kinds sought blessings from monks, and corporations became crucial donors for the sangha (Tambiah 1973: 10). Sangha members throughout history have played an immensely important

---

[29] For a translation of the *lokanīti*, see Gray 2000 [1886].

role in Myanmar society, being materially provided for by the laity, and functioning for them as a 'field of merit' (meaning they provide laypeople with the opportunity to gain merit by accepting their donations), as teachers, and as moral examples. Ideally every male Burmese should join the sangha at least once in his life, and many young boys become part of the sangha as novices, through the important ceremony of novitation (Burmese *shin pju.*). Joining the sangha can sometimes be an opportunity to receive an education and achieve upward mobility, especially for rural boys from poorer backgrounds. Men can live as monks however long they want, from a few days to a lifetime. Men and women also spend time in monasteries as lay meditators, and a number of women join monasteries as nuns (Burmese *thi-la. shin*). Their status is much lower than that of monks, and they cannot become fully ordained because full ordination is not possible for women in Myanmar, unlike in Sri Lanka (see Kawanami 2013, on nuns in Myanmar; and Falk 2008, on Thailand). It is safe to say that today's sangha is a fragmented group in terms of organization (it is organized into nine official main sects), as well as in respect of activities and perceptions, for example, concerning the extent to which they engage in political affairs or social welfare. Most monks are linked to a monastery, but there are also many who act individually outside the monasteries: some concentrate on meditation, some run welfare projects, and others act as astrologers or offer other spiritual services. The state maintains an interest in controlling the monks and their involvement in political processes (see Crouch 2015: 7–8, on relevant laws).

Theravāda Cosmology

The cosmology of the Pāli canon includes a range of beings. Humans, animals, gods, ghosts, and spirits are part of a cycle of endless rebirths, which can only be 'exited' by reaching *nibbāna* (Burmese *neikban*). The cosmos has a distinctively hierarchical arrangement. The universe is thought to be made up of thirty-one planes of existence (*loka*), of which only eleven are defined with reference to perception through the five senses. Of these, the four lowest planes include those of demons, ghosts, animals, and hells. The plane of hells alone consists of many different hot and cold *narakas* (hells). Unlike in Christianity, one is not sent to the realms of hell by a superior god as a punishment, but is instead reborn there as a result of one's own *kamma*. The period of staying in a realm of hell before a new rebirth is thought to be very long, measured in millions of years. Above those four low planes marked by suffering comes the plane of men, marked by a specific balance of pleasure and suffering. It is assumed that existence in one realm is temporary, so that beings can eventually leave their current realm through rebirth. Rebirth into a better state demands the accumulation of good *kamma*, which is a privilege of humans alone. According to the *sutta*s, rebirth as a human being is not only extraordinarily rare but also special in so far as humans possess the wisdom and ability to act on their *kamma*, making the human the 'fundamental acting agent' (Tambiah 1970: 40) in this cosmos. Those in higher planes cannot lose their status anymore through bad *kamma*. And those in the planes below cannot generate merit on their own but rely on humans to share their merit with them and help them escape their suffering.[30] This indicates interconnectedness and one's responsibility for others, both in the human realm and beyond. Above the plane of men are six planes mostly marked by delight and bliss, which contain realms for the *deva* (gods), including some gods more usually worshipped in Hinduism. Above these six planes come another sixteen planes of form without sensual enjoyment, and above that there are four heavens with no form at all (Harvey 2013: 33–37).

The Three Gems and Moral Action

It may be less this cosmological order in its totality that is relevant for moral ideas of Buddhists today than some of its more widely known key components, such as *kamma*, the Four Noble Truths, the ten *pāramitā* (including *dāna* and *mettā*), and the Noble Eightfold Path. These concepts are among the most prominent ideas in the doctrine, and I have encountered them in Pathein as ideas that people know and to some extent see as guidelines for their actions and decisions. Buddhists in Myanmar usually have shrines in their houses, where many place daily offerings. In the morning, believers turn to the altar and recite Pāli verses to 'take refuge' in the 'three gems' of Buddhism: the Buddha, the *dhamma* (the Buddhist teachings), and the sangha (the community of monks). This act is meant as a daily reminder of the nature of things and one's own responsibility for their course. It may also be a moment for expressing gratitude for the sangha or the wish to remain protected from evil (Walton 2017a: 38). Some people commit themselves specifically to abstain from harmful and immoral actions by taking the 'five precepts', which are: 1. to abstain from the taking of life, 2. to abstain from taking what is not given, 3. to abstain from sexual mis-conduct, 4. to abstain from lying, and 5. to abstain from taking intoxicants. Breaking these rules is believed to create demerit. Monks, nuns, and occa-sionally lay meditators take more precepts than those listed above. Sangha members are also supposed to follow the *vinaya*, the monastic code of

---

[30] For instance, people who encounter a ghostlike being might react frightened at first, but later they sometimes go to the pagoda to perform rituals and pray for this being, assuming that it has shown itself in order to ask for help, as it is 'trapped' in its cosmic position.

conduct. The precepts, like other practices which have the aim of reaching *nibbāna*, are seen as expressions of *sīla* (Burmese *thi-la.*) which translates as 'morality', emphasizing actual moral practice, rather than mere thought or understanding (Walton 2017a: 46).

To understand how actions are judged, one has to know that in Theravāda Buddhism there is a fundamental distinction between what could be called the mundane realm and the supramundane realm.[31] The former, in Pāli known as *lokiya* (Burmese *law:ki*), consists of all physical and mental perception and all material things. In contrast, *lokuttara* (Burmese *law:kou'tara*) consists of all actions only devoted to attaining *nibbāna*. Actions in both of these realms have to be adequately balanced. Some actions might be forbidden in the realm of *lokuttara*, but they cannot be avoided in the realm of *lokiya*, where they do not in all circumstances pose a moral problem (e.g. dealing with money or the killing of animals; see Spiro 1982: 450).

The Four Noble Truths and the Noble Eightfold Path

According to Buddhist doctrine, all existence is marked by three characteristics: *anicca* (impermanence), *dhukka* (suffering/ unsatisfactoriness), and *anatta* (no-self). *Anicca* refers to the idea that all things are impermanent and will ultimately cease to exist. *Anatta*, the notion of no-self, has also been translated as 'no ownership of the self' or 'no control' over what we perceive as the self. The third element, *dhukka* (suffering), results from people's ignorance of the other two: because we do not accept that everything will cease to exist and that we have no control over our self or over anything else, life consists of permanent suffering or 'unsatisfactoriness' (Walton 2017a: 41–42). Respectively, the things commonly listed as the 'three poisons' or 'three defilements' are greed, hatred, and ignorance, all of which are morally condemned. To convey the nature of things and the way out of suffering, the Buddha established the Four Noble Truths. The first of these Truths states that all life is suffering. The second one states that the cause for this suffering is craving, for pleasure, for material possessions, and 'for the continuation of life itself' (Walton 2017a: 43). The third Noble Truth is that suffering will end when cravings end, thus pointing to the possibility of overcoming suffering. The fourth Noble Truth

---

[31] Walton notes that this description is not entirely correct. *Lokuttara* is difficult to translate, or to describe for that matter. It can be understood as a method of perception that is consistent with the Buddhist ideas of right view and right understanding (seeing the true nature of things). It can also refer to the path toward this insight or understanding (2017: 54–56).

states that the way to overcome suffering lies in the Noble Eightfold Path. The latter consists of

1. Right view (or 'right understanding')
2. Right intention (or 'right thought')
3. Right speech
4. Right action
5. Right livelihood[32]
6. Right effort
7. Right mindfulness
8. Right concentration

The Noble Eightfold Path outlines eight important aspects of correct practice that lead one to attaining *nibbāna. Nibbāna*, the ultimate doctrinal goal of Buddhist practice, constitutes a state of complete detachment and an exit from the cycle of rebirths (*saṃsāra*). In practice *nibbāna* is not actually seen as a desired aim for most people, including monks (Walton 2017a: 44). Spiro stated that 'the average Burmese villager [...] desires, rather, to remain in the wheel of life and to experience pleasure, luxury, and enjoyment' (Spiro 1966: 1169). Moreover, people's 'very notion of salvation consists in being reborn as a wealthy male, with the means to satisfy his desire for worldly pleasures, or even better as a *deva*, for whom these pleasures are both greater and of longer duration' (Spiro 1982: 460). *Nibbāna* remains an abstract ideal for most, even though those who actively attempt to attain it are highly admired, and the teachings surrounding this aim lay down a general moral conduct for leading a life of virtue. People's concern with a beneficial rebirth brings the notions of *kamma* (Burmese *kan*) and merit (Pāli *kusala*, Burmese *ku.tho*) to the fore.

'Kamma' and Merit

Kamma refers to the Buddhist law of cause and effect that sustains the whole cosmos. According to this law, people's current situation, including its physical, social, and economic aspects, is a result of their *kamma*, which is determined by their actions in past lives. Respectively, one's actions in the present and the merit (*kusala*) one gains from them will influence one's future rebirths. While *kamma* is a theory of causation, the effects of past deeds are not directly foreseeable: they can be manifested quickly or only after billions of years (Bunnag 1973: 21). *Kamma*, for its believers, can be understood as a sort of 'quasi-natural life order' in the Weberian sense. Such life orders are perceived as having a nature-like quality, appearing to be governed by 'uncontrollable forces' (Terpe 2018: 16). It is not uncommon

---

[32] I will address Buddhist teachings on livelihood and wealth below.

for Buddhists to regard their socio-economic situations as resulting at least partly from the *kamma* they were born with into their current lives, and thus as a result of an inescapable law of cause and effect. As such orders cannot be altered, 'one can only live with it and try to make the best of it by acquiescing to its rules' (ibid.).[33] Another parallel with other such 'quasi-natural life orders' is the potential of *kamma* to function as a constraint in questioning or challenging socio-economic conditions and inequalities. Sylvia Terpe refers to Moore's research on German factory workers in 1914 (Moore, 1978) to argue that 'the perception of inevitability is one of the main obstacles against the emergence of a sense of injustice' (Terpe 2018: 15). Moore explained the lack of protests among the workers, despite hardships such as hunger, inadequate shelter, and the like, with reference to a perception of circumstances as inevitable and uncontrollable for the individual. In this case these circumstances were the capitalist economic system governed by market forces, which can equally be perceived as an 'unalterable order of things' (Weber 1992: 19).[34] When circumstances are seen as quasi-natural, they will be endured without sparking moral outrage. In his political writings, Burma's independence hero Aung San criticized the ease with which many Buddhists (rich as well as poor) justified social inequality. He did not question the logic of *kamma* as such, but he felt that most people base their ideas on overly simplified notions of the concept (Walton 2017a: 111).

There are, however, also important differences from the example described by Moore. While the factory workers in his study saw their situation as a result of 'natural' and uncontrollable market forces, Buddhists might understand their situation as an equally unalterable result of *kamma*, for which, however, they were personally responsible. The latter aspect might result in a perception of not only an unavoidable but perhaps even a 'just' or deserved condition. The aspect of deservingness adds a moral dimension that might strengthen the acceptance of adverse circumstances even more. The *kamma* doctrine puts a lot of moral responsibility on the individual, compared to outside forces. In Moore's example, any dimension

---

[33] However, some people believe that good deeds in the present will also make good *kamma* from the past dominate over bad *kamma*, so one can to some extent influence the effects of accumulated merit and demerit from past lives.

[34] There have been a range of protests throughout the country in recent years, for instance, against people's relocation due to big infrastructural projects or against working conditions in garment factories (see, for example, Zaw Zaw Htwe 2018). Such actions surely result from people's perceptions of specific treatments as unjust, which entails a moral assessment of the situation. It must be noted that condemning concrete treatments does not have to stand in contradiction to the belief in *kamma* as a reason for one's general position. Accepting general economic inequality does not mean generally accepting abusive or unjust treatment by others.

of self-responsibility is lacking. However, regardless of their differences, in both cases there remains the perceived inevitability of the natural *order* of things (in Buddhism the law of cause and effect). Like other religious doctrines, *kamma* posits an explanation for the ultimate conditions of human existence and offers 'a resolution to the problem of unequal suffering' (Keyes 1983b: 6). In precisely this context Weber himself described the *kamma* doctrine as representing 'the most consistent theodicy ever produced by history' (1958: 121).

What I have just discussed is a generalized and simplified version of the *kamma* idea. In practice the extent to which people attribute economic differences to *kamma* varies. Often, *kamma* is seen as certainly playing a role, but aspects such as personal failure (e.g. laziness or a lack of discipline), as well as political mismanagement, are considered as well. Also Buddhist doctrine does not see *kammic* inheritance as the only factor responsible for the individual's situation. Instead, it combines with *paññā* (Pāli, intelligence or wisdom) and *vīrya* (Pāli, effort) (Jaquet and Walton 2013: 59). Furthermore, *kamma* 'is fatalistic neither in practice nor in doctrine' (Keyes 1983c: 264). The individual is not obliged to wait for the manifestation of his fate shaped by past *kamma*, but instead has the responsibility for conducting meritorious deeds to improve his present *kamma*. Many lay followers believe that merit-making can also bring about good consequences in the near future of one's present life. Moreover, acts of merit-making are an outward and visible sign of one's spiritual concern and virtue.

This leads us to the importance of merit and *kamma* for the social hierarchy. Like the overall cosmos, the human realm is itself seen as inherently marked by inequalities and hierarchies. Merit-making not only promises a better rebirth, but also a good standing in one's current life. Concepts such as *parami* (Burmese 'virtue') and *hpoun:* (Burmese: a certain type of power of which it is often claimed that only men possess it), *ana*, and *awza* are seen as resulting from merit gained in past lives. They serve as measures of one's standing in social hierarchies and thus are relevant for ideas on politics and political leadership (see Houtman 1999; Harriden 2012). Moreover, there are other status-related concepts like prestige (Pāli *guṇa*, Burmese *goun*) that are important for making livelihood decisions (see Chapter 4).

'Dāna', 'Mettā', and Sharing Merit

One of the most prominent ways to gain merit (and thus enhance one's *kamma*) can be found in the concept of *dāna* (Burmese *dana*), which is also the one concept that is linked most directly to publicly observable economic transactions such as donations and other kinds of gifts. The practice of giving, or *dāna*, is the first of ten qualities (*pāramitā*) that need to be practised and mastered on each person's spiritual path to attaining enlightenment. By practicing *dāna*, people gain merit and thus directly work towards a better rebirth. The Buddhist gift has been studied quite extensively. With reference to the work of Marcel Mauss, several scholars have discussed the question of reciprocity in Buddhist gift-giving processes.[35] However this theoretical question might be answered (opinions differ here), it is undeniable that in Myanmar the act of giving is seen to bring many returns, even if these returns should not be the motivating factor behind a gift. Donations continue to play an enormous role for Buddhist lay people of all social strata, and thus for their household budgets. Religious donations especially are publicly observable on a daily basis in all Buddhist areas in Myanmar. The stark contrast between the impressive amounts of gold and money in pagodas on the one hand and the material poverty of large parts of the population on the other hand can be striking for visitors. People offer food to monks on their morning alms rounds, and many regularly visit pagodas to worship and to donate. At big donation events, the principal donors will receive a lot of admiration from other attendees. People also donate their labour, for example, to organize pagoda festivals or to teach in monastic schools.

Earlier studies (Tambiah 1970; Spiro 1982) have focused mainly on *dāna* as transfers from the laity to the monastic order. The sangha materially relies on donations from the laity. What is also crucial here is the duty of every Buddhist to protect and promote the *sāsana* (Burmese *thathana pju. de*). Many lay followers believe that the ultimate donation in terms of merit-making would be for an individual to build a whole pagoda. However, several later studies have emphasized that *dāna* also occurs in gifts between lay people, including those of lower standing, as well as in gifts directed at other beings, such as animals or spirits (Burmese *nat*) (Bowie 1998; Kumada 2004). While *dāna* is a specific process of giving something away, the particularities lie in a certain mental state of the giver rather than in specific rituals. *Dāna* can mean giving money, objects or food. Ideally, for *dāna* to create merit, the gift should be made with a pure intention (*cetanā*), with no expectation of a return from the recipient, and in a state of full detachment from the object (the giver should not regard it as a loss) (Kumada 2004). Despite this ideal form of *dāna*, in practice things are more complicated. It is often not easy to distinguish an act of *dāna* from an ordinary gift, or from

---

[35] For a more recent set of papers, see the special issue of the *Religion Compass* edited by Nicolas Sihlè and Bénédicte Brac de la Perrière (2015).

social obligations and social work activities (Burmese *luhmu.ye: parahita)*. The boundaries between them are blurred.

Spiro (1966: 1168) found that his informants held that the amount of merit generated depended on how much a person gave and on the spiritual standing of the receiver. Naoko Kumada's (2007: 16) informants, conversely, stressed the importance of the right intention (*cetanā*) of giving, which they saw as more important than the actual amount given. In other examples, the level of need of the receiver was thought to matter for the amount of merit that will be generated (Jaquet and Walton 2013). Discourses on *dāna* thus not only exist in scholarly debate, but also among practitioners themselves, and like all religious concepts, ideas about *dāna* are not static but subject to change. *Dāna* can take the form of charity and donations to welfare projects, and perhaps a growing need for such projects has reshaped ideas of *dāna* (e.g. the reaction to Cyclone 'Nargis'; see Jaquet and Walton 2013), thus putting more emphasis on *dāna* as gifts to the disadvantaged. In Theravādin societies, there is also a certain social pressure to donate. Those who experience personal economic success are expected, to some extent, to share it with the local community (see Bowie 1998, on Thailand). In that regard, gift-giving also plays a major role in redistributing wealth, albeit without ultimately altering socio-economic inequalities. In the coming section, I will engage with the worldly aspects of *dāna*.

Generally, the donation of money for religious purposes must be seen as having many other returns besides spiritual gain. Using a significant part of their income for religious purposes not only lets people gain merit, and therefore make an investment for their next life, but also allows them to have worldly pleasure from it, for example, in the forms of food and enjoyment at temple festivals. Moreover, the community is strengthened through public events, and the donors gain social prestige, as donations are very often public acts (Spiro 1966). In a context that emphasizes modesty and generosity as opposed to greed and materialism, donations here fulfil a function similar to 'conspicuous consumption' elsewhere (Veblen 2007: 49–69). In practice, despite the often heard claim that the intention matters more than the amount given, those who make particularly large donations will often also enjoy particularly strong admiration and prestige. What is admired in a wealthy donor is not only, or not necessarily, that person's wealth as such, but more the presumed good *kamma* of which it is seen as a proof. At the same time, such worldly attributes make it easier to increase one's merit even more, as one has more resources to make donations, and perhaps easier access to greater 'fields of merit', like powerful monks. F. K. Lehman stated that, 'just as in the market economy, it takes money to make money, so it takes merit to make merit' (1996: 29), outlining merit-making as a 'competitive game' (ibid.) in which each player wants to increase his merit to gain a better rank in the hierarchy and in society, as well as in the whole cosmos. As a result, people try to persuade others to accept their gifts and hospitality. For those accepting gifts (or even depending on them), this signals a position of weakness, as their acts of receiving gifts allows others (the givers) to move up in the social hierarchy. Lehman mentioned the Thai notion of *kreng jai* and the Burmese *a: na de*, expressions of shyness or reluctance (for example, over receiving a gift), which, according to Lehman (and Kawanami 2007: 4, mentions a similar meaning of *a: na de*; see also Keeler 2017: 141–146), actually express the anxiety of becoming obliged to someone because this would place one lower in the social hierarchy in relation to the giver.[36] This paints a picture of a sort of Buddhist *homo economicus*, who not only tries to acquire as much merit (and thus status) for himself as possible, but even shows a reluctance to enable others to make merit, for example, by trying to refuse gifts. Such notions need to be nuanced further. Lived Buddhism is very much a 'collective religion' (Tambiah 1973: 12). Its collective social dimension can be found, for example, in the fact that merit can and should be shared and transferred to others, allowing the practical tradition of Buddhism to account for social realities and individuals' connection to society (Tambiah 1968; Keyes 1983a).

Merit transfer is possible in a number of ways and directions. It may occur from members of the sangha to lay people, from sons to parents through an ordination ceremony, between lay people, from the living to the deceased, and also from humans to non-humans (see Ladwig 2011, on Laos). It happens through specific rituals, usually in the context of Buddhist ceremonies in monasteries. The fact that merit can be shared lets merit appear almost as the 'common property' of a social group (Gombrich 1971: 219). Merit transfer is often linked to the wish and duty to help others, like the concept of *mettā* (loving kindness). Like *dāna*, *mettā* is one of the ten perfections (*pāramitā*) that one has to master on the way to enlightenment. The respective teaching, *Mettā Sutta*, is among the most popular sermons.[37]

---

[36] These arguments match with Keeler's (2017) analysis of autonomy as a key value in Buddhist Myanmar, in which he argues that those who are more autonomous, who are less obliged to others, and less trapped in social demands and constraints, are ranked higher in the social hierarchy. This is most clearly exemplified through highly admired forest monks who detach as much as possible from worldly demands and desires. In contrast, being attached, unfree and bound may be interpreted as a sign of bad *kamma* and additionally these worldly constraints lower one's potential to make new merit (see also Lehman 1996).

[37] *Mettā* is a widely used concept in public discourse. It has given one of Myanmar's best known local charitable foundations its name (*Metta* Development Foundation). Furthermore, the *Mettā Sutta* was chanted by monks who opposed the military in the 2007 protests that later become known as the Saffron Revolution. The recently growing discourse around rising

It preaches kindness towards all beings. People also talk about sharing or sending *mettā* to others. Inherent here is the idea of a responsibility that one has for others, not only economically, but also spiritually.

Beyond *Dāna*: Buddhism and Economic Action

It seems sensible to begin with Max Weber when looking at scholarly engagement with the theme of Buddhism and economic action. Weber, although not having done fieldwork in Asia himself, wrote about Buddhism as a tradition of world renunciation and its adherents as incapable or at least extremely unlikely to develop a spirit of capitalism (Weber 1958). Weber had, directly or indirectly, a crucial influence on Buddhist studies (Gellner 2009). His writings on Buddhism have since been criticized (e.g. Tambiah 1973), but as Gellner (1982, 2009) has pointed out, in general much of the criticism of Weber had resulted from a misunderstanding of his writings. Weber did not think that Buddhists would necessarily make bad capitalists once they lived in a capitalist system, nor did he see any specific religion as the direct and sole cause of the emergence or non-emergence of capitalism. His theory was rather that Buddhist communities had at least one (insufficient, but necessary) factor lacking for developing capitalism *before* they came in touch with it through outsiders, namely the *spirit* of capitalism. Weber drew his conclusions from secondary sources on doctrines. As a consequence, he overestimated individual practice and underestimated the extent to which monks were integrated into the sangha, as well as the many connections between monks and the laity (Gellner 1982: 538–9).

There have been other studies, some based on empirical research, that saw in people's strong Buddhist beliefs a potential hindrance to economic development: '[T]he aspiration of the Burmese for worldly pleasures in a future rebirth, and their consequent concern for merit and *dāna* has been a serious obstacle to a better standard of living in their present life' (Spiro 1970: 461). Mya Maung, a former finance professor at Boston College, wrote in 1964 about the attempts of the Burmese post-independence govern-ment to foster economic development and extend the welfare state. He saw the leaders' (and people's) strong desire to preserve their cultural heritage as being at odds with such attempts, arguing that Burmans would not be willing to pay the price of cultural change that far-reaching economic shifts would require (1964: 764). People's interpretations of Buddhism, he argued, have been crucial in all moments of political emancipation, such as the nationalist

---

islamophobia and attacks on Muslims has also seen many references to *mettā*, mainly by those advocating peaceful coexistence, who urged that the principle of *mettā* should be applied to everyone, including non-Buddhists (Tin Yadanar Htun 2016).

movements against the colonial occupation. People would accept change only if it was reconcilable with religious ideas. If this were not the case, even opportunities to better one's living conditions might fall on stony ground among the population.

Without going too deeply into doctrinal sources, it is worth noting that Buddhist teachings do not at all condemn the accumulation of wealth by laypeople, especially given that Buddhism is often reduced to notions of non-materialism and detachment by outsiders, as well as some of its practitioners. There are several *suttas* dealing with wealth.[38] Wealth itself is presented as an enjoyable and legitimate thing to gain for lay people, who are living in a world of economic constraints and demands.[39] The Buddha also specifically listed ownership, wealth, and debtlessness as particular joys in life.[40] *Suttas* also mention how wealth can and should be gained by the right means, stating that people should not engage in five types of business, namely business in weapons, business in human beings, business in meat, business in intoxicants, or business in poison.[41] The Buddha further condemned pursuing gain with gain. It is, however, not completely clear if this relates specifically to usury or rather to greed in general, especially given that this particular talk was directed at monks.[42] For lay people, there are teachings on how wealth should be used and which responsibilities come with it. The teachings encourage a skilful organization of one's business[43], strategic improvement of wealth[44], and balanced spending[45], as well as the avoidance of debt.[46] The teachings warn that wealth can be lost through debauchery, drunkenness, gambling, and friendship with evil-doers.[47] One must also protect one's property from fire, water, thieves, the king, and unfriendly relatives.[48] Economic inequality is not generally seen as prob-lematic, as long as the wealthy give to others (including relatives, friends, servants, religious orders, the king, *devas*, and the dead)[49] and as long as

---

[38] English translations of *suttas* can be found under http://www.accesstoinsight.org. For Buddhist teachings on prosperity, see also Rahula (2008).

[39] *Aputtaka Sutta,* SN 3.91.

[40] *Anana Sutta,* AN 4.26.

[41] *Vanijja Sutta,* AN 4.79.

[42] *Mahā Cattārisaka Sutta,* MN 117.

[43] *Mangala Sutta* Khp 5.

[44] *Dhammapada* Verse 155.

[45] *Dighajanu Sutta,* AN 8.54.

[46] *Anana Sutta,* AN 4.62.

[47] *Dighajanu Sutta,* AN 8.54.

[48] *Sappurisa Dāna Sutta,* AN 5.148.

[49] *Adiya Sutta,* AN 5.41.

they do not grow greedy for sensual pleasure and mistreat others.[50] The teachings further warn against indebtedness, stating that the inability to repay a loan is worse than mere poverty due to the pressure and conflicts it creates.[51] Similar attitudes toward indebtedness can be found in the *lokanîti*, (No. 87; No. 141). Conditions such as indebtedness are seen as a consequence of moral misconduct, such as an excessive desire for sensual pleasure, greed, or improper thought, speech, and action. The *Sigālovāda Sutta*, a sort of code of conduct for lay people, contains several ethical and social duties with livelihood implications, including how to treat one's employees. It also warns against gambling.[52]

While core ideas like those of *dāna* and *mettā* are widely known, the teachings listed above are not necessarily known in detail by lay followers. Furthermore, even many of the more widely known religious ideas appear complex and abstract, and some seem hard to reconcile with worldly everyday demands. Teachings of non-attachment, the emphasis on suffering, the non-existence of a soul, and the non-existence of a main god come to mind. But anthropological studies have also shown how Buddhist ideas are interpreted and deployed in everyday matters not only by monks but also by lay people, without the direct involvement of religious institutions (Gombrich 1991; Cassaniti 2015), even though many lay people consider themselves not very knowledgeable on Buddhism, something they see as the concern of 'experts', i.e. monks. We must therefore generally avoid producing rigid cultural-deterministic views on religious influences or completely ignoring religious factors in a specific setting. Instead we must explore the nuanced and complex ways in which religion and economic thought saliently interact, and which other factors are at play.

Implicitly or explicitly informed by Weber, empirical research has been carried out on the actual connection between Buddhism and economic activities in Asia. Notable early contributions were made by Tambiah (1970), Keyes (1983a), and Spiro (1966). Comparisons between Buddhism and village economic behaviour in two villages in Thailand and Myanmar, roughly comparable in terms of size and economic profile, showed striking similarities concerning the influence of religious norms on economic ethics (particularly the centrality of merit making), against the background of the very different historical and political conditions of the two countries

---

[50] *Appaka Sutta,* SN 3.6.

[51] *Iṇa Sutta,* AN 6.54; *Anaṇa Sutta,* AN 4.26.

[52] Gambling is nevertheless popular in Myanmar. Rozenberg (2005) argues that there is a link between the ways in which people try to increase their odds for winning in the illegal lottery (e.g. by analysing, through complex calculations, monks' words as hints to the winning numbers) and their interpretations of specifically Buddhist ideas on numerology.

(Pfanner and Ingersoll 1962). Buddhist concepts are also deployed in order to understand concrete life situations and make sense of emotions. Examples of *anicca* (impermanence) were seen in life-cycle events or body-related issues, as well as in livelihood matters (Cassaniti 2015). Buddhism also contributes to an ambiguity toward business ownership as form of livelihood (Tambiah 1973: 19; Keyes 1990: 182). This ambiguity stems from the impression that doing business is linked to materialism and greed, and entails the risk of breaking Buddhist precepts, which include not stealing and not lying (see also Pyi Phyo Kyaw 2017). Another factor that might have contributed to shaping ambiguous attitudes is the strong presence of minorities in business and trade that has historically occurred in many Southeast Asian regions. Attitudes towards doing business and their implications for status will be further addressed in Chapter 4 in describing my ethnography. Having considered the links between Buddhism and economic action, I will now proceed to investigate the implications of Buddhism for matters regarding the family and gender.

Morality in Family and Gender Relations

Scholars of the Theravādin countries of Southeast Asia have made different attempts to make sense of the cognatic kinship system more generally, and of the status of women more specifically. Earlier studies of unilineal kinship systems in Africa or East Asia had not equipped them with the right tools to analyse kinship in these cases (Keeler 2017: 27). Soon, the term 'loosely structured', which Embree (1950) had coined for the Thailand (in contrast to Japan), 'became a catch-all for what conventional kinship theory failed to explain' (Kumada 2015: 83), including in the Burmese case. Ward Keeler (2017) has recently revisited the debate briefly to argue that kinship ties in Myanmar can indeed be extended as well as disengaged from rather easily. He sees kinship ties as entailing only 'lightly carried burdens' (p. 126) with relatively few obligations and instead considerable room for manoeuvre for individuals.[53] Like others (Spiro 1986: 71–71), Keeler observed that kinship ties have to be actively cultivated, otherwise they might dissolve. And while relatedness may be selectively and temporarily mobilized as a basis for support (e.g. finding jobs and shelter in the city), the categories of 'kin' and 'neighbour' or 'fellow villager' (someone sharing territoriality) can be rather blurred and flexible in many contexts (p. 126).

---

[53] Such room for manoeuvre should not be confused with 'individualism'. Bunnag has argued that this term was used mistakenly to characterize Thais in their 'loosely structured' social system by Embree and others. However, individualism in the sense of diverging considerably from social norms was rather disapproved of. Instead, behaviour in interactions was defined by strict status considerations (Bunnag 1971: 20).

A relative lack of concern with descent and lineage has also been analysed with regard to a specifically Buddhist understanding of relatedness, in which the idea of rebirth becomes paramount.[54] Naoko Kumada pointed out that through rebirth biological family ties are not transferred to future lives, but instead are disrupted. This makes it unpredictable to whom one will be related in a future life: in fact, it is not even clear whether one will be reborn as a human or as something else, such as an animal, a spirit, or another being.[55] All this depends on a person's *kamma*. *Kamma*, as explained above, can be positively influenced through merit-making. It is merit, rather than blood ties or genes, that is seen as a substance transferred to a future life. And it is also through merit-making rituals that Burmans understand relatedness beyond one's current life. Making merit together with another person (fulfilling rituals and good deeds together) is believed to increase the chances of meeting again in a future life, and conversely, being related in one's current life is seen as a consequence of having done joint merit-making rituals in one's past lives.[56] A bond created through shared merit-making is stronger than mere biological ties, as the latter is only valid in one's current existence. However, even though people can try to increase the likelihood of reaching physical proximity to others in future lives through rituals, it cannot be known in which form one will be reborn, and it certainly does not have to be as relatives (Kumada 2015).[57] Such ideas might contribute to the fact that Burmese kinship is ego-oriented rather than ancestor-oriented. Burmans do not usually remember ancestors beyond people who were present during their current lives and thus who they can remember in person – there is no transgenerational lineality beyond that (Kumada 2015: 80, 82). While a certain room for autonomy in the kinship system cannot be understood to simply originate from Buddhism, it seems that the two go well together. On the other hand, Buddhism offers just as much a basis for cooperation and mutual support (see Chapter 6).

---

[54] In the following section I rely heavily on Kumada (2015), who explored ideas on kinship, birth, death, conception, and relatedness among Buddhist villagers in Myanmar.

[55] While the Theravāda doctrine denies the existence of a soul, many Burmans believe in a kind of soul (*winnyin* or *leikpya*) as an essence that will be transferred through rebirth (see also Brac de la Perrière 2015).

[56] Kumada (2015) identified the pouring of water together as the most important ritual in that context.

[57] Kumada gives the example of two friends who pour water together often. It is believed that they may be reborn in physical proximity to each other. However, it depends on their *kamma* whether they will both take the shape of humans. It could be that one of the two friends has not gained enough merit, so that her soul will enter the womb of a dog that lives close to her friend's house. The physical proximity would still be given, just that she would be reborn not as a human but as a dog in the friend's neighbourhood (Kumada 2015: 95).

Within the family, people certainly make a distinction between distant relatives and close relatives, that is, ego's parents, siblings, children, and spouse. This group usually constitutes a domain of moral and economic obligations.[58] Earlier studies (Nash 1965; Spiro 1986) have focused on relatively endogamous village communities, a context in which distinctions between close kin, distant kin, and non-kin were perhaps not crucial for everyday economic matters and thus difficult to observe. However, Spiro already described that, if a person was in serious trouble (such as sickness), it was not primarily fellow villagers who helped: instead, relatives had to come from afar to support the person in need (Spiro 1986: 76). The moral importance of parents has always been emphasized in particular, often with reference to Buddhism. Parents are listed (together with teachers) as one of the five objects of worship, directly following the Buddha, his teachings, and the sangha. Many religious activities circle around the family as well. Lay people who donate parts of monastery buildings or religious events often dedicate these publicly to their parents (see Chapter 6). In the economic realm, even young children are actively encouraged to help their parents with economic tasks, and teenagers sometimes engage in full-time work, more and more often far away from their families (see Chapter 5). Newer developments such as growing urbanization allow us a new perspective on kinship ties, as they further disclose their relevance for economic, logistic, and social support. Migration made systematic kinship support necessary (and visible) over geographical distances (see Turnell et al. 2008, on remittances from abroad), and with neoliberal developments, the importance of securing property, capital accumulation, and inheritance strengthens the role of inter-generational ties for purposes of property transmission. Socio-economic changes are likely to influence both practices of support and ideas of descent and inter-generational belonging, perhaps increasingly beyond the relatives whom one can remember personally.

Jane Bunnag (1971: 10–12) argued that it might have been the abundance of land and rice that was responsible for a lack of systematic cooperation in the ethnographic examples from the 1950s and 1960s, rather than certain Buddhist ideas, as some have claimed (e.g. Phillips 1967: 363–4). After all, in Sri Lanka, where economic conditions were challenging, but the religious tradition similar, corporate groups around kinship had been documented for the same time period (Leach 1961). Newly emerging

---

[58] Spiro quotes the saying *qayei gyi thwe ni* ('in matters of urgent importance, blood is closest') (1977: 54). He also mentions the joke that the first part of the word for relatives (*hsweimyou*) should rather be pronounced as *shwe* – gold – indicating that people value relatives most when they are rich (1977: 48) [transliteration style adopted from original source].

economic challenges in Myanmar since the early 1990s have coincided with
an increase in community-based support arrangements (McCarthy 2016:
315–316), which further supports Bunnag's argument. Once systematic
cooperation was needed, it appeared.[59]

Inherently connected to kinship is the topic of gender. Gender norms
in Myanmar are generally more restrictive for women than for men. They
usually circle around behaving in appropriate ways before marriage (most
importantly not engaging in any sexual activities) and fulfilling care
obligations within the family. Gender relations are crucially influenced by
the concept of *hpoun:*, a specific spiritual power associated with masculinity.
Hpoun: is thought of as an actual substance residing in the male body. It is
seen as a sign of good *kamma* from past lives and therefore as proof that men
are inherently spiritually superior to women. These conceptual hierarchies
shape everyday actions in manifold ways. Women's laundry, for example, is
associated with a pollution that can potentially weaken a man's *hpoun:* and it
must therefore always be washed separately from men's laundry. Women are
expected to remember that they might weaken a man's *hpoun:* when they
move and act around men. Monks are believed to have specifically high
amounts of *hpoun:* and therefore are referred to as *hpoun: gyi:*, *gyi:* meaning
'great' or 'big'. Despite their assumed spiritual inferiority, women have important roles as lay donors and lay meditators, and some become nuns.[60]
Women, as well as transgender people, also fulfil important roles as
astrologers and spirit mediums (*natkadaw*).

Regardless of their assumed spiritual inferiority, depictions of women
in Myanmar enjoying high status or even equality with men prevail. To
understand their origin, historical considerations need to be taken into
account here. The position of women has been severely weakened through
centuries of masculine and patriarchal politics, under colonialism as well as
military rule (Ikeya 2011; Harriden 2012). Even before that, women were
not supposed to acquire significant political power and apart from some
noticeable exceptions, they could assert political influence only through their

---

[59] Looking at pre-colonial Burma further underlines the importance of socio-economic and
political factors for the role of kinship and kin cooperation. Back then, descent might have
played a larger role among the Buddhist communities, since class (or rather, belonging to a
certain order) and occupation were hereditary, although this organization was far less rigid
than, for instance, the Indian caste system (Furnivall 1957: 29–35).

[60] The status of nuns is lower than that of monks. Also, the act of joining the monastery for a
longer period, or lifelong, is a choice that is more readily permitted to men. Women who want
to become nuns may receive criticism for neglecting their social roles at home (Kawanami
2013). However, women usually make up the largest share of the audience in public religious
dhamma talks, women hand donations to the sangha more often than men, and by far more
women than men join meditation retreats for laypeople (Jordt 2007).

husbands (Harriden 2012). However, women had important roles in the household and the economic sphere, for example, being heavily engaged in weaving and trading. They also acted publicly in ways that Western observers were not used to. Consequently, prevailing images of the supposed high standing of women in Myanmar have their roots in descriptions by Western observers from pre-colonial or early colonial days. Furnivall, for example, remarked that, '(…) by the common consent of all observers, the women of Burma enjoyed a position of freedom almost unparalleled in the East and, until recently, exceptional in Europe' (Furnivall 1957: xi).

This, however, was for the British a possible hindrance to modernization, and they put a lot of effort into 'civilizing' women (for example, in institutions of secular education) and preparing them for their roles as wives and mothers, or for 'appropriate' jobs such as teaching or nursing. The colonial economy and the disruption of social patterns further altered women's roles (Ikeya 2011). The military dictatorship after 1962 was also a period of decidedly masculine and patriarchal politics. Nevertheless, there is, at least in theory, a relative equality between women and men in legal terms (same access to inheritance or divorce as men, for example). Nowadays, women graduate from universities in higher numbers than men (Myanmar Department of Population 2017b: XII)[61], and there are also more female than male professors (Asian Development Bank et al. 2016: 77). Status enhancement through education and a respectable job seem to be of particular concern to women. Since they occupy a superordinate position to men in the spiritual hierarchy, worldly status and prestige might be a way to balance this subordination, at least to some extent. In politics, women's role remains less than that of men. Furthermore, some of the presumed markers of women's high position have to be re-evaluated with regard to Buddhist ideas, for example, the fact that women usually control the household finances. Handling money is linked to pollution and greed in a Buddhist framework, and material attachments are seen as a source of suffering (Kawanami 2007: 11). In this logic, instead of being a marker of high status, handling the household money, like selling goods in the market, constitutes a lower task that men should not concern themselves with if possible.

Overall, women cannot undermine general hierarchical arrangements (in which men are, after all, still in the higher position) without negative

---

[61] Women in Myanmar are increasingly found in the role of leaders, managers, and professionals. The majority of doctors, nurses, and teachers are women, and women are also employed by many government ministries (however, top-level government positions remain dominated by men). Additionally, Myanmar has the highest proportion of female science researchers in the world (85.5 percent, UNESCO 2018: 4).

consequences.[62] Gender norms entail restrictions for many women in everyday life. For example, unmarried women are not supposed to be left unattended for long periods, especially overnight. It remains unthinkable for most women to go out after dark, or for unmarried women to live alone. Single women often live with relatives or colleagues. 'Dating' nowadays often consists of chatting via Facebook or other social media apps, and in most cases it no longer includes any unsupervised periods of being together physically. If a young couple run away from home overnight, it is not unusual for a marriage to be arranged quickly, as this is the only way to prevent the shame associated with the suspicion of premarital sex. If a woman breaks gender norms, concepts of 'losing face' or 'ruining one's name' are evoked (*name pye'* Burmese for 'name destroyed'; *mye' hna pye'* Burmese for 'face destroyed').

As mothers, women find respect and authority in the household. Children are considered to be indebted to their parents, especially the mother. The Buddhist ordination ceremony (Burmese *shin pju.*) is primarily meant for sons to create merit for their mothers, to compensate at least for a part of this debt. When parents grow older they often move in with their children, usually with a daughter. Traditionally, the youngest daughter had the obligation to care for her aging parents, and in return she would receive the largest bulk of property, normally the house. However, such patterns are now mere tendencies, and today, especially in urban areas, different kinds of living arrangements exist. While unmarried adult children usually contribute to their parents' households financially, the period after marriage is occupied by setting up one's own household, and many people start a small business in this phase. In most cases, married partners have separate incomes. A relatively high number of women remain unmarried and childfree (roughly 15 percent of women between the ages of 45 and 49 according to the 2014 census, see Shwe Aung 2016). As elsewhere in the world, some women consciously choose this way of life, while in other cases the reasons lies in

---

[62] Much of the anti-Muslim rhetoric in Myanmar, for example, circles around the issue of interfaith-marriages and the fear that Muslim men are persuading Buddhist women to convert. Buddhist women who marry men from other religions often face serious criticism. Several laws have been implemented and updated since the 1930s with the aim of protecting Buddhist women's property in cases of marriage with a Muslim man (Crouch 2015: 3), indicating that the fear of losing property to Muslim communities through such unions is one aspect of the criticism. Keeler adds another dimension to this debate when he suggests that, by marrying a Muslim and converting, a woman would leave (and thus fundamentally violate) the Buddhist hierarchy and thus rob Buddhist men of their superior standing in relation to her by choosing other, non-Buddhist superordinates (2017: 236–37). As a result, she would be suggesting the 'other' men's superior standing over Buddhists, something that the latter might experience as offensive.

outside circumstances. These women, referred to as *apyo gyi:*, fulfil important and respected social roles as aunts for younger nephews, nieces or students, and some pursue professional careers. They are not necessarily looked down upon or pitied. In fact, some people openly envy them for not having to deal with the trouble that marriage and motherhood can bring. They are even respected for their ability to resist sexual temptation. This constitutes an interesting parallel with Buddhist monks, who are sometimes envied and admired for the same thing (Kawanami 2001: 146).

Nun-human Members of the Buddhist Cosmos

Myanmar may seem like the orthodox Theravāda Buddhist country *par excellence* to the outside world. However, its religious landscape is much more diverse and complex. First of all, a variety of other religions are practised among the population, such as different branches of Christianity, Hinduism, and Islam, as well as a range of animist beliefs and more. Several of the decade-long wars in Myanmar's border areas have been fought along religious lines. Furthermore, the Buddhist belief system in itself contains a range of non-human beings such as *nat*s, guardian spirits, *deva*s or *weikza*s (also written *weizza*), many of which are acknowledged in statues and pictures on pagoda grounds. Some people worship these beings. People also make use of astrology, healing practices, and different mechanisms of protection, for example, tattoos and amulets.

In everyday practice, some beings play a larger role than others. *Nat*s (spirits) are very present. Most people in Myanmar are familiar with the most famous *nat*s, the myths surrounding them, and their typical appearance. *Nat*s are not inherently either good or bad: they can be moody and cause suffering if people disrespect them, but they can also protect and assist humans. Communication with *nat*s happens through a *natkadaw* (a *nat* medium). *Nat*s can be propitiated in private or at public festivals (*nat pwe:*) (for detailed analyses of *nat*s, see Spiro 1976; Brac de la Perrière 1989). Besides *nat*s there are other spirits, like pagoda guardians, or specific spirits who protect the pagoda's treasures. In rather more recent emerging cults that could be labelled 'prosperity religions', these guardians of the treasure trove are the focus of possession rituals and offerings (Foxeus 2017b).

As for the *weikza*s, they are usually not thought of as spirits but as supernatural beings, much higher than *nat*s, but lower than *arahat*s (saints) in the cosmological hierarchy. A *weikza* is a supernatural being, a master of Buddhism who has acquired supernatural powers, often through the practice of alchemy. *Weikza* cults became popular in the later phase of British rule and around independence, and *weikza*s are still worshipped today by their followers.[63] When a *weikza* disappears from this world, he does not die but only 'exits' this realm. He then remains in an immortal state to wait for the next Buddha to appear. From this plane, the *weikza* can still communicate with and influence the human realm. The *weikza* path to spiritual progress is an alternative to long years of studying and meditation (on *weikza*s, see Brac de la Perrière et al. 2014; Rozenberg 2015; Patton 2018). Many Burmese people believe in these beings, cater to them, respect them, and sometimes fear them. They are seen as part of the complex Buddhist cosmology, in which they interact with people and with each other. While some cults or practices are more popular in certain areas, or among certain strata or classes, it is important to acknowledge in general the complexity of the religious landscape. People may also consult astrologers to determine auspicious dates for important events such as a wedding or the opening of a business. Astrologers may tell their clients to perform protection rituals (Burmese *yadaya*) to prevent bad things from happening. Consulting astrologers for important decisions has been reported among the highest political elites of the country (Murdoch 2015).

While spirit and *weikza* worship is not suppressed in the same way as in the early Ne Win period, opinions differ as to the extent to which such practices are acceptable to Buddhists and whether or not they are part of Buddhism or outside (or even contradict) 'pure' Buddhism. Some Buddhists doubt the existence of, for instance, *nat*s, *weikza*s and genuine astrologers altogether, while others acknowledge their existence but see them as inferior to Buddhism and thus frown upon those who worship them. Others have integrated such practices of worship into their own lives and see in them no contradiction of their identity as Buddhists. Scholars have also differed in their views on how such practices relate to Buddhism. While Spiro saw such 'Burmese supernaturalism' (1967) decidedly as a religious system outside Buddhism, later studies have challenged this perception, arguing that they constitute one dimension of an overarching framework of Buddhist belief (Brac de la Perrière 2009: 193). After all, spirits, other supernatural beings, and astrologers have a strong presence in Buddhist legends, and many of the cults surrounding them have the inherent task of protecting Buddhism

---

[63] A religious resurgence, including the re-emergence or new emergence of spirit cults, has been observed in many parts of the world, including Southeast Asia (Hefner 2010; Endres and Lauser 2011). Here, as well as in other regional contexts, such developments have been linked to modernization phenomena and the rise of capitalism (see, for instance, Comaroff and Comaroff 1999; 2002). While the turbulent times of independence and the formation of the new nation gave rising popularity to phenomena like the *weikza* cults, newer publications suggest that the relatively recent expansion of the market economy brought about new forms of 'prosperity Buddhism' from the 1990s, such as cults surrounding the guardian spirits of the pagoda treasure trove (Foxeus 2017b).

(Foxeus 2013: 71). Spiro, despite seeing such practices as separate from Buddhism, nevertheless analysed their function with reference to Buddhist ideas. 'For if it is true that Buddhism makes the *nat* cults necessary, it can also be argued that the *nat* cultus renders the persistence of Buddhism possible' (Spiro 1996: 279). The argument here is that lived Theravāda Buddhism is '*accretive*' (Gombrich 1991: 58, emphasis in original) and thus can only exist with other (or attached) religious structures that provide for worldly needs. Since in the Buddhist logic suffering is the *kammic* consequence of previous sinning, one can do nothing to avoid it. If, on the other hand, suffering is seen as caused by *nat*s and other harmful beings, one can combat it more easily by proper propitiation of these spirits (Spiro 1967). For many people, spirit cults, astrology, and healers seem to offer more ways to improve one's immediate living conditions than traditional 'orthodox' Buddhism, and thus such practices are appealing, in addition to making merit for a better *kamma* in hope of a better rebirth. While I find it important to acknowledge this dimension of Buddhism, it will not feature prominently in my ethnography. The people I interacted with in Pathein mostly acknowledged the existence of non-human beings and occasionally consulted astrologers about business or family matters. Otherwise, they usually confined themselves to relatively 'mainstream' practices surrounding the Buddhist sangha, like attending sermon readings, donating, and meditating.

This chapter has been designed to provide context and background information on important concepts that influence moral considerations in Myanmar. We have to understand concepts like *dāna* and *mettā*, but also other characteristics held in high regard such as *pyinya* (knowledge, from the Pāli word *paññā*) and *goun* (prestige, from the Pāli word *guṇa*), as values in themselves. While they are technically understood as means leading to a higher goal, namely the accumulation of merit, in practice they function as values that are also seen as desirable for their own sake. As already mentioned, moral concepts are not static but stand in mutual construction with the socio-economic world, which is rapidly changing in some parts of present-day Myanmar. It must be anticipated that these changes may influence notions of values and morality. Changing ideas and practices have been recorded already in ideas of *dāna* (Jaquet and Walton 2013) and community-level cooperation (Bunnag 1971: 10–12). It can be expected that other attitudes will change as well. Rising consumerism and material demands might change attitudes toward greed and materialism. Foreign-sponsored initiatives for the promotion and support of 'SMEs' (small and medium enterprises) might help to render them an increasingly attractive livelihood option, stripping them of some of the moral ambiguities that I was still able to encounter in Pathein. Certainly a lot is happening in the realm of the political. Ideas about democracy, equality, and human rights are being discussed among parts of the population, leading to altered understandings of power, governance, and the state. Such influences will continue to play a role, perhaps increasingly so in the near future. However, ideas from the outside never land in an empty space. They will always be taken up, understood, analysed, and altered against the backdrop of existing world views and the moral considerations these entail. In the following chapters, I will present my ethnographic materials and analyses, outlining how the thoughts and actions of business owners in Pathein are both embedded in social relations and subject to moral considerations, some of which are anchored in the concepts outlined above.

Chapter 4
The Family

Introduction

I begin the ethnographic part of the book with the intimate sphere of the family. I explore how business owners (Burmese *hsain pain shin*) and their families navigate different values in family and economic matters, and how these matters are closely intertwined. I will look specifically at the desire for prestige (Burmese *goun*) and at the value given to autonomy (Burmese *lu'la'hmu.*[64]), both of which matter for livelihood choices. I argue that both take the function of values, since they are seen as generally desirable by many. I will show how such values coexist and how one sometimes outweighs the other, depending, for example, on a person's socio-economic situation and the opportunities this provides, and thus also how values stand in interaction with the material world. By studying people's considerations over value, I aim to shed light on processes of business foundation, management, and succession, thus helping to explain why, for instance, some businesses endure while others die out. I will show that such processes are not merely the 'natural' consequences of economic developments, but that they also result from inner-family negotiations. Social reproduction is selective, and what is worth being reproduced and what is not needs to be negotiated (Narotzky and Besnier 2014: S5). It is not always a business that is regarded as worth maintaining. Thus, such negotiations affect not only the family itself, they are also relevant to larger processes of class-making and self-making (Yanagisako 2002: 174) as well as to the overall business landscape of the town. In order to show how this is the case, I will portray two businesses that exemplify different modes of interaction between kinship and business, respectively with different consequences. While I regard these businesses as typical cases, I will account for multifaceted realities by

---

[64] *Lu'la'hmu.* can be translated as 'freedom' or 'independence'. The expression can be used to describe personal freedom. It thus captures the meaning of 'autonomy' in some contexts.

referring to other examples along the way in which things have been played out differently.

I study values such as autonomy and prestige here primarily through perceptions of intergenerational social mobility. I suggest that social mobility, rather than being measured in quantifiable factors like income and education, must be understood with reference to emic perspectives and locally specific contexts. Thus, I will take into account in what terms my informants describe upward mobility and achievements, both for themselves and for their children. What gives them a sense of pride? Are sources of pride to be found within the realm of the family, or the business, or both? How are kinship demands reconciled with the requirements of the business? Which occupations do business owners regard as desirable for their children? What do they see as the best option in pursuing one's livelihood? Which is the safest, the most profitable, the most prestigious choice? How are factors such as status, income, and education interlinked?

Before I arrived in Pathein I had read Yanagisako's ethnography (2002) on inter-generational family firms in Italy, where family members of different generations pooled their efforts to run a firm and in which the families she portrayed identified strongly with their businesses. However, in Pathein I could hardly find any similar businesses, at least not among the majority ethnic group, the Burmans. Their businesses had rather short life-cycles, often lasting no longer than one generation. This chapter will explain why business owners usually did not pass the business on to their children and why the latter were instead encouraged to pursue formal education and find more prestigious forms of employment. I outline these arguments in my first case study, a business run by a married Burman couple. The workshop produces the handmade bamboo parasols for which Pathein is famous.

However, one also finds larger, multi-generational firms in the city that match more closely the idea of a 'family business' in the sense of family members sharing efforts and capital, intergenerational business transfers, and portrayal of the business as a family legacy. Many of these businesses are located downtown and are run by members of minority groups, primarily ethnic Chinese (Sino-Burmese) and to a lesser extent Burmese-Indians. By portraying a Chinese-owned rice-trading business in the second half of my chapter, I will show how this is a consequence partly of historical developments, but also of different values and kinship structures. I compare the two cases with regard to the business owners' reasons for starting a business, their responses to expectations of kinship, and their utilizing of family labour and capital. Despite operating in very different sectors, these two businesses are typical of Pathein and other urban areas of Myanmar in the sense that they both benefited massively from the economic opportunities of the early

1990s, after the government had abandoned socialist policies and adopted a market-oriented economic trajectory. In that period the number of small businesses in the whole country increased dramatically, as private investment was encouraged (Kudo 2009: 70).[65] Both businesses now employ a similar number of workers, around twenty-five. By looking at three generations, I was able to see that the businesses have led to considerable upward mobility for both families, measured in terms of material wealth as well as educational degrees. Such business histories prove that it was not only big tycoons close to the military who benefited from the business opportunities after 1988. The many private small businesses that appeared (or emerged from the black market) throughout the country have often been overlooked in scholarly discussions of this period (e.g. Crouch 2017b; Jones 2018).

My aim in portraying the parasol workshop on the one hand and the rice-trading business on the other hand is not primarily to paint a contrasting picture of the contemporary business strategies of different ethnic groups. Rather, I want to show how certain historical socio-economic circumstances have played themselves out differently for the two families over the course of several generations, and how these circumstances interact with their prevailing kinship structures, values, and moral considerations. This allows me to point out that generalized comments on the shared values of a 'society', as well as more specific questions, such as whether such values are monist or plural (e.g. Robbins 2007, 2013), become especially problematic in places of great diversity, which urban areas often are.

Autonomy and Obligations in the Family

To understand why my Burman informants run their businesses the way they do, it is crucial to pay attention to their kinship system. The Burman kinship system is bilateral: Burmans do not have family names, and property is usually inherited in equal parts by all the children, though the latter can also be disinherited altogether.[66] In Chapter 3 I have described how Burmese

---

[65] Unlike in the early 1990s, setting up a business today (at least when land is needed) requires a large amount of capital that is almost impossible to accumulate through locally available employment options. The bigger businesses that have been set up only recently in Pathein have typically been financed by their owners through periods of working abroad, e.g. in Thailand, Malaysia or Singapore, or by money that had been in the family already.

[66] I have heard of quite a few conflicts among siblings involving inheritance. This can occur, for example, if property cannot be divided easily, or if one child feels he or she deserves more than the others for some reason. Traditionally, the largest share of the property was given to the youngest daughter, who had the obligation to care for the aging parents. With changing economic conditions and more mobility and migration, such expectations and practices are weakening.

kinship has been interpreted with reference to the 'loosely structured' debate
on kinship in Thailand (Embree 1950) between, for example, Spiro (1977:
72) and Nash (1965: 73). I have also mentioned how Kumada (2015)
explained the lack of concern with descent and the absence of transgenerational lineality with reference to the prominent idea of rebirth, since
rebirth leads to a disruption of kinship ties (Kumada 2015). It is clear
through that the close family constitutes a domain of moral obligations
among Burmans.

With these ideas on Burman kinship in mind, I will now discuss how
family relations interacted with business matters in my field site. Among my
informants, some room for children's choice and autonomy when looking at
plans for business succession was very evident. Burman business owners
rarely planned to pass on their businesses to their children, nor did they
typically rely on regular (paid or unpaid) family labour, which is of great
importance elsewhere (White 1994; Yanagisako 2002; Smart and Smart
2005: 6). Instead, they preferred to hire non-relatives or distant relatives
from rural areas as workers. In these latter cases, business owners tried to
make use of kinship ties and kinship morality[67] to obtain workers, but in the
workplace these distant relatives would often not be treated much different
from non-kin. While sometimes one or two family members feel obliged to
stay for longer periods, it is more common that relatives leave after a
relatively short time to seek new opportunities. There were no clearly
defined expectations of working together among relatives. If close relatives
like the owners children helped in the shop it happened on an occasional
basis, with relatively few feelings of obligation. And even if children
pursued business activities themselves, they would rather start their own
ventures than become involved in their parents' businesses.[68] That was even
the case when children became involved in exactly the same sector as their
parents. For instance, the owner of a pottery business told me that his parents
and grandparents had run pottery businesses as well. However, while

---

[67] One will sometimes see the word 'family' in business names (on signs outside the business
and often in English). This is yet another way to present the business as a family-like entity in
terms of social and moral closeness. It might result from a genuine wish for a harmonious
work environment as well as constitute a promotion strategy (see also Chapter 5, in which
employers refer to non-kin workers by saying 'we are like a family'). It should not mislead
the observer to think that these businesses are actually projects of larger families, since this is
rarely the case among the Burmans.

[68] Pathein's most well-known parasol shop, Shwe Sar, is an exception insofar as it has been
run by the same family for several generations and the owners have started to actively
advertise it as a 'traditional family business' to outsiders, including foreign tourists.

learning some skills from their relatives, each generation had opened a workshop of their own.[69]

Despite the fact that Burman children usually were not expected to take over the business and were free to form their own households after marriage, the family consisting of one's spouse, parents, children, and to a lesser extent siblings nevertheless clearly constitutes a domain of moral and economic obligations. Assistance is expected in times of need including after family members have left the household (see Chapter 3). Newer developments, such as the growth in urbanization, provide us with a new perspective on the importance of kinship ties for economic support. Increasing migration, urbanization, and rising prices made the centrality of family support visible, including over a distance. Migrants often send money home (see Turnell et al. 2008, on remittances from abroad) and are expected to return if problems occur, or when their parents grow older. In Pathein, many workers in the large garment factories of the 'industry zone' were young unmarried women from the surrounding countryside. Each month on their pay day, the streets around the factories were crowded with women preparing food or holding lunch boxes. My initial interpretation of the situation was that these women were exploiting a new business opportunity by selling food to the workers. However, I quickly realized that in fact they were the workers' mothers, come take home the salary and leaving the workers with only a minimal sum for the weeks ahead. This exemplifies the fact that the household constitutes a budgetary unit of which working children are a part until they marry and leave the household. Clearly, marriage remained a central precondition for setting up a household and having children.[70] Although, as already noted, in many marriages each partner pursued their own incomes, if one enterprise turned out to be very promising, they might pool their efforts to run it. This was the case with the

---

[69] This individualistic attitude toward means of livelihood within one family is similar to what my colleague Anne-Erita Berta has observed among Danish entrepreneurs (Berta 2019).

[70] The moral implications concerning marriage as an institution became clear when I visited an 'orphanage' (I use inverted commas because not all of the children's parents were dead) on the outskirts of Pathein. The orphanage, run by a group of Buddhist monks, hosted around sixty primary-school children who received education and shelter here. Next to the building that served as the school was another room where female volunteers cared for around ten babies, some of which were only a few weeks old. I was told that some children had been given away due to their family's poverty, while in other cases their mothers were not married, having given birth in secret and then giving the child away soon afterwards. I talked about this with a group of university students. They generally expressed sympathy for the mothers' decision, and some claimed that for the children it was better to grow up in an orphanage than with an unmarried mother. Abortion is illegal and is also seen as a great sin, therefore being judged the worst of all options. Nevertheless, hospital staff confirmed to me that abortions happen frequently, often performed in secret.

parasol business I describe below. Outsiders too understood such businesses to be the shared projects of the married couple only, rather than of the whole family, even if some relatives would help out in the shop here and there. Daughters who remain unmarried might stay with the parents, while ageing parents may be invited to live with the children's families later in life.

As elsewhere, growing migration, especially to distant locations, creates dilemmas for people. Those working in Yangon or abroad often support their parents financially, but they may still feel guilty for not being with them as they grow older. Besides migration, securing property, capital accumulation, and inheritance are becoming increasingly important in the light of economic changes and rising land prices. Such property transfers indicate the role of intergenerational family ties. With socio-economic changes having made practices of support visible, and perhaps having created new ones, they may in turn also influence ideas of descent and inter-generational belonging. If property inheritance increasingly matters beyond two generations this could change, for example, the current relative lack of concern with descent and transgenerational lineality. On the other hand, older informants especially expressed regret over the erosion of family bonds through increasing migration. Like the comments on employer–worker relations I shall look at in the following chapter, which were also seen as fluctuating increasingly and becoming more and more impersonal, even inner-family relations were deemed to be at risk of becoming weaker. In rural areas, I was told, more and more old people were being left behind to look after themselves and were unable to retire from working in the fields due to a lack of younger people staying at home to do the work.

The crucial point here is that the immediate family is a domain of economic support and obligations, despite the autonomy it leaves for individuals to pursue their own means of livelihood. Furthermore, not expecting children to become involved in the parents' business fits the Burman kinship system, which leaves considerable room for manoeuvre to individuals (Keeler 2017: 27). However, this cannot be seen as a sign of indifference from the parents' side concerning their children's future, as their expectations just take different forms. Parents were often concerned with matters of prestige, often hoping their children would receive an education and find employment that would offer more status and prestige than continuing the business. To explain the underlying considerations of parental expectations over several generations in more detail, I will now present a concrete ethnographic family history of a Burman couple that owns a traditional parasol workshop. I shall describe patterns of support, parental expectations, and what they mean for the firm.

Case 1. Making Parasols: Family and Business, but not a 'Family Business'

Myo Aung and his wife Thu Zar were in their forties when I met them. They both come from ethnic Burman families with small-scale business backgrounds. Myo Aung's parents sold cosmetics, while Thu Zar's family manufactured and sold window frames and other construction materials. When the couple met, neither of them had an interest in working in their parent's businesses, nor was it expected of them. By the time of their marriage in 1991, new opportunities to set up private enterprises had emerged in the country, as the government had introduced a market-oriented economic trajectory. It was in this phase that Myo Aung and Thu Zar decided to start their own venture. They knew they would have to work as labourers first to save up enough capital to buy land and materials, as they did not qualify for bank loans. Myo Aung recalled that their parents had hoped that their children would receive an education and find respectable employment. Seeing them work as labourers for someone else would have constituted a disgrace for their parents, said Myo Aung. Nonetheless the need to save up money required them to spend a period as workers. The only possibility they saw to avoid confrontation with their parents and embarrassment was to carry out such work far away from home. Myo Aung and Thu Zar thus left their home town in central Myanmar without informing their parents and through a friend came to Pathein. It is important to remember here that at no point did the parents expect them to continue their (the parents') businesses, but nor would they have been pleased to hear that the couple had chosen to start one of their own. From their parents' perspective, neither of these options could compensate for the status that formal higher education and prestigious employment would have brought.

Aged only twenty-one, and without any savings, Myo Aung and Thu Zar started working in someone else's parasol workshop, where they learned every step of the production process. When their child was born, Myo Aung and Thu Zar returned to their parents for a period of one and a half years. From there, Myo Aung went to work in the ruby mines in northern Myanmar to earn money. After his return, the couple knew that they had saved up enough money to buy a plot of land and hire some workers. However, they were reluctant to leave their families right away to return to Pathein, so they stayed in their home town for a few more months and set up a small chicken farm. When one of the chickens pecked at their baby's cheek, Myo Aung read this as a sign to abandon that work and finally start their parasol shop. Here, he brought in a moral aspect to means of livelihood, saying: 'My religion condemns the killing of animals, so I never felt comfortable with the chicken husbandry anyway. We packed our things. I "sold" the chicken farm to a friend. I knew he would not give me money for it, but I did not mind; I decided to regard it as a gift. We left [the town] again without telling our parents. Back in Pathein, we worked for another few weeks to refresh our parasol-making skills. And then we got a small plot of land and hired our first two workers'. This was in 1995.

Plate 3. Parasols drying in the sun in Pathein.

The founding story of this parasol business shows how Myo Aung and Thu Zar carefully negotiated the need of the business for capital (working as labourers) with parental expectations (carrying out the actual work some-where else to avoid confrontation and parental disappointment), while still remaining close to the parents for some time when their child was still small. Over the years they found they were able to employ more and more workers, and at the time of my research they had around twenty five. These workers made the parasols from bamboo, wood, and cotton or silk, which was masterfully painted. In its first years the shop produced mainly parasols for monks and nuns. The parasols were part of the usual 'donation package' that laypeople offered to monks on certain religious occasions. When, in 1996, the Ministry of Religious Affairs permitted monks to use smaller ready-made umbrellas, that market declined. Myo Aung and Thu Zar started focusing more on parasols for purposes of decoration, for which they tested new designs and materials.

While many other parasol businesses have closed down over the years or switched to other products, Myo Aung and Thu Zar soon had difficulties in keeping up with the demand. They could not easily find more workers, and good bamboo is scarce in some seasons. All over the country, and even abroad, restaurants, hotels, but mostly resellers were ordering their parasols. 'I stopped accepting large orders that I could not fulfil. I want to be able to guarantee high quality. Sometimes I am afraid to pick up the phone because then I have to explain why again an order is delayed', Myo Aung said. He had no intention of expanding the business, for example, by starting a new branch under the supervision of someone else. Instead, he wanted to keep it at a size he could control. Not wanting to let the business grow does not mean that there was no profit motive. Instead of expanding, Myo Aung invested his profits in plots of land that could later serve as an inheritance for his daughter.[71]

Their daughter had meanwhile grown up, completed a degree in medicine and was working as a doctor in Yangon, to the great pride of her parents. At the time of my research, Myo Aung and Thu Zar did not have anyone to take over the business. While to a certain extent they regretted the possible disappearance of the parasol-making craft and of the parasols as a traditionally Patheinian product, they did not cling to the business itself as an institution that needs to be maintained. They were relatively content with the fact that their business might die with them. Thus, they had repeated a pattern that their own parents had already displayed of not expecting their children to continue the business. But unlike their daughter, Myo Aung and Thu Zar did not fulfil their own parents' hopes of continuing their education and finding respectable employment when they were young. Instead they had opted to exploit the newly emerging business opportunities back in the early 1990s.

As mentioned earlier, the couple had left their home town without informing their parents in order to avoid confrontation with them and shame. I have seen this pattern repeatedly, including with people who decided to migrate to Thailand or Singapore to work as housemaids, in factories or on ships, all of which might be considered degrading from their parents' perspective. I came across several cases where people had informed their parents only once they had reached their destinations. This strategy was also a way to free parents from any responsibility – not being informed, there was nothing they could have done to prevent their children's migration. Such actions sometimes led to short-term disputes, but usually not to serious

---

[71] Purchasing land, even only small plots, has played a role in all cases of considerable wealth accumulation that I learned about. Land prices have risen dramatically in recent years, making it a crucial object of investment (Franco et al. 2015; Okamoto 2018: 195, 198).

conflicts that would disrupt the 'long term morality of kinship' (Bloch 1973: 195). In fact, leaving, in this case, was a way to avoid anger, confrontation, and open disputes. It was thus something respectful to do. Withdrawing at least temporarily from relationships is something that seems to happen with relative ease, for example, between workers and employers (as we will see in Chapter 5), and even within families. However, the fact that children can decide their economic pathways relatively freely did nothing to reduce the obligation to provide mutual support with other family members. Accordingly, children working abroad or in the urban areas of Myanmar usually sent money home to their parents.

Support can also be extended by inviting ageing parents into the household, as Thu Zar did. Thu Zar is the only daughter, so the caring responsibility was hers. Her mother did not come alone, as she also brought Thu Zar's two brothers, one with a family of his own. The brothers had had no economic success comparable to that of their sister. As a result, many of Thu Zar's relatives now lived with her and her husband in Pathein. Thu Zar and Myo Aung could offer them a relatively comfortable life thanks to their own economic achievements. The kinship norms in which they were embedded granted Thu Zar and Myo Aung the autonomy to move out and open their own shop, but when the shop was successful, they acknowledged their family obligations by bringing Thu Zar's mother and other relatives into their household. Among Burmans, extended families remaining in the same house together in the first place were rare, but it was not uncommon for ageing parents to move into the households of their children, whom they often relied on in later stages of life. The fact that Thu Zar's family ended up living together again constituted a different situation than it would have been had she simply never left home: it constituted a difference in authority. The main decisions in the house were now made by Thu Zar and Myo Aung, not the other family members (Thu Zar's mother and brothers). By setting up a household and business activity of their own, they were in a position to fulfil their kinship obligations to support their parents without losing authority when it came to decision-making because 'authority within the house is with the one who owns it' (Spiro 1986: 117).

Plate 4. Manufacturing parasols in Pathein.

The fact that Myo Aung and Thu Zar's daughter, Wai Wai, was not expected to take over the business requires further analysis. While it could be thought that parents might want to spare their children from physically hard labour, this was not an actual concern for most business owners: as soon as they employed workers, they themselves usually resorted to administrative and management-related tasks. Hierarchies within the workplace manifest themselves very quickly in the division between manual and non-manual labour. One could further argue that a traditional parasol workshop might not be worth passing on, as a number of its features reduce its future prospects: bamboo is becoming more and more scarce, and the work demands skills that few workers nowadays are willing to learn. In fact, many of Pathein's parasol shops have already closed down. However, for Myo Aung and Thu Zar's business there was more demand than they could fulfil. Moreover, this pattern was not specific to the crafts sector. My ethnographic data contains cases of successful tea shops, restaurants or small-scale factories whose owners did not plan intensive expansion and did not want their children to take them over. As a consequence, many businesses have rather short life-cycles, often no more than one generation, as shown in the diagram below. If we understand autonomy as a value, we can trace its meaning for people in approaches to work and family and point out the consequences for the business landscape. Like what Yanagisako called sentiments, values too are reproduced through culturally shaped everyday practices. For Yanagisako

(2002: 11), sentiments function as *Produktivkräfte* within family firms. Yanagisako uses Marx's German term, making the point that for Marx too human capacities, meaning things (such as sentiments, knowledge, and skills) *within* humans, rather than only outside factors, were crucial 'productive powers'. The latter term is an alternative translation of Marx's term to the more usual 'forces of production' (see also Cohen 1978, on Marx, as cited in Yanagisako 2002: 11; Donham 1990). It seems more appropriate to grasp these 'inner' factors and acknowledge their role in the shaping of actual material production.

Yanagisako includes a range of different things in her discussion of *sentiments*, among them ideas of selfhood and identity. I have touched on these as well by outlining what people see as achievements and what they are proud of. The desire for succession by a son is one such sentiment, present in Yanagisako's Italian examples, as well as among my Chinese informants, as I will describe below. Yanagisako opted against the term *desire*, which to her sounded too much like a physical yearning, as well as *goal* or *idea*, because these terms imply too much mental calculation (Yanagisako 2002: 11). While values can be either personal or shared, the word generally seems to imply more of a shared nature than Yanagisako's 'sentiments'. Values and sentiments have overlaps, and both matter to businesses. Yanagisako lists trust and betrayal as sentiments which, while they are not necessarily values in themselves, can certainly trigger moral judgements and responses. In the Como silk industry, the desire for capital accumulation is induced by the sentiments of family unity and com-munalism, as well as individualism, independence, and competition. In this case, as certain sentiments *incite* capital accumulation, they function as *Produktivkräfte*. I will describe similar observations in relation to my Chinese informants.

However, in the case that I have just presented I have identified the value of autonomy within the family and the value of prestige that does not come with business, but is rather weakened by it. These values, which were present particularly among Burmans, act rather as a constraint on business growth, thus posing a counterforce to production, which results in the setting up of a separate small firm by the younger generation. Studying values among business owners allows us to go beyond Marx to show that capitalists too try to realize values other than profit maximization. The exploitation of capital and labour does not work in the same way everywhere, and we can essentialize neither in accordance with class position or cultural background. Instead we must analyse qualitative data against the background of both historical and current socio-economic conditions.

Case 1: Manufacturing bamboo umbrellas

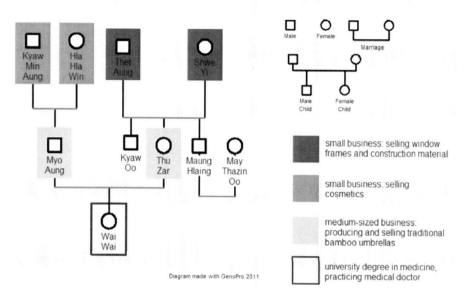

Diagram made with GenoPro 2011

Figure 1. Kinship diagram with occupational information, case 1.

Myo Aung and Thu Zar's case is an example in which parental hopes for status enhancement have been fulfilled, as their daughter became a doctor. The fact that she was unmarried and childfree did not seem to bother the parents, and they did not put much pressure on her regarding these aspects. Instead they asked my help to gather information about stipends to allow her to work or upgrade her education abroad, which could earn her a promotion upon returning home. Pursuing professional careers is not something generally seen as unsuitable for women. In fact, acquiring formal educational degrees and prestigious jobs can even be a way for them to achieve authority and prestige, which might at least partly compensate for their perceived lack of *hpoun:* (a type of power that men possess), which keeps them inherently spiritually subordinate to men (see Chapter 3).

However, if work demands too much of a woman's time and attention, this could interfere with care obligations if they are mothers. Thu Zar herself had repeatedly mentioned to me that she felt bad because she and her husband barely had time for their daughter when she was small and the business was growing in the 1990s. They gave their daughter to a kindergarten. When the parents told me that Wai Wai had some trouble with her co-workers at the hospital where she was working, and sometimes generally tended to avoid people, they wondered whether this was 'because

we somehow neglected her when she was little'. Even though their
relationship with their daughter was close, Thu Zar especially displayed a
sense of shame and regret for having compromised her caring duties for the
sake of running a business, and the business success could not morally compensate for her perceived failure to care for the child properly. This indicates
the different social roles people assume and the need to fulfil expectations
from different sides. Thu Zar continued to doubt whether she had chosen the
right priorities. In the following section I shall analyse more closely the
different values that many business owners subscribed to, namely the value
of being one's own boss, but also the concern with prestige, and how these
are weighed against each other.

Business Ownership: Autonomy without Prestige

While their business did not really serve as a source of pride for them, like
many business owners Thu Zar and Myo Aung appreciated being their own
boss. When they talked about their work, they often phrased it as a
'negative' form of freedom. Rather than saying 'it is good to do your own
business', I often heard 'it is good that I don't have to work for someone
else'. They stressed freedom *from* working for someone else, rather than
freedom *to do* one's own thing, which would have indicated a stronger
identification with their business. While in this chapter I have focused
mainly on autonomy in the family realm, the role of autonomy in work
contexts will play a greater role in the coming chapter. What is important
here is that the autonomy of being their own boss that business owners enjoy
comes at a price: not obtaining much prestige from what they did. This is
true even in cases like that of the parasol workshop, which makes products
that are well known throughout the country and are popular as souvenirs
with Burmese visitors to Pathein. The proud 'self-made man' identifying
himself primarily through his business achievements barely existed among
Burman business owners in Pathein. Many business owners then found
themselves in a seemingly contradictory situation in which they definitely
valued their own autonomy in the sense of not having to work for someone
else, but at the same time pressured their children to find high-level
employment in an environment characterized by strict workplace hierarchies.
This situation shows that people can subscribe to contradictory values simultaneously. Only empirical research allows us to disentangle these contradic-
tions and understand how they affect families. Are the values here incommensurable, forcing people to make 'tragic choices' (Robbins 2013: 102)? I
suggest that, while a conflict of values can certainly occur, for most
business-owning parents I met the concern with prestige outweighed their
appreciation of their autonomy at work.

Sometimes parental expectations concerning status enhancement go against the preferences of the child, and respectable jobs do not necessarily result in individual pleasure or happiness, as was the case for U Thet Naing Soe, an elderly man with whom I became friends. He had worked as a school headmaster all his life. Now that he was retired, he fixed printers. 'It has always been a dream', he explained. He always liked to fix things and was fascinated with technology. However, unlike Thu Zar and Myo Aung, he did not act against his parents' will by starting his own shop. Running small businesses themselves, his parents wanted to see him educated and convinced him to become a teacher. 'I was never happy. I liked the children and I did my best, but my salary was so low that I could barely survive on it'. When he retired, he taught himself how to fix printers. As more and more shops in the town purchased printers, his services were in great demand, and U Thet Naing Soe stated that he felt more satisfied now than he had ever been as a teacher. Livelihood choices thus entail inner-family negotiations that revolve around different individual and shared values like autonomy and prestige, as well as one's personal preferences. The two are not always compatible.

Moral ambiguity does not only concern the business activity itself but also the wealth attained from it. In fact, in a society where displaying generosity (*dāna*, see Chapter 6) is of such great importance, one might argue, as Kumada (2001: 109) has, that renouncing material objects is a stronger way of asserting status through moral virtues than possessing them, especially if these things were accumulated through business activities.[72] In the case of Thu Zar and Myo Aung, I only learned about the extent of their accumulated wealth after I had known the couple for several months. Only then did they show me the new big house they had recently built just around the corner from their business. The house will serve as an inheritance for their daughter and maybe for the couple to move into when they are older. For now they were still living in the upper floor of their workshop. The new house was largely empty, the king-size bed untouched, the mattress still wrapped in plastic. 'It is not good for our backs, this mattress', said Thu Zar. 'I prefer to sleep on the floor'. Material assets were not something they saw as achievements worth mentioning to me in the beginning. The couple tried to convey modesty, perhaps also because they live in a neighbourhood where

---

[72] The opposite of downplaying, namely conspicuous displays and mentions of material wealth, can also generate admiration from others in certain situations. As discussed in Chapter 3, different values and measures of 'success' are at play in different circumstances. In the example here, modesty expresses a rather morality-based value orientation amidst the outlined circumstances.

most people are poorer than they are, and also the economic gap between
them and their employees was considerable.

Negative attitudes toward business activities were especially strong
against small-scale trade like market-selling. 'I feel sorry for these people
who sit here all day and have to praise their goods', said one informant when
we visited the market. Where do such views come from? Older sources have
already described entrepreneurship in pre-colonial Burma as lower in status
compared to those who served the king, ordinary civil servants, and even
cultivators (Mya Maung 1946: 760). In respect of the Buddhist societies of
Thailand, Burma, and Ceylon (now Sri Lanka), Tambiah (1973) too
mentioned the 'the suspicion and base motives attributed to the trader,
middlemen, and moneylender by all levels of society – from the peasant
farmer to government economist (…)' and that 'private accumulation of
property and wealth, especially through trade and manufacture as an exclusive orientation, has always been devalued as signifying excessive self-
interest, greed, and exploitation' (p. 19). Some of my informants linked
entrepreneurship to dishonest behaviour, and more specifically to breaking
the five Buddhist precepts for lay people, which include no stealing and no
lying. Some business owners or traders admitted that the market persuaded
them to break these precepts, for instance, by exaggerating the quality of
their products (see also Pyi Phyo Kyaw 2017) or by not telling the truth to
tax officials when negotiating their turnover tax (see also Bissinger 2016:
32). While business owners appreciated the fact of being their own boss and
avoiding subordination (see Chapter 5), they refrained from admitting this
preference for autonomy too openly. Thus, another reason why doing
business does not generate much respect is that it shows too clearly people's
opting for autonomy, a value that certainly matters but does not necessarily
help to show a person in good light as a member of a social collective. Thus,
as I shall discuss later, business owners would often stress their role as
family members, supporters of the sangha, good employers, or otherwise
valuable community members almost to balance out their role as business
owners.

Besides religious ideas, historical developments have played their part
as well. The country has experienced a century of colonial rule in which
entrepreneurs were mostly foreigners, a period of independence in which no
considerable Burman entrepreneurial class emerged (Brown 2011), followed
by almost three decades of socialism that discouraged private business
activities and forced many into the shadow economy. Doing business
became a risky undertaking, as businesses were always under the threat of
being confiscated by the government (as it had happened in large numbers in
the 1960s), and this fear is still in the back of the minds of business owners

today. Moreover, in the transition years after 1990 a crony capitalism emerged consisting of alliances between business tycoons and military elites, which linked the image of large-scale entrepreneurship to fraud and exploitation. None of these factors did anything to foster positive attitudes towards entrepreneurship. In addition, in Pathein today, many of the businesses in the inner parts of town are owned by members of minority groups. A prevailing negative attitude towards entrepreneurship among Burmans might also have been framed in relation to other groups, such as the Chinese. Trade appeared to be the realm of 'others'.

Keyes (1990: 182) mentioned the ambivalence of north-eastern Thai villagers (a minority group linguistically and culturally closer to the Lao than to the Thai) towards people doing business in rice-milling, shop-keeping, trucking, and brokering in agricultural and craft products. Moreover, in Keyes' field site most traders and merchants were historically from different ethnic groups, usually Chinese and to a lesser extent Vietnamese. When more local people began to engage in these activities they were given a morally ambiguous status, and even very wealthy businessmen were not treated with much respect, unlike, for instance, government officials. In response to their ambivalent status, however, many actively and generously participated in religious events in the village. In that context, wealth was acknowledged as advantageous for increasing one's merit, and people's ambiguity towards wealthy businessmen did not mean that villagers declined opportunities for wealth improvement. Many went to Bangkok for better earnings and tried to work their way up. What is particularly interesting is that when more and more villagers encountered successful Chinese business people in Bangkok, some saw in them a new model for a different way of moving 'up', that is, in economic terms. Some villagers took that as an inspiration to start engaging in business themselves. However, the important difference for my informants is that these villagers were fully aware of their minority status within Thai society, and they perceived themselves as being in a subordinate position to the Thais. Imitating what other ethnic minorities (the Chinese) did constituted a way for them to enhance at least their economic position in the light of their already subordinate status. In Pathein, in contrast, my Burman informants are part of the ethnic majority, so the dynamics at play here are fundamentally different. No perception of inferiority would bring the Burmans to alter their attitudes toward entrepreneurship and lead them to orient themselves toward the Chinese traders. While Burmans would acknowledge that the Chinese are 'good at doing business' (see below), and even admire their skills as such, this does not put the Chinese in a morally superior position – if anything, the opposite.

Due to the morally ambiguous and unprestigious image of doing business, many Burman business owners presented their work activities merely as a means to get by, without specifically emphasizing their wealth accumulation. However, this does not mean that *all* employment situations were regarded as morally superior to business ownership. Prestige from employment comes mainly from jobs that demand certain educational degrees. Moreover, the question of which jobs bring prestige cannot be answered with reference to simple distinctions between employment and self-employment or the public versus the private sector. At present the private sector offers only a very few attractive and respectable employment options in places like Pathein. Therefore, a large number of people saw it as desirable to obtain employment as a civil servant. Employment in the public sector also often comes with advantages such as a stable income, pensions and free or subsidized housing. Furthermore, it may enable access to influential people, potential patrons who could bring further benefits. However, this does not mean that public-sector jobs *per se* are prestigious and respected. While some jobs, such as teachers, enjoy great respect, there are other moral discourses against, for example, corruption in the state ministries. Some public-sector jobs, such as police officers, seem to be rather disrespected by many. The daughter of Myo Khine, an egg trader I got to know in Pathein, became a lead engineer in a private company in Yangon, which has made him very proud and serves as an example that private-sector jobs can bring prestige as well.

In fact, business owners who abandoned employment to start their own shops (often financially more profitable, but that was not mentioned as a reason) would also phrase their decisions in moral terms. Myo Khine was one who had traded employment for business ownership. In 1980, at the age of twenty, he started to work as a cashier at the Myanmar Economic Bank after finishing grade ten at school. He stayed in this job for four years, but then decided to train as a goldsmith in a shop where his uncle was already working. Myo Khine said that he resigned from the bank because the salary was low, but also because he did not agree with the bank's and the government's policies, claiming that 'these people were not honest; what they did was not good'. He was referring to different strategies the bank used to obtain money from customers. He said his salary and position remained low because he refused to engage in dishonest activities, and he condemned his colleagues' and superior's greed.

It is impossible to know whether what Myo Khine said is true or if there were other reasons for him not receiving promotion. In any case, it is telling that he now emphasized the moral aspects of his decision. Myo Khine worked as a goldsmith for some years, but as the business environment became tougher when people started buying less gold, he changed tack again and is now trading eggs. However, rather than talking about his trade in eggs, he prefers to talk about the Buddhist school where he volunteers, and he was always eager to show me photos of the building's progress on his phone. While business activities were regarded with ambiguity and do not offer much prestige, they are sometimes the only and often the most profitable option for many. Myo Khine's example makes it clear that a move toward business ownership is seen as something that has to be justified, and such justifications often take the shape of moral arguments. Opting for autonomy, as Myo Khine did, is something that happens frequently (see Chapter 5), but especially if it leads to a loss of prestige, it needs to be explained and balanced with taking otherwise valuable roles in the social collective, such as making donations.

Myo Khine's case also serves as an example showing us where business owners in Pathein found a sense of achievement and pride. In his case it was his daughter's prestigious job and his own religious activities. Women who run small shops in Pathein were often quick to mention that the shop is actually more of a hobby, as their husbands hold good positions in the public sector. Even the owners of bigger businesses would often change the topic of conversation from business to other aspects of their lives, such as their charitable and donation activities, or their children's education, indicating that these aspects were deemed more valuable. This should not be mistaken for a rejection of 'hard work', since many self-employed people, especially business owners, like the parasol workshop owners presented here, have been working hard for decades, often rarely making time for leisure. Yet, they did not emphasize business ownership but instead drew on other realms of life as sources of pride that the economic sphere does not offer them in their view. Some business owners, especially women, stressed that they wanted to focus on religious practice when they get older, for example, by joining meditation retreats and attending *dhamma* talks. They also explained that keeping the shop a controllable size instead of letting it grow makes it easier to focus on religious practice and thus on one's spiritual progress. In these cases, the businesses guaranteed the necessary economic security needed to focus on religion, meaning that here they served as a means to spiritual ends.

I have now outlined the moral ambiguity with which business activities are viewed – one of the reasons why children of business owners were often encouraged to pursue more prestigious professions. In the following section I will take a closer look at a certain form of prestige – *goun* – and show why it matters in obtaining one's livelihood.

Trading Autonomy for *Goun*

Among Burmans, status considerations play a role in all social interactions because society is perceived to be hierarchical. However, it would not be enough to understand status as just an end in itself. A higher social status indicates dignity, security, and empowerment, understandable wishes given the country's particularly unstable economic and political history. There are different 'avenues' to status mobility, for example, by gaining political, moral or spiritual influence. One obvious path for men is to join the sangha, whose members are understood to be inherently spiritually superior to all laypeople. In the worldly realm, considerations of status in Myanmar have often been addressed with reference to different concepts of power, like *ana*, *awza*, and *hpoun:* (e.g. Houtman 1999; Harriden 2012; Walton 2017a). Such concepts, which are crucial for the ideal leader, are largely believed to be given at birth, a result of the *kamma* of past lives. I have been struck by how much attention has been paid to *ana*, *awza*, and *hpoun:*, while almost no one addressed the concept of *goun*. This is probably because scholars have concentrated on understanding political developments in Myanmar, these former three concepts being primarily relevant for questions of leadership and political power.

I suggest we pay more attention to *goun* because a desire for *goun* matters for many life decisions among Burmans, including those concerning work. *Goun* (from the Pāli word *guṇa*) has been translated as 'prestige' (Spiro 1966: 68; 1982: 446) or 'virtue' (Nash 1965: 76), and online dictionaries also give glosses like 'dignity' and 'honour', although here the term *thei'ka* seems closer. Some of my informants also found the English word 'pride' appropriate. *Goun* can be either religious or secular. I argue that, for the average Burman person for whom the prospect of receiving any relevant political leadership position is remote, the idea of *goun* is of much more immediate importance. Another factor that makes *goun* so important is that it is not innate, not (unlike *hpoun:*) a result of deeds in past lives, but instead can be acquired during a person's present lifetime (*goun ya. de* which means 'to get *goun*'). *Goun*, which has the function of a shared value here, is important with regard to issues of livelihoods. Thin Zar, a tea-shop owner I will describe in more detail in the following chapter, kept her employment as a teacher alongside running the shop for fifteen years. This constituted a double burden and required her to get up extremely early in the morning to get the tea shop ready before leaving for her job as a teacher. The shop was much more profitable than the teaching, and it was not financially necessary to continue the latter. Why did she keep doing it? '*Goun shi. de*', she replied. Running a tea shop, no matter how profitable, would never result in *goun*. *Goun* is part of the answer to the question why business owners want their children to pursue an education and certain forms of employment, so that they may acquire the prestige they themselves never had, even though their work allowed them to be their own boss and accumulate wealth.

My observations contradict what Spiro wrote (1966: 68; 1982: 238, 446, 474) because unlike Spiro I do not think that many people automatically recognize other people's *goun* through their mere possession, display or even sharing of wealth – at least this does not seem to be a very dominant understanding of *goun*. Wealth might be recognized as proof of the possession of good *kamma* from past lives, and generous donors receive gratitude and admiration, but this is because their wealth enables them to gain merit through acts of *dāna* (generosity), rather than because it is automatically recognized as *goun*. Thin Zar, the tea-shop owner, is the best example proving this point. She kept her low-paid job as a teacher precisely to acquire *goun*, instead of focusing fully on her much more profitable tea shop. We thus need to complicate the notion of *goun* and look for other potential ways to earn *goun* that influence people's decisions and assessments. If material possessions were really so decisive for *goun*, it would make no sense that entrepreneurs and traders enjoy so little respect, with some even trying to downplay their material possessions. We acquire some more systematic insights from Nash (1965), according to whom *goun* (which he transcribed as *gon*) has strong moral connotations. *Goun* constitutes a virtue that can stem from different sources, such as 'a sterling personal character, social religious learning or piety, or even the trait of impartiality in dispute' (p. 76). As Nash studied *goun* in connection with the political authority of village leaders, he focused primarily on the importance of *goun* for respected and legitimate leaders. However, *goun* does not only, nor even primarily, manifest itself in political contexts. Nash viewed *goun* more widely as the 'moral content of social relations' (p. 271).

Discussing *goun* with Burmans revealed that the concept can be understood in a variety of ways. Some stripped it completely of its moral component and saw it in physical beauty or material wealth, or other aspects that individuals may value or be proud of. Others saw *goun* as primarily linked to high social status through education and certain professions. Yet others said that such interpretations of *goun* were misunderstandings of the concept, insisting that *goun* requires a moral component and that every person can earn *goun* through moral actions. One informant who held this view quoted the saying '*alou' huthamya. goun shi. so*', that is, 'every kind of work contains *goun*' or 'every kind of work is valuable', stressing that *goun* stems from morality much more than from the status gained through certain occupations. However, people would also mention that *goun* can have a negative dimension as well. For example, it can be used to discriminate against others, those who are not seen as having it. Also, if people are over-confident or too proud of themselves, it is regarded as negative (*goun mau'*, *mau'* literally meaning 'overflowing'; can refer to boastful or bragging behaviour). Here, the importance of modesty and respect for others becomes evident.

This ambiguity concerning current interpretations of the concept should not lead us to doubt its analytical usefulness. *Goun* might be similar in nature to religious knowledge, spiritual purity, and the power that monks acquire by practising meditation. In theory these qualities are attainable for everyone, and it is not necessarily obvious to others who possesses them, since theoretically they cannot be directly linked to certain measurable or visible factors. In practice, however, these qualities will rarely be publicly recognized if conspicuous markers are lacking (see Houtman 1990: 193). For one's religious status such markers could be belonging to a certain monastery, attracting many lay followers, having passed Buddhist exams or regularly sharing one's wisdom (ibid.). For *goun* among lay people, important markers could be knowledge, a respectable job or being known for one's positive personal qualities. Thus, people aspire to achieve these markers. The fact that *goun* can be earned during one's lifetime makes it important for everyday considerations. Nash outlined certain types of *goun* that seemed to be collectively recognized. He mentioned three major types: *goun* coming from a recognized moral and good character (*thi-la.goun*), being modest, incorruptible and beyond self-interest (*thamadi. goun*), and *goun* stemming from worldly or religious wisdom (*pyinya goun*) (Nash 1965: 271).

I want to focus here specifically on *pyinya goun*. This form of *goun* is probably the most easily grasped and regarded as 'measurable', as people see it nowadays as something one can attain through formal education.[73] *Pyinya* (from the Pāli word *paññā*) means knowledge or wisdom, and is an important concept in Theravāda doctrine. In Myanmar today, *pyinya* can refer to the spiritual wisdom of monks, but it is also the common term for secular education. Words for 'education system', 'ministry of education' or 'higher education' all contain the word *pyinya*. A combination of the Buddhist roots with the historically emerging importance of formal edu-cation and white-collar jobs (mainly developed under the British) have both

---

[73] This is the case at least for its worldly version, *law:ki pyinya*. There is also *law:kou'tara pyinya*, which refers to the spiritual wisdom needed to attain *nibbāna*, which is not gained through worldly education but by studying Buddhist scriptures, gaining religious insight, and meditation.

contributed to people's high concern with formal education degrees.[74] Formal education remains a goal and an ideal, even in the absence of any realistic job prospects for most people in their respective fields of study.[75]

When people in Pathein talked about themselves or others, the level of someone's education was often seen as a person's main feature, one that required mentioning, whether directly relevant for the respective conversation or not (phrases such as 'he/she is not educated' are often uttered quickly when talking about someone). In many houses graduation photos were hung on walls, and when a couple married, their university degrees were mentioned on the wedding invitations. People pursue degrees even when they are not planning to work in the respective field. As in Maung Maung's case, to be presented below, Chinese entrepreneurs also send their children to university, despite knowing that they will take over the family business. This shows that among entrepreneurs, as well as among non-Burmans, a formal university degree is highly desirable. The value placed on formal educational degrees does not contradict the fact that many people saw serious flaws in Myanmar's educational system. Informants criticized the quality of the teaching, the methods of rote learning, and the fact that the teaching materials are in English, even though hardly anyone has an adequate knowledge of the language. People who can afford it send their children to private schools or to study abroad. Moreover, final degrees are not the only formalized measure of a certain form of prestige or status. People in fact collect all sorts of certificates, and schools now issue written certificates for all kinds of things and assignments, including having produced poems or paintings. It is not uncommon to find several different certificates on the wall of a home, especially if the family has children who are currently attending school or university. If children are formally educated, this also creates *goun* for the parents.

Ideally, education should lead to high and respectable positions in either the public or private sector. Especially in the public sector, this can mean a relatively low income. To understand how out of kilter status and income can be, it is illuminating to look at the role of teachers more closely. Teachers are among the most highly respected members of society. People talk of them as one of the Five Infinite Venerables, alongside the Buddha,

---

[74] On the growing enthusiasm for education in India and young people's negotiation of educated under- and unemployment, see Jeffrey et al. (2008).

[75] The high regard that people have for education should not obscure the fact that formal education, let alone prestigious employment, are not easily available for most of the population. The vast majority of Myanmar's population aged 25 or over, 61.3 percent, either had no formal education at all, or had only attended primary school, but not always completed it, according to the 2014 census. Only 7.3 percent had a university degree (Myanmar Department of Population 2017b).

the *dhamma* (Buddhist teachings), the sangha, and one's parents. The term used in addressing a teacher, *hsaya*, is also used for superordinates or experts (masters) in other contexts. As we have seen, Thin Zar, the tea-shop owner already mentioned here, kept her employment as a teacher to infuse *goun* into her life and thus ensure herself a high social status. I was impressed by the number of people in Pathein who claimed to be 'teachers', many of whom had even designed their own business cards, referring to themselves as '*hsaya* [name]' to advertise the classes they gave. Often these were private tuition classes in the evenings, something that is not actually legal but widely practised. Parents, despite the additional costs, often have no choice but to let their children participate in these tuition classes, as participation is often mandatory in order to pass a course.[76] This informal tuition system can also be a way for actual teachers to make extra income in the evenings.[77] However, as many people giving tuition classes are not actually employed as teachers elsewhere, I argue that this practice also constitutes a way for people to gain a teacher-like high status.

The imbalance between status and income is striking also in other cases. A snack-seller on the road-side near my home in Pathein sold savoury pancakes from a stall each day from early morning until the night time for 500 kyat each. He told me that he earns at least 30,000 kyat per day, sometimes more. As he works seven days per week, this would result in a monthly income of something like at least 900,000 kyat (ca. 653.00 EUR). Even deducting the cost of renting a space for selling and the salary of one worker, this is still an income considerably higher than what a teacher earns. A high-school teacher's monthly starting salary is 175,000 kyat, which is around 127.00 EUR.[78] The teacher's status, though, is one of almost unques-

---

[76] As a result, all over Pathein I met people who saw themselves as capable of teaching a certain subject, offering evening classes to students. For parents it is often impossible to judge the actual quality of these classes. The effectiveness of such tuition classes is questionable for different reasons (see also Lorch 2007).

[77] If teachers try to make too much money through tuition classes they appear greedy, which lessens people's respect for them. A delicate balance must be kept in which conveying modesty remains crucial. Sometimes, retired teachers are financially supported by their former students, who collect donations for them. This is an indication of both the respect teachers enjoy and their often dire financial situations after retirement.

[78] Public-sector employee's salaries have nonetheless been rising. In 2012, a teacher earned only between 47,000 Kyat and 64,000 Kyat (Davidsen et al. 2018: 126). Furthermore, the public sector comes with some more structural benefits. Those employed in it (civil servants, military and political personnel, employees in state-owned enterprises) are the only ones who receive pensions and sometimes other in-kind allowances, such as free or subsidized housing, and fuel or vehicles, under certain conditions. Such in-kind allowances are not available to all employees, and granting them seems rather variable and discretionary, in contrast to salaries, which are clearly laid down by official regulations (ibid.: 15). In the fiscal year 2015/2016,

tionable authority, and it evokes respect and admiration; the snack-seller, by contrast, is looked down upon.

Weber's theory of stratification (1946: 180–194) emphasized that class in economic terms is not the only criterion according to which people will be ranked in a social hierarchy: what he labelled 'power' and 'status' are just as important. One might rank very high in one domain and very low in another. Moreover, these factors all influence each other, can take different forms, and might stem from different sources. Both power and prestige, for example, can stem from worldly factors in the case of political power, or from spiritual factors, as in the case of monks. The sangha is a striking example. It has always been a refuge for people from poorer backgrounds. Rural families would give children to the sangha when they could not feed them. People who have lost all their material possessions often still have the option of going into the monastery as a monk. While these people do not come from the 'high classes' in terms of wealth, as soon as they wear the robe they leave everyone else behind in terms of status, not as a person, but through the moral role they assume as monks. Their status here even increases precisely because of their rejection of material wealth. As mentioned, teachers are another example of the mismatch between prestige and income. They may rely on donations from their former students to give them a living after retirement, but these students kneel before them as a sign of their great respect. That respect comes from prestige, not from power, nor from material wealth.

Since business ownership is often more profitable than, for example, low-level public-sector jobs, we are dealing here with an imbalance between income and status. This can have several consequences. It can keep those without access to prestigious employment, among them business owners with a high income, in positions where they are not seen as particularly respectable. It can also hinder entrepreneurial ambition and capital accumulation if a preference is given to low-paid employment that entails a higher status. However, attitudes toward business ownership might change with the growing attention being given to small and medium enterprises as potential drivers of economic development. Increasingly, foreign organizations and local government authorities are promoting and supporting the

---

public-sector salaries ranged from 120,000 Kyat (ca. 87.00 EUR) to 500,000 Kyat (ca. 363.00 EUR) according to rank. Reforms from 2012 have also expanded benefits for public-sector employees concerning housing, unemployment insurance, disability, and survivors' pensions. Furthermore, a monthly allowance for civil servants working in 'hardship areas' has been introduced (ibid.: 109). Public sector jobs are also seen as attractive because the incomes are stable and predictable. However, many employees are expected to rotate and thus have to move to new locations every few years. Furthermore, despite the benefits mentioned here, financial payments such as pensions remain very low, especially for those of lower rank.

development of small and medium enterprises in Myanmar, and media outlets portray successful entrepreneurs positively as role models in Yangon or Mandalay.

I have outlined how the low regard for business ownership on the one hand and the concern with prestige (specifically in the form of *goun*) on the other hand, as well as the importance of autonomy within the family and as business owners, influence people's attitudes to work and livelihood choices. However, people generally do not choose between alternatives (if they can choose in the first place) based on one single measure of comparison. Factors such as stability, income, autonomy, and prestige all play a role. In the world of jobs, it seems to be often the case that there is a certain tipping point after which stability, security, and the prestige of certain forms of employment outweigh the independence of being one's own boss and even the potentially higher income of self-employment. At least among those for whose children access to higher education and respected employment were a realistic prospect, enhancing status and prestige had priority over the advantage of being one's own boss that business ownership would entail. Here, positive inter-generational upward mobility was understood as the conversion of financial capital gained through the parents' business into cultural capital and ultimately symbolic capital (Bourdieu 1986). I have also shown that, even though many Burman-owned businesses in Pathein did not resemble the type of 'family firm' depicted in Yanagisako's well-known ethnography from Italy (2002), this does not mean that the family does not matter for Burman business owners in Pathein. In fact, precisely because of the specifics in their kinship system and certain values they hold, they favour separate means of livelihood for each generation. Thus, although the situation is different from that described by Yanagisako for Italy, in Pathein too family negotiations shape the business landscape in crucial ways.

If all this is the case, then at this point one is bound to ask who are those who display different patterns, namely the owners of the slightly bigger inter-generational businesses in Pathein, many of which can be found in prime downtown locations? The answer is that most of these businesses are owned by members of minority groups, such as the descendants of Chinese and Indian immigrants. Their role in the business sphere is so prominent that they deserve some attention here. The question then becomes what leads these families, contrary to those I have presented so far, to invest in building up inter-generational family businesses? In order to explain this, I shall contrast Thu Zar and Myo Aung's business with a rice-trading firm run by an ethnic Chinese family located only a few minutes driving time away.

Case 2. Maung Maung's Rice Trade: A Chinese Family Business

One of the Chinese business owners in downtown Pathein is Maung Maung, a rice-trader.[79] When I first met him, I had no idea about his ethnic affiliation – we just had a quick chat to make an appointment for a longer meeting. As I went away with a student, Zarni, who had accompanied me, the student casually said, 'He is Chinese'. I was puzzled. Had I missed something? 'Do you know him?', I asked. 'No', Zarni said. 'Did he say that he is Chinese?', I asked. 'No', Zarni replied, 'but he said he owns some houses downtown'. Zarni's logic was to attribute a certain ethnicity to Maung Maung based on his wealth and business activities, as well as on the location of his houses. In doing so, Zarni followed a pattern that was not uncommon among Patheinians. Half-jokingly they would refer to the downtown area as 'Chinatown'. My interaction with Zarni indicates how certain economic aspects may be linked to ethnicity and made manifest in stereotypes and sometimes in prejudices. One of the most popular sayings, known to virtually everyone, is *Tayou'-lo lou', Kala-lo su., Bama-lo ma' hpyoun: ne.* – 'Earn money like the Chinese, save money like the Indians[80], and don't waste it like the Burmans'.[81] The saying may function as advice which parents would give their children. In fact, often it was Burmans themselves who quoted the saying in a humorous way, almost as an excuse for their presumed inability to succeed in business, as in 'it is just not something we are good at'.

Burman as well as Chinese informants linked the success of some Chinese families mostly to factors they saw as typically 'Chinese'. This included habits such as hard work and frugality, as well as specific business knowledge and certain network structures, within which 'the Chinese always support each other'. In a more negative fashion, some Burmans described the Chinese as greedy and 'crazy about money'. Some also mentioned that they felt that the Chinese in downtown Pathein 'look down on us'. In return, some Chinese I spoke with described the Burmans as 'lazy' and as unwilling to take on opportunities. One informant said that Burmans 'don't think about tomorrow' (see Tong 2010: 157–158 for similar data). In that sense, people in Pathein themselves voiced different stereotypes which linked the values and social factors of specific groups to economic performance in a rather deterministic way. I have described negative attitudes toward entrepreneur-

---

[79] There are also many business owners of Indian descent in Pathein, but due to a lack of data I cannot systematically engage with these communities here.

[80] The term *kala* for Indians has derogatory connotations.

[81] Karen friends knew the saying as well, but in the version they were familiar with, 'Karen' replaced 'Burmans'.

ship among Burmans earlier in this chapter. We must consider the possibility that these attitudes might have been shaped or strengthened precisely in relation to other groups, such as the Chinese. Burmans may see entrepreneurship as an arena of 'others'. Some Burman informants mentioned that it is difficult to build successful businesses because many buildings in attractive locations are owned by Chinese. While the prominence of minorities among business owners was not the only reason for Burmans' ambiguity about these activities, it probably did play a role. While the socialist period had the official aim of making private property irrelevant and levelling people's social and economic conditions, it did little for the abolition of traditional attitudes, stereotypes, and 'typical' roles in the economic sphere, many of which are still organized along lines of ethnicity. A large black market had kept people active in the private economy, and even though the accumulation of wealth was hindered, trade and business activities were always taking place. In contrast to the Burmans, among the Chinese business owners, their business ownership and success appeared to be much more highly valued in themselves, being presented as a sign of intergenerational cooperation, discipline, and business intelligence.

A person's ethnicity is registered by the Myanmar state, and for many people of Chinese (or other, such as Indian) descent, their ancestry will be displayed on their identity cards, no matter for how many generations their family has been living in Myanmar. The same goes for people of mixed descent. A certain 'otherness' is thus institutionalized and often makes it impossible for these people to attain full citizenship. Ethnicity can be experienced as a rather fluid category in everyday matters, and many Chinese in Myanmar, as elsewhere in Southeast Asia, display a 'portfolio of identities' (Farrelly and Olinga-Shannon 2015: 9)[82], with some families

---

[82] There are many similarities here to Burmese-Indians, many of whom practice forms of Hinduism, Islam or Sikhism. Usually, their places of worship function as a community centre just like monasteries do for Buddhists. Like Chinese, Burmese-Indians have undergone a process of 'Burmanization', and yet many (some communities more than others) retain a lot from their original traditions and belief systems, and their ancestry continues to play a role in their self-identification. Like the Chinese they have been able to maintain and strengthen low-key but valuable commercial networks throughout the socialist period, which has helped them focus on petty trade (see Egreteau 2011). Burmese Indians are often regarded as successful traders (or smugglers), thus having to deal with economic labelling just like other groups: Burmese-Indians in general, especially Islamic ones, are confronted with discrimination on the institutional level and in day-to-day interactions. Nevertheless, in socio-economic terms they have been described as a 'lower middle-class of urban merchants, shopkeepers, traders, restaurant managers and pharmacists' (ibid.: 45) In Pathein Burmese-Indians act as business owners, market sellers and traders, and Muslims of Burmese-Indian descent run quite a few of the larger businesses downtown, such as teashops and hotels, even though my impression was that the Chinese still had a larger presence here.

following Chinese traditions and practices more than others. Chinese often have a Burmese as well as a Chinese name, and some display both of them on their business cards. They may use either their Burmese or Chinese identities in interaction with others or in official processes, depending on what serves them better in a particular context. People of mixed ancestry often explain their identity as a patchwork made up of different parts. They would say, for example: 'I am one quarter Chinese, one quarter Karen, and half Burmese'. Many Chinese arrived in Burma with a degree of 'religious flexibility' (Farrelly and Olinga-Shannon 2015: 19). Some were Mahayana Buddhists, while others were not. However, over the generations, most Chinese in Myanmar have embraced Theravāda Buddhism, but combine it with a range of Chinese beliefs (Roberts 2016: 139).

The Chinese have been careful to fulfil certain local expectations and have often strongly assimilated to the Burmans in respect of names, language, and religious practices. Besides assimilating to the main religion, Chinese also intermarry more frequently with Burmans than, for example, Muslims or Christians tend to, and such unions are met with much less resentment, possibly because the offspring of such marriages will be raised predominantly as Buddhists (Farrelly and Olinga-Shannon 2015: 18–20). As a consequence of all these factors, the Chinese are not considered a threat to Buddhism, unlike Muslims, who have faced increasing hostility in recent years (ibid.: 16).[83] In Maung Maung's home, as in most Chinese homes, one finds a Buddhist shrine alongside Chinese religious objects. However, the extent to which my Chinese informants performed and actually identified as Theravāda Buddhists varied. A number were very quick to stress that they were 'not actually Buddhists', or 'not in the same way as the Burmans'[84], while others saw themselves as serious believers.

Maung Maung was in his sixties when I met him. He was married and had three grown-up children. His house was located on the inner town's Strand Road, with a balcony overlooking the river. Two of his children were

---

[83] There have been anti-Chinese sentiments as well, sometimes expressed in cultural and media work (Zin 2012). However, these sentiments usually refer to newly immigrated Chinese who have come since the early 1990s to invest in the country. Some of these investments have had severe effects in the bigger cities, first and foremost Mandalay. A number of large-scale infrastructure projects in the country have been set up by Chinese as well, and some of these projects, such as the planned construction of the Myitsone dam, have sparked public protests by residents.

[84] Maung Maung first stated that he was not a strict Buddhist when we talked about *kamma*, but on a different occasion he pointed to Buddhism as a unifying factor with Burmans, in distinction to Muslims. He said: 'We, Burmans and Chinese, are different from Muslims, because our religion is the same'. Religion is deployed flexibly here, either to set boundaries or to form unions with others.

still living with Maung Maung and his wife, and they all worked together in the business. The third daughter had married and settled in Yangon, where she worked in her family-in-law's gold shop. Maung Maung bought rice from rice-mill operators or from other brokers and traded it to different parts of the country. Most of his customers were resellers who ordered larger amounts, but some customers ordered only three or four bags of rice, which they sold directly to consumers or served in restaurants. The administrative work took place on the ground floor of Maung Maung's house, where a number of rice bags were stacked around the desks. Most of the rice, however, was stored in three big warehouses further down the river. Maung Maung had started this business in the early 1990s. Technically he had not inherited the business itself from his father, but he had inherited the land for his house from him, as well as some starting capital and had gained business experience through his parents' activities.

Maung Maung's father had come to Burma from China's Fujian province during the years following independence, having arrived by ship with a group of others. When his friends went back to China, he decided to stay. While Pathein had been a multicultural trading hub for centuries, large-scale migration had taken place to Burma from India, and to a lesser extent from China, in the colonial period. Under British rule, Indians as well as Chinese were able to secure important roles in the economy. However, during World War II hundreds of thousands of Indians fled the country. As they left behind positions in the economy as well as houses in the inner cities, the Chinese filled some of these gaps, for example, as rice-mill owners (Roberts 2016: 104). In the post-independence period, the Chinese were able to continue running their economic enterprises, as well as Chinese schools, associations, and temples (Mya Than 1997: 132). However, their situation worsened considerably after the military took power in 1962, and many had their businesses taken away after the introduction of the 'Burmese Way to Socialism'. Later, the promulgation of a Citizenship Law in 1982 hit the Chinese community once more. As a consequence of these legal changes, Chinese were not given full citizenship, which limited their rights and opportunities, for example, to work for the government (Arraiza and Vonk 2017). It also affected their children, who were not allowed to attend certain professional tertiary educational institutions, including medical, engineering, agricultural, and economics colleges (Mya Than 1997: 133). Some discriminatory policies and practices also extended to persons of mixed ancestry (ibid.: 136). As elsewhere in Southeast Asia, entrepreneurship was thus a logical path to pursue for marginalized minorities.

Before Ne Win took power in 1962, Maung Maung's father was running a small business in Pathein selling pagoda utensils for donation purposes. Under the new rulers, this business was nationalized. Many others too lost their profitable rice and salt mills, and those without full citizenship lost prestigious positions in larger, now state-owned enterprises. In their efforts to reduce foreign influences on the country the military introduced a range of policies aimed at 'Burmanization', which included the shutting down of Chinese newspapers, schools, and associations. Those Chinese who did not leave the country were forced to keep a low profile, taking on Burmese names and dress and adopting Theravāda Buddhism. Many secured their livelihoods through small-scale business activities or black-market trade. As these were both crucial for the survival of the population, they were largely tolerated by the government.

After losing his pagoda utensils business, Maung Maung's father started selling Chinese snacks, and since he and his wife had two children by then, he also decided to sell his last asset: a boat. From the money he received for it, he bought the piece of land in Strand Road where Maung Maung's family were still living at the time of my research. The couple survived from small-scale trading activities. When the children had grown up, Maung Maung's older sister got married and settled in Yangon, where she built up a coconut oil business with her husband's family. Maung Maung's parents decided to follow her to Yangon after the economic changes of the early 1990s, as business opportunities seemed better there. Maung Maung himself chose to stay in Pathein: he said that if he had followed his family, he would have always remained their subordinate, as his sister's husband controlled the coconut oil business. In Pathein he could build up his own business. Maung Maung deliberately decided to part from his family to ensure a certain authority in business and in family matters in the years to come. When his parents left Pathein, Maung Maung inherited the plot of land as well as a sum of money that would serve as initial capital for his own business ventures. He was now married to a Chinese woman. They first opened a licensed pawnshop, but switched to the rice trade after a few years.

Plate 5. Bags of rice ready to be transported in Pathein.

Maung Maung received a bank loan from the newly established Asia Wealth Bank, for which he had to prove ownership of a house and a business. This distinguished him from the parasol workshop owners Myo Aung and Thu Zar, who did not fulfil these criteria when they decided to open a business, and thus had to save money through a period of working for someone else. Maung Maung and his wife started their rice trade and had three children. Over the years, as the rice business grew, Maung Maung paid back his loan to the bank and renovated his house. He attributed his success to *kamma*, which he thought had somehow been 'stimulated' by the birth of his children: 'I am not a university graduate, and I am not even a strict Buddhist. But it seems that I have good *kamma*. Whenever I had another child, my business became more successful'. Maung Maung thus linked business success and kinship in his rationalizing process.

At the time of my research, his rice trade business employed twenty-five workers. Administrative tasks and managing orders were done by Maung Maung himself, his son, and to a lesser extent his wife and youngest daughter. The family had diversified their capital. They were also trading in fertilizers, did small-scale money-lending, and had invested in some stocks and plots of land. Maung Maung had his table full of books on business management and investment, from China, Japan, and America. He regularly met with other Chinese businessmen to exchange knowledge, experience, and contacts. When pointing to the photos of his children's graduation ceremonies, Maung Maung said: 'Now, all my kids have graduated. But none of them is educated', a criticism of the country's education system, which he (as well as other informants) regards as inefficient. He was not the only one to make such sarcastic comments. Since the quality of education has dropped so much under the military, quite a few people maintained that having a degree does not actually mean much in terms of education. Maung Maung's cynicism concerning the education system may also have been a way to counter the high regard many people have for formal education, while business ownership, the path that his family took, does not enjoy similar respect. In his social circles, however, which mostly consist of other Chinese business people, running a successful business was indeed a way to gain recognition, as well as being a source of pride.

Since 2008, it has essentially been Maung Maung's son, Naing Lin, who has managed the business. Maung Maung explained that it was best for his son to take over the already established business. He continued by saying that Naing Lin had not been one of the best students in his cohort, and therefore prestigious careers in medicine or engineering seemed unrealistic anyway. This indicates that Maung Maung had, or wanted to give the impression that he had, at least considered alternatives for his son, but in any case, he made it clear that he as a father had had a lot of say in the decision on Naing Lin's future. Naing Lin himself said that taking over the business happened 'automatically' for him. He identified with the shop and saw it as a family heritage, referring to its formation and expansion as an achievement of his father which deserves to be honoured and preserved (similar to Yanagisako 2002: 40). In that sense, just as in the case of Thu Zar and Myo Aung, Maung Maung too had his hopes concerning the son's future fulfilled, even though the results took very different shapes. While in the first case the daughter pursued formal education to become a doctor, in Maung Maung's case the son willingly continued the family business.

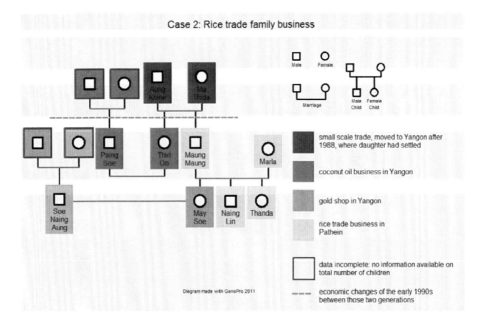

Figure 2. Kinship diagram with occupational information, case 2.

Many of the Chinese business-owning families I got to know followed this pattern of a son continuing the business, with children starting to take over management tasks often in their mid-twenties, after completing a university degree. For example, one of Pathein's biggest outlets for clothes and furniture items, a five-storey shop with more than seventy employees, was managed by the twenty-three-year-old daughter of the founder. Despite being very good at her tasks, she knew she would not stay in her parent's shop. She was engaged and was expected to work in her husband's business after marriage. For her, it was clear that it would be her younger brother, still in school for the time being, who would later run the parents' shop. This sheds light on specific gender roles among these families, according to which women rarely become firm leaders but rather work in the background of the firms of their fathers and later their husbands.

Diverging from such patterns can sometimes lead to conflicts, as in one case where the son refused to take over the parent's business. The parents ran a rice-trading business, very similar to that of Maung Maung. Their son, however, wished to open his own motorbike shop, which he eventually did. But it took years of negotiation and struggle, a time that he described as very unpleasant and distressing for himself and his younger brother, as well as for the parents. The latter were unhappy with their son's plans. They feared for the future of their own business, they did not agree with the son's economic strategies and visions, and they wanted to avoid losing control over him. They made it clear that they wanted their son to take over the responsibility for the rice business under their authority. When his younger brother died in a traffic accident the pressure on him as the only remaining heir became even larger. Referring to some Burman friends, the son told me that they were 'freer' than he was when it came to deciding on their future. Unlike this case, we have seen that Maung Maung was successful in placing his son in the role of the business manager. When I was living in Pathein he was barely at home but instead was enjoying the fruits of his efforts. He had discovered a passion for travel and had visited fifteen countries, including some in Europe, since his son had taken over the business in 2008. His wife, also in her sixties, was less adventurous and preferred to spend her days in Pathein's brand new air-conditioned 'Ocean' Shopping Center, only a few minutes' walk from their house.

For Maung Maung's business history, his Chinese descent mattered because it precluded his father, himself or his children from acquiring public-sector jobs. They might have experienced discrimination in other attractive employment positions as well, which are rare in any case. Such families had often been active as entrepreneurs for generations: some managed to accumulate considerable wealth, and they felt it was best for their children to continue along this path. Maung Maung's Chinese identity also mattered because it enabled him to insist on what he saw as 'traditional' Chinese values, those that are often said to stem from Confucian influences, such as hard work and filial piety, as well as on typical inheritance and succession patterns for the benefit of building his business. Such values do not simply persist automatically: instead, they were actively reinvented and instrumentalized by the business owning father. In this way, inequalities of gender and generation could be justified by the family patriarch in order to utilize unpaid family labour in building and maintaining the firm (Greenhalgh 1994: 748). The opportunity to reinforce such values and maintain patrilineal structures had put the father, who is also the head of the firm, into a position of strong authority. It is worth noting here that, due to the wide-ranging economic changes of the early 1990s, Maung Maung himself was able to escape these structures. When his parents moved to Yangon he had the opportunity to open his own business, in which he again resorted to 'traditional' patterns of work and succession.

Maung Maung's descent also mattered for his identity. One of his trips took him to China's Fujian province, where he visited his father's relatives. Later he also took his children there to pay their respects at the grave of Maung Maung's grandmother. Communication with their relatives was difficult because Maung Maung himself could not speak Chinese very well, while his children have no knowledge of the language at all. Those same relatives asked Maung Maung for financial help a few years later, as one aunt had fallen sick in China. Maung Maung's family was now in a far superior economic position to them, a result of his father's migration to Myanmar and their economic efforts over three generations. Since the father had passed away, however, contact with their relatives in China remained very limited. Nevertheless, Maung Maung emphasized his family's Chinese identity: 'My father was purely Chinese. My mother was a Burman who grew up in a Karen village. And my wife is purely Chinese. So my children are pretty much Chinese', he stated. The fact that a concern with ancestor worship and descent was stronger among Chinese than among Burmans fits Chinese families' rhetoric of the firm as a family heritage, worth preserving for the sake of the founders, which I did not encounter much among Burmans.

Conclusion

This chapter has presented two main case studies of business-owning families, one of Burman and one of Chinese ethnicity. Both cases are typical 'success stories' of the post-1990 period of market liberalization in Myanmar. Both have served to foster wealth accumulation and social mobility for their families. However, they show considerable differences in terms of initial resources, the utilization of family labour, and business succession. These differences stem partly from historical developments and the respective opportunities and constraints they entailed.

The considerations, conflicts, and expressions of pride outlined in this chapter reveal a lot about shared values, but also about conflicts of value, both between individuals within one family and between groups. The two portrayed families acquire their sense of achievement through different factors. Burmans rarely planned to pass on their businesses to their children. Three factors contributed to this. First is the Burman kinship system, which encourages members of every generation to set up their own households and means of livelihood. Second, among many Burmans, business activities are not held in particularly high regard, for reasons I have explored in the chapter. Third, and connected to the second point, formal education and high-status jobs create prestige instead, and are thus preferred over business activities. In many cases, the fact that a business was not passed on leads to the venture being entirely discontinued. As a consequence, it was rather difficult to find Burman-run family businesses that had existed as a single entity for more than one generation.[85] Similar patterns have also been observed elsewhere in Southeast Asia, for example, in the Philippines (Szanton 1998: 263) and on Java, where small businesses run by Javanese owners rarely continue to exist after the withdrawal of their founders. If these business owners employ close family members, they will pay them, and 'Javanese "family heads" have little de facto economic authority over their wives or adult children' (Alexander 1998: 216). Clifford Geertz (1963) studied economic processes in Indonesia much earlier, in a period in which he saw a shift from a peasant society to an industrialized nation. Among different communities, Geertz linked aspects of social organization, belief, and values to the setting up of firms, more specifically outlining how they function as a hindrance to firm growth. For him, the readjustments of older patterns that he was still able to observe were insufficient to capitalize systematically on emerging opportunities in the new industrial order (Geertz 1963: 140–1).

The Burman case of the parasol-makers makes a contrast with the rice-trading business run by the Chinese family. In the latter case, the son had never moved out, his father therefore also becoming his employer. Steps towards greater independence are usually only possible without initiating conflicts when they happen within certain boundaries defined by kinship norms. In many Chinese families, daughters are expected to get married and then become involved in their husband's business, while sons are expected to take over the business of the parents. Maung Maung, the Chinese business owner who had not been in a position to pursue prestigious employment under military rule, had utilized family labour and built up a family firm by instrumentalizing a patrilineal kinship system and 'traditional' Chinese family values. His case is a typical example of the 'rags-to-riches' stories that many (but definitely not all) Chinese business families experienced. Naing Lin, his son, said that taking over the business happened 'automatically' for him, and he sees the business as a heritage of his father, the business founder (similar to Yanagisako 2002: 40). For Maung Maung and his family, prestige through formal education (as a way to gain *pyinnya goun*) mattered to a certain extent just as it did for Burmans – that is why Maung Maung, like many Chinese business owners, had insisted on his children going to university, while actually anticipating that they will become involved in entrepreneurship thereafter. But within their community,

---

[85] There is nonetheless a parasol workshop in Pathein that has existed for several generations. This shop is featured in several guidebooks for foreigners, and the owners have learned to use the label of a 'Family business since [year]' to attract customers. Labelling one's business 'a family business' is not too uncommon, but the existence of a business for several generations is unusual.

status could also be gained by doing successful business. These values differ from those that Burman informants voiced, for whom business ownership was often viewed as morally suspect.

While the Chinese Maung Maung ensured the reproduction of both firm and family through succession to the business by his son, Myo Aung and Thu Zar took pride in the fact that their daughter managed to leave the entrepreneurial section of society to become a doctor. She moved 'upwards', as they consider it. As a consequence, their firm is likely to disappear with them. Responding to parental expectations, whether to pursue education and earn *goun* through prestigious employment, or to take over the family firm, is a process that I see as a navigation of values. The different kinship systems stress certain values to different extents, making it easier, for example, for Burman children to leave the parental household and set up their own households and businesses after marriage. The children in both main cases fulfilled parental expectations, displaying an example of an almost Durkheimian morality of reproduction (Robbins 2007: 296). Kinship obligations thus go beyond the choice of profession. I have also emphasized that the family usually constitutes the main economic support unit in life. Complemented by a complex of non-state social protection structures, including religious institutions, charity, mutual help among neighbours, and informal financial saving and credit arrangements (see Chapter 6), in moments of adversity the family is seen as being primarily responsible for offering support.

Struggles within families constitute struggles over the control and ownership of resources, such as capital and property, as well as over intangible productive powers, including practices of kinship and gender, but also norms and discourses (Yanagisako 2002: 178). Taking into account the different firm histories over several generations, I have shown that expectations as well as actual business strategies differ among families of different ethnicities, underlining the fact that studying values demands a specifically nuanced approach in spaces of great diversity. This chapter has also shown that considerations of value and family systems can work either for or against the emergence and growth of businesses. They are thus crucial for our understanding of economic processes, as they not only affect individual fates, but also shape socio-economic realities.

While the two main cases presented in this chapter had a sort of 'ideal-type' character in the sense that the business founders' wishes and hopes, fuelled by their respective value considerations, were fulfilled, I have also referred to examples in which children resisted their parents' wishes and chose a different path. Certainly, not all families subscribe to overarching values: sometimes Chinese families might deem daughters an acceptable long-term heir, and perhaps increasingly, young Burmans will achieve successful entrepreneurship with pride, especially since self-optimizing literature that defines success mostly through business achievements is becoming more and more popular. Yet, certain value tendencies and expectations have appeared as rather typical of specific groups in Pathein, as illustrated through the main cases here. In the next part of this work I will take up the value of autonomy beyond the realm of the family, exploring further the role it plays with regard to self-employment versus employment and to social relations within the workplace by looking at business owners' relations with non-kin workers, i.e. workers who are not their relatives.

Chapter 5
The Workers

Introduction

The previous chapter has outlined how business owners' family relations matter for business formation, management, and succession. This chapter looks at another sphere of business owners' social embeddedness: their relations with non-kin workers, i.e. those who are not their relatives. It explores the responsibilities and obligations that exist on both sides and investigates how these are negotiated. I shall begin with a problem that business owners repeatedly mentioned, namely how difficult it is to find workers, especially ones who are reliable and are willing to stay for long periods. Employers complained that workers frequently change jobs or leave at the slightest inconvenience. A high labour turnover has also been identified as a main obstacle for business owners in several large surveys which focused on different cities and towns in Myanmar (Abe and Molnar 2014; DEval 2015; UNDP and CSO 2015; World Bank 2016). Moreover, the problem has not only been reported for local small businesses but also for large and quite recently established factories (Bernhardt et al. 2017: vii). Economic analyses had identified Myanmar as 'Asia's final frontier' (Parker 2016) for investors, whose young demographics and cheap labour costs looked particularly promising. Indeed, the problem is not necessarily a general lack of potential workers, as urbanization is increasingly attracting people from the countryside into the cities (Kraas et al. 2017: 74–78). Instead, I argue that business owners' difficulties in hiring people stem partly from a preference for autonomy among potential workers. In many cases the available jobs do not offer enough for them to renounce this autonomy. Such value-related factors are often left out of economic calculations and predictions that are solely based on quantitative measures such as population size and age structure.

Many workers or potential workers in Pathein found that the jobs that are available to them do not offer more structural benefits, more income nor a rise in status than small scale self-employment does. Furthermore, several people reported negative experiences with employers or labour contractors, including abusive behaviour and withholding wages. This was said to happen especially in short-term and rather impersonal employment situations, such as road construction work, where workers are only hired for a few days. Not least due to such disappointments (or rumours thereof), many people become what the Myanmar census classified as 'own account workers'[86], which includes all those who run a one-person workshop or stall, mobile vendors, and trishaw and motorcycle taxi drivers.[87] I take the reluctance of workers to become employed and their consequential preference for small-scale self-employment as my starting point in this chapter. Following the perspectives of the workers, I will then discuss which strategies business owners use in order to find workers and bind them to the business. For business owners, as for the owners of larger factories, these problems create constant 'anxieties about labor commitment and reliability' (De Neve 1999: 230). One common procedure to resolve the lack of workers that has been described for other regional contexts is to hire specifically vulnerable people such as undocumented workers (Kim 2012), foreigners, ethnic minorities, and in some cases women (De Neve 1999: 94). In Myanmar, arguably the most vulnerable workers are children, who constitute a major element in the workforce. I will describe a tea shop that employs children as a case study in the second half of the chapter.

Autonomy and Work

Ko Ko was pushing his wooden cart loaded with six plastic containers along the sandy roads near Shwezigone Pagoda in central Pathein. He had just filled the containers with water from a well in the monastic compound and was setting out to sell it to people on the road, or on their doorsteps. Ko Ko was in his forties and lived together with his wife May Wah and their nineteen-year old son in a simple, one-storey, half-open wooden house in one of Pathein's northern wards. Ko Ko never complained, but I knew that he could barely make ends meet. While his wife, who produced and sold

---

[86] In the 2014 census, 38.8 percent of the total working population stated they were 'own account workers', making this the largest group among the respondents. This includes the many small-scale traders, providers of services or owners of stalls and businesses that do not employ workers (Myanmar Department of Population 2017a: 40).

[87] Referring back to the topic of informality (see Chapter 2), being an 'own account worker' does not necessarily mean working in the informal economy. The line between formal and informal does not run between own account workers and owners of big established businesses. The former might have a license to ride a trishaw or sell goods in a market (in fact, many do), while the latter might refrain from registering all of his workers, making him act partly informally.

small pottery items, was originally from Pathein, Ko Ko had grown up in Labutta Township, in the south of Ayeyarwady Region. His entire family had 'gone with "Nargis"', as he put it, the devastating cyclone of 2008. Ko Ko and his wife owned a tiny piece of land on which their house stood, but they had no savings. They had been able to let their son to finish high school and start a course at Pathein University. However, during my fieldwork, they had to ask him to suspend his university education, to his great disappointment, as they needed him to find work and contribute to the family income. The Chinese-brand motorbike they had recently purchased on credit would take them many months to repay. They figured that a motorbike was needed for transportation, for example, for visits to the doctor or to buy groceries in areas where the prices were lower than in the small market next to their home.

'Our neighbour's daughter has started to work in the industry park', Ko Ko told me while pushing his cart, referring to the big garment factories on the edge of the town. 'She cannot rest when she feels tired. She cannot go home when her child needs her. She cannot even take a few minutes to go to the toilet sometimes. Because the employer does not arrange transport, she loses a part of her income to pay for transportation to the factory in the morning and back home in the evening. Actually, she already thinks about quitting again', he continued, pushing his cart further on. Ko Ko liked to decide himself when to work and when to pause. He sits down in the shade of a tree when the afternoon sun gets too hot, or when the rain starts pouring in the monsoon season. 'We are not educated. We don't have many options', he said, describing his economic and social standing in society. With prestigious and secure occupations in government, engineering or medicine out of reach, Ko Ko could only choose between various low-income, low-status jobs, such as factory work, carrying salt bags, unloading ships, and stocking up shelves in corner stores. Alternatively, he opted for small-scale self-employment and had been selling water to people for several years. This was one of the few things he had the power to decide over. After all, self-employment allowed him to maintain a certain autonomy. He added a moral dimension to his work by saying: 'Water is pure. And important.[88] In my work, I don't break any rules, I don't need to engage in any illicit activities'. When I asked him if he found it more pleasant to work for himself instead of for someone else, he turned his response into a generalized claim by simply saying: 'I don't think it is in our nature to say "Yes, boss. OK, boss"'.

Having to work for someone else in the low-status manual jobs was seen as degrading by many. The reluctance of workers to subordinate them-

---

[88] On the significance of water in Burman Buddhist rituals, see Kumada (2015).

selves to a boss brings the value of autonomy (Burmese *lu'la'hmu.*) back into focus. Here autonomy functions roughly in the sense of self-determination. In Chapter 4 I dealt with autonomy mainly in the family context, showing that, while economic support within the family is expected and practised, Burman businesses owners (unlike Chinese) do not usually hire their own children or expect them to take over the business. Instead, children move out and pursue their own means of livelihood. In the following part, I explain how autonomy plays itself out with regard to work choices and social relations in the work place. In this context, socio-economic conditions and opportunities constitute a crucial factor. The Burman business owners I presented in the previous chapter ran larger businesses with several employees – they were not one-person ventures. For them, the fact of being one's own boss could not compensate them for the lack of prestige that business ownership entails. As a consequence, they hoped that their children would be able to leave the world of business and find prestige through formal education and, ideally, respectable employment. In some cases the wealth they had accumulated made this a realistic option.

However, when we talk of those who could potentially be hired as non-kin workers in businesses, like Ko Ko, we are usually dealing with people for whom higher formal education and prestigious employment seem far out of reach. These people belong to those parts of society affected most by grave economic problems, often they are struggling to make ends meet and many face indebtedness. While Ko Ko at least owns a small plot of land, things are even more difficult for the many landless people who have been struggling increasingly since the onset of market liberalization, which has not yet created a lot of new and profitable employment options for them. People are very much aware of their options and limitations. When informants talked about themselves, they would often self-identify through their origins (rural/urban), religion, or ethnicity (e.g. Karen/ Burman/ Chinese), and people would fairly quickly mention what they had studied (whether it played a role in their current work or not), or, like Ko Ko, say that they are 'not educated' (*pyinya ma' ta' bhu:*). This factor as part of self-identification functioned almost as a label of one's social standing, as well as an assessment of one's opportunities. While the high regard for formal education and its importance for upward mobility is also clear to those who do not have it, it seems that not everyone thinks of him- or herself as being entitled to it, and many feel it is simply out of their reach.[89] I argue that for

---

[89] Additionally, people said that for good jobs one also needs a certain amount of social capital, namely contacts with influential people. Education alone is no guarantee of an attractive job. In fact, most people with a university education do not find jobs in their respective fields, and many resort to self-employment as well.

them, since gaining a high social status through a job seems impossible, opting for autonomy or small-scale self-employment over working for someone else can bring more freedom, pleasure, and dignity (*thei'ka*).

This shows that when we analyse values such as autonomy and prestige, and how they relate to each other, it is crucial to take into account an individual's actual options and constraints since these realities shape which values will come to the foreground. While being one's own boss was valued by the self-employed from all socio-economic strata, based on what I have outlined above, I argue that the value of autonomy changes its function and importance depending on one's socio-economic standing and opportunities. By acknowledging how the meaning of a specific value varies across classes and ethnicities, as shown in the previous chapter, it becomes clear that values stand in a dialectical relationship with people's particular socio-economic situations.

In Pathein, avoiding the subordination of working for someone else was easier for locals than for newcomers. The former were familiar with the available options and had a place to stay and good networks, making it easier for them to engage in small-scale self-employment such as selling or trishaw-driving. Migrants from the surrounding countryside, by contrast, were more likely to take jobs in factories, the shipyards, or small businesses. They often had no networks and were more reliant on shelter provided by their employers. I visited one group of women who worked in Pathein's big garment factories, and they all expressed to me a clear wish to open their own sewing businesses, thus taking a step towards autonomy, once they had acquired enough money and experience. While the garment factories offered stable and relatively high wages[90] (at least compared to other available employment options), workers felt that their subordination to supervisors, combined with negatively perceived working conditions, made the job unpleasant. On another occasion, when I talked to a woman whose two daughters had gone to Yangon to work, I asked her which daughter had the better job, as one worked as a housemaid, the other in a factory. 'It's the same', the mother said; 'they both have to work for someone else'. To her, the defining feature of these very different jobs was the element of subordination. Feelings of humiliation (Burmese *thei'ka kya.de*) became stronger when workers experienced belittling or otherwise rude treatment from superiors at work.[91] This recalls Keeler's understanding of autonomy as a key value in Myanmar's Buddhist population that entails people's attempts

---

[90] At the time of my research the daily wage in the garment factories was 3600 kyat per day (ca. 2.60 EUR) plus extra pay for work during holidays.

[91] One informant who had spent many years working in Singapore said that he found it easier to accept his subordinate status abroad than at home, among his 'own' people.

to avoid the problems and demands of hierarchical social relations[92] (Keeler 2017).

    Other recent studies have also addressed the topic of autonomy specifically in relation to communities in Southeast Asia. Motorcycle taxi drivers in Bangkok consciously choose self-employment over low-wage employment, with all the instability and insecurity that brings. Based on his ethnography, Claudio Sopranzetti questioned certain Marxist and Foucauldian approaches to freedom and capitalism for displaying 'passive subjects and dismiss[ing] their ability to understand the paradoxical nature of the political-economic and hegemonic processes, while also deciding to take part in them' (2017: 71). Instead, the motorcycle taxi drivers had made an active choice. Their perceptions of freedom have been shaped through a mixture of local economic conditions and individual as well as locally shared values, experiences, and options. Other sources have dealt with autonomy and work in Myanmar. As was pointed out earlier, in the colonial period, the urban industrial economy was dominated by Europeans, Indians, and Chinese at all levels. However, Michael Adas pointed to Burman agency as another factor contributing to the systematic exclusion of Burmans from industrial employment. His study of colonial documents revealed that in many cases Burmans preferred agriculture over industrial employment in the cities, partly because the latter were regarded as low in status, while agriculturalists, at least those who owned their land, could remain their own masters in the countryside (Adas 2011: 120). Urban industrial tasks were here linked to a loss of autonomy and status alike.

Flexibility and Dignity

To disentangle the importance of autonomy with regard to work, it is necessary to differentiate several aspects of it that can be roughly grouped into the aspects of flexibility and dignity. These aspects become differentiable if, in each specific situation in which autonomy appears to be of importance, we ask: autonomy from what or whom, and for what purpose? As indicated by Ko Ko at the beginning of the chapter, choosing self-employment over employment offers people more control over their tasks and time, and hence the freedom and flexibility to fulfil individual desires (such as resting on a hot afternoon). However, this flexibility also enables people to respond more easily to kinship demands or emergencies,

---

[92] While Keeler (2017: 88) stated that one's autonomy, or freedom to act (e.g. through wealth) directly functions as a marker of one's social standing, Lehman (1996: 25, 29) held that only merit, not autonomy as such, was the actual criterion that ranks people in the social hierarchy. Autonomy (freedom to act) is seen here merely as a means to gain more merit and not as something admirable in itself.

such as caring for a sick child, thus offering what Millar calls 'relational autonomy' (Millar 2014). Such 'relational autonomy' is more relevant for women than for men, since women are usually primarily in charge of caring for children or the elderly. The fact that care obligations are gendered needs to be considered when looking at people's work choices. Women usually tried to find work they could do from home if they had children and no one else could care for them. For example, they engaged in handcrafting fans from leaves, preparing snacks for sale from their houses or doing small craft work. 'Relational autonomy' indicates that in certain situations a desire for autonomy can be 'tightly woven into other desires for sociality, intimacy, and relations of care' (Millar 2014: 47). A preference for autonomy thus cannot be equated with a general avoidance of social obligations. Paradoxically, the flexibility of precarious informal and instable self-employment may even enable people to manage family demands better, in comparison to full-time employment, for example, as a housemaid or in factories.

All the aspects mentioned above are related to flexibility. Analytically, we have to distinguish them from another important dimension when looking at people's preference for autonomy, namely, not having to obey a superordinate in the workplace. These two different aspects of autonomy, those related to flexibility and dignity respectively, which I have just disentangled analytically, are in reality often intermixed. This becomes clear in the following statement by Ko Ko's neighbour, whom he had mentioned to me. As he had anticipated, she quit her factory job after just a few weeks working there for the following reasons: 'I did not like working there [in the factory], because the supervisors were always shouting. We constantly had to follow their orders. It was tiring; we had almost no breaks. Also, I had to give my child away to someone else to care for her, and I prefer to do that myself'.

With these sentiments of the workers in mind, I will now shift the focus to the employers. To make their businesses run smoothly, business owners have to restrict the autonomy of others, specifically those whom they want to work for them. In the following section I will explore work relations between business owners and their non-kin workers. I will touch upon the questions of how employers attract workers, what my informants regarded as a 'good' employer, and how responsibilities and demands are negotiated in the workplace.

The 'Good' Employer: Incentives, Responsibilities, and Obligations

Keeler speaks of 'elective subordination' (2017: 156) when describing how lay Buddhists become followers and material supporters of a specific monk, preferably one with great spiritual potency and purity, in order to gain access to spiritual power. I see a process of 'elective subordination' in the work sphere as well, albeit with a different purpose. For workers to take a job in a workplace, the conditions must be good enough for them to give up their autonomy. Put differently, the employer needs to be an employer worth submitting to. Another factor that would make it hard to refuse a job offer is pressure through social links, for example, having other relatives who already work for the same employer. As a consequence, to attract workers, business owners need to guarantee stable incomes and fairly attractive conditions, ideally leading workers to develop feelings of loyalty towards the business. The opening of several big garment factories in Pathein a few years ago added to the difficulties of smaller businesses like restaurants, retail shops, and craft businesses in finding workers, as they now have to compete with factory-level wages.

Hiring Strategies

Legally, businesses in Myanmar that employ more than five workers are required to register them at the Social Security Board and pay contributions to health insurance. In reality, many employers register fewer workers than they actually employ and do not regularly update the register when workers change. According to my observations, even though most employers have an official license to run their businesses, a lot is organized informally when it comes to the workforce. Formal job advertisements, like written work contracts, were almost non-existent among Pathein's small businesses. Rather, employers tried to find workers through social links. They asked friends, relatives or current employees if they knew of anyone who would be interested in working for them. If possible, employers tried to hire workers who had some connections between them, such as coming from the same family or from the same village. Not only does this make it easier to replace workers or recruit additional ones, it also invokes a higher degree of social control among the workers when they know each other's families, friends, and histories. In one rice mill in Pathein's Strand Road, the owners employed more than seventy workers who came almost entirely from the same village outside Pathein. Hiring people who have a connection with one another is one way of countering the high turnover of labour.

However, hiring new workers through current employees means that employers need to care about their reputations. Before entering into an employment position, workers will try to find out whether an employer is good or not. For instance, restaurant waiters told me that they had been warned not to work in a larger, more frequented downtown restaurant. They had heard that those who worked there were not treated well, and that they had to pay if they accidentally broke a cup or a plate. Moreover, the work was said to be very stressful in the restaurant because it was always busy. Larger and busier shops were here linked to a less satisfying work experience, while smaller shops were associated with a more intimate and pleasant work experience.

In fact, some work agreements turn into long-term relations between an employer and a family when the former employs several of its members. Zin Moe Aye, a middle-aged woman, lived in a village about forty-five minutes' drive from Pathein. Both her daughters had found employment as seamstresses in the same small garment-processing factory in Yangon. After they had proved reliable, the employer also hired Zin Moe Aye's son as a security guard and a cousin to maintain the machines. The connection between the two parties had lasted for more than eight years when I talked to Zin Moe Aye. The rural family became a source of the recruitment of reliable workers for the business owner. These workers are less likely to resign than other workers because they know that the firm is responsible for a large part of the family's income. Moreover, when workers have worked in a business for longer, a certain affection and sense of loyalty can evolve. This is an example of how obligations grow through histories of transactions between two parties (Carrier 2018: 30–31). For Zin Moe Aye, even though the wages may be low and the work hard, it was comforting to know that all her relatives work in the same place, where they could pool their incomes, look after each other, and work under an employer whom she trusts. This is especially valuable in a migration context, which comes with a great deal of uncertainty and the danger of unpleasant experiences and exploitation for workers. In other instances, feelings of obligation occurred when workers learned that their employer relied heavily on their specific skills, for example, in craft businesses. Some workers were very reluctant to leave a job in such a situation even when better opportunities arose. Affection and feelings of obligation can thus also become a constraint for individuals. It was therefore in the interest of workers to avoid becoming too attached to a workplace and an employer – a difficult balance, given that a certain degree of attachment can also provide benefits.

If employers fail to recruit workers through social connections, they might need to use the services of a broker (Burmese *pwe sa:*). Such agents approach villagers occasionally or regularly and place them in suitable workplaces in town, for which they receive a commission from the employer. Hiring through such agents has its pros and cons. Employers do not have to search for suitable workers themselves, and if a worker leaves the workplace earlier than was agreed, they can ask the agent to find a replacement. Workers might have some security through an agent, who can act as a buffer or mediator between themselves and the employer in situations of conflict. In rural areas labour contractors are the contact persons for landowners wanting to hire seasonal labourers. This also became common in urban contexts, for example, in construction work. Conflicts would then appear primarily between labour contractors and workers, which spared the employer from having to deal with them.

Moreover, some agents specialize in placing people in employment abroad, for example, in Singapore or Malaysia. While they can be of crucial help for people seeking work, these agents often charge a commission not only from the employer, but also from the workers. This means migrants have a debt to pay right from the beginning of their period working abroad (see Constable 2007: 63–86, on migrant workers in Hong Kong). Besides full-time agents, some people in Pathein acted as agents on a more informal and occasional basis. I saw how one elderly and well-connected woman in a poor ward in Pathein was occasionally asked by neighbours if she knew a good place for them to work. She would then put workers in contact with business owners of her acquaintance, with the promise that the worker was reliable. For this service, she usually got a small amount of money as recognition from the shop owner. Such a connection, even though rather loose, allows both worker and employer to feel more comfortable about the deal. I have now described hiring strategies and will continue by looking at the expectations and obligations between employers and workers once the employment has started.

More than Wages

What takes place between employers and workers corresponds to what Carrier identified as a specific type of 'moral economy' in which the moral force arises directly from a specific economic interaction between people (2018: 24), that is, through 'mutuality' (Gudeman 2008).[93] Here, 'moral' has to do with obligations arising from interactions more than with values (Carrier 2018: 23). While a lot has happened to the concept since its emergence, this understanding comes close to the original idea of a 'moral

---

[93] Other examples of economic interactions that Carrier mentions are those between co-workers, between landowners and tenants, and between shopkeepers and customers.

economy' (Thompson 1971; Scott 1976). This obligation-focused approach is a crucial part of the general idea of this book, namely that people's economic activities and thoughts are shaped by a wider, overarching ethical and moral context in which not only values but also norms and obligations appear. There are culturally shared assumptions about how the parties involved should behave and what their reciprocal duties are. These assumptions have been shaped through a history of economic transactions between specific people and groups. If such expectations are disappointed, a person's behaviour might be regarded as immoral. In Myanmar, apart from the salary, many employers offer additional benefits and support. Such non-monetary duties were usually strictly limited to the period of employment: thus obligations were clearly bound to this specific process of economic transactions.

In different settings in Pathein, such as craft workshops, rice mills, and grocery shops, or retail shops, workers were provided with lunch, and often also with simple shelters inside or close to the work compound. Business owners also sometimes gave loans to workers when they were expecting a child or planned to build a house. I have also seen employers offer refuge to workers whose homes had been affected by severe flooding in the monsoon months of 2016. Employers tried further to establish social bonds to instil loyalty. I have noticed how the owner of a watch shop tried to set aside time to introduce himself to the families of some of his young female workers, who were adults but unmarried and living away from home for the first time. He also provided shelter for his workers and adjusted the wages he paid to what the big garment factories were offering. On special occasions, such as Buddhist New Year, he gave small presents to his workers and their families. Some employers took into account the different levels of need among their workers. One rice-mill owner explained to me that he calculated the salary of his seventy employees according to each family's needs. Thus someone with more children received more money than someone who was single. 'If they have to worry about their family, they will not be happy at work. If they are not happy, they won't put much effort into their work. So I support them, which is good for both sides. A businessman who only thinks about himself will not be successful'. The rice-mill owner's statement clearly shows how treating one's workers well is linked to hopes for business success, revealing the profit orientation in his motivation. Nevertheless, it was very important for employers to present the employer–worker relationship as socially close, going beyond the monetary dimension, for instance, by repeatedly stressing, 'we are like a family here'. Even though actual hierarchies and socio-economic differences were great, as I will shall show below, this rhetoric of 'embedded' work relations was crucial, not only to make workers feel indebted, but also to present oneself in morally good terms, and perhaps because there was a genuine wish for close, loyal, and good relations in the workplace. These attitudes counter images of mere profit maximization and stress the responsibility and obligations not only of the workers, but also of oneself as an employer. They are also as a way to balance the fact that one withdraws from social obligations by working independently instead of in employment.

Apart from workers' physical needs, some employers also see it as their duty to support their spiritual well-being. In many businesses workers will be invited to participate in blessing rituals, for which monks come to a business at least once a year. Small firms may provide leave to their workers if they want to attend a meditation retreat for a few days. Once, on a visit to the parasol business described in the previous chapter, I saw its owner doing the work that was usually carried out by his employees. I had not seen this happening before, as the owner usually did only the managerial tasks. On that day, however, he was sitting on the floor, together with his wife, and the two of them were preparing bamboo and wood for a handmade parasol. 'Our workers asked for leave to go to the monastery, for meditation', he explained, 'so we have to do their work'. Looking at his hands, he said: 'When our hands are dirty from the mud, we have to wash them. The same applies to the mind'. Here the employer interpreted meditation as a purifying process, perhaps beneficial not only for the workers' *kamma* but also for their productivity.

Employer–worker relations in Myanmar in some ways resemble patron–client relations, which are important in the social organization of Southeast Asia more generally (Scott 1972). Such relations are characterized by inequality between the two parties, but their relationship nevertheless contains a degree of reciprocity and cannot be based on pure coercion or force. The two parties rely on each other, and loyalty is not only based on material exchange, but often also on some degree of affection. While the employers may seem to be in the more powerful position, the growing competition for workers actually reduces their power. Workers often try to avoid a 'debt of obligation' (Scott 1972: 93, 99) so that they can change work places easily. As a consequence, many work relations are not very durable. Furthermore, the reciprocal duties implied in these relations remain limited only to the period of work. The differentiation of the economy in industrializing contexts has further contributed to making such relations less comprehensive and less stable over time. Nevertheless, around five decades ago patron–client ties still represented 'diffuse personal bonds of affection when compared to the impersonal, contractual ties of the marketplace' (Scott 1972: 107) and this is still true today, although to a letter extent than in the past. Ongoing changes in the labour market keep altering such interpersonal links but employers continue trying to insist on interpersonal connections to evoke feelings of loyalty among workers, while many workers continue to expect more from an employer than the mere pay of wages.

While the far-reaching responsibilities of employers like those I have described above seem far from today's reality in many new private companies in the transformed metropolitan centres of Yangon and Mandalay, they were deeply rooted in the moral perceptions of my informants. This became clear when these perceptions clashed with new work experiences. Such clashes, and the respective disappointment of expectations on how the other party ought to behave, are likely to appear in moments of striking economic change, more precisely the rise or in-tensifying spread of capitalism, as has been shown by the original contributions to the concept of 'moral economy' (Thompson 1971; Scott 1976). On one occasion I arranged a group discussion with young female workers from one of the big new garment factories in Pathein, outside working hours and away from the factory setting. Most of the factories had only been operating for around four years at that time. The workers ex-pressed discontent with their working conditions. They specifically em-phasized that no lunch was provided at the factory and that they had to pay for their own shelter and work clothes. Some referred to a Japanese-run factory in Yangon that reportedly provided lunch vouchers to workers as a positive example.

The garment workers were also outraged about the supervisors' and employers' reactions when recently one of their colleagues hurt her hand on a sewing needle. With disapproval they recalled that, instead of receiving proper care, their colleague had to organize her own transport to hospital. Additionally, she was blamed for the incident by her supervisors, who accused her of having been chatting with her colleagues and not paying enough attention to her sewing – that is, she caused the accident herself. The young workers had started working in the factory only recently. They contrasted these new work experiences with other jobs in small businesses, where lunch, shelter, and support in times of need had been provided. In reply, I mentioned that the size of a business might influence the relationship between employers and workers. Surely, I said, in a factory employing three thousand workers, an employer cannot look after all the workers in the same way that a small business owner can. However, the garment workers had a different take on the matter: 'The employers in our factory don't know anything', they said; 'They are foreign investors who are new to our country.[94] In the small businesses that you talk about, everyone is from Myanmar'. The garment workers linked the treatment of employees, including responsibilities that go beyond wage payments, to familiarity with Myanmar customs and norms, rather than to the massive difference in business size. Their idea was that a *good* employer from Myanmar would naturally care for his workers and display concern and empathy in difficult times, such as sickness. These judgments show how moral considerations underpin opinions about proper employer – worker relations. A 'good' employer cares for his workers. In the eyes of these women, a tea-shop owner employing eleven-year old children, like the one I describe later in this chapter, might act in a morally better way than a foreign investor offering regular and relatively high incomes to thousands of workers. Perhaps more structural explanations, like the one I had offered by pointing to the difference in business size, were also rejected because they left little room to hold someone specific responsible, which can more easily serve as a ground for resistance (see also Chapter 3 on *kamma*).

From the side of the employers too, there were occasional complaints that referred to a continuing erosion of bonds beyond the monetary aspects. Especially when discussing difficulties in hiring workers, shopkeepers would note a growing fixation on money as a sole criterion for accepting or rejecting a job. 'Nowadays, all people care about is the salary. That is the first thing they ask if they consider working here. If another shop offers only slightly more money, they will switch work places', said one restaurant owner. Workers and employers alike negotiated the tensions between older patterns and newer developments in line with their own respective responsibilities and expectations towards others.

Sometimes, keeping up good relationships in the work place has to be weighed against economic demands for profit. Myo Aung, the owner of the bamboo parasol workshop I described in the previous chapter, had purchased bamboo from the same merchant for several years. The quality of the bamboo decreased year by year, as good bamboo was simply more and more difficult to get. One day, Myo Aung showed me an entire room full of completed parasols that he does not dare to sell because of their low quality. Why did he keep producing parasols from batches of bad bamboo instead of waiting until he received better quality bamboo again? After all, making parasols is a complicated process that includes several steps and takes a long time. Given the low quality of the bamboo, these finished products are economically useless to him. 'I cannot let the merchant down', he replied. 'We have been working together for many years, so I buy the bamboo any-

---

[94] Investors came from China, Hong Kong, the Philippines, and Japan and often some higher level foreign staff were present in the factory.

way. And my workers get paid by the piece – the work is important for them, too. I have to offer them regular work. So I let them produce the parasols anyway'. Accumulating a number of products that have no economic value to him functions to keep good relations with a business partner, as well as providing his workers with an on-going opportunity to earn money. Myo Aung's decisions may mean a short-term loss in economic terms, but they are part of long-term economic circulations, reflecting important social values and institutions and thus ensuring their reproduction (Parry and Bloch 1989). As in many other cases, the moral and social aspects cannot be separated neatly from economic considerations. Myo Aung knows that offering a regular income to workers is the key to keeping them. Offering work even when the products turn out to be substandard in quality might thus be important for long-term business success, especially as Myo Aung relies on his workers' specific skills.

Another case in which economically rational decisions contrasted with an employer's perceived moral obligations is the story of Cho Lwin. Here, however, the shopkeeper chose short-term profit over keeping her worker. Cho Lwin was planning to open a small restaurant. I helped her in the weeks ahead of the opening. Together we designed the menu, bought the furniture, decided on the wall colours, and finally organized the shop's opening, for which a monk came to give his blessing. As the restaurant was new, Cho Lwin did not yet have a stable group of customers. She was nervous about how the start of the business would go. She decided to offer a traditional Myanmar breakfast (*mohinga*), and hired an elderly woman to prepare it. The woman had a misshapen hand, a condition she had been born with. After a few days had gone by, Cho Lwin decided that she could no longer employ the woman. She suspected that her employee's hand was scaring off customers, who might have thought she suffered from leprosy. Cho Lwin felt sorry for the worker and hoped to find some other way of rehiring her soon. Such examples show how moral expectations and responsibilities that clash with demands for profit can create dilemmas in work relationships.

Payment

Businesses with fewer than fifteen employees are exempt from paying the minimum wage. But even working for the minimum wage (which during the time of my research was set at 3600 Kyat, which converts to ca. 2.6 EUR a day) often brought less income than many forms of small-scale self-employment. The salary in small businesses is in most cases too low to sustain a family. However, employment can have financial advantages over self-employment in the sense that the income is more stable, and it sometimes comes as a relatively large sum all at once. This is the case with advance payments, a common payment scheme in small businesses in Pathein. Advance payments mean that workers received their salary at the beginning of their employment for several months ahead. Different forms of advance payments occur in many places in the world, and while they constitute a form of debt bondage, advance wages, or loans additional to wages, are also actively asked for by workers (De Neve 1999). In fact, workers in Pathein often made it a condition for accepting a job that they would receive the salary in advance, and employers stated that they had no other choice, saying, for instance: 'I *have* to give the salary in advance'. Employers mentioned that they would actually prefer instead to test first whether a worker is good and reliable or not.

Receiving bigger sums at once allows people to make crucial purchases or repay loans, something that would be more difficult if one had to save up from one's small daily earnings. Breman (2010) described a system of 'neo bondage' in India which characterized work relationships between low-caste cane-cutters and sugarcane factory owners. It was a mixture of an extra advance loan that needed to be paid back and the holding back of actual payments until the end of the working season. Breman used the term 'neo' to describe the contrast with earlier forms of debt bondage, which came with a range of responsibilities for the employer and were passed on from generation to generation. The 'neo' form of bondage occurs in an industrial setting, is only seasonal, and lacks the earlier patronage elements, such as providing long-term security for the worker's family. In urban settings in today's Myanmar, there is usually no long-term pattern between employers and workers that lasts several generations and provides comprehensive security. Work relations therefore resemble more the second kind of debt bondage that Breman described for industrial settings, in which agreements are strictly limited to the work period. Also, support that goes beyond salaries remains restricted to the period of employment, and thus to the point in time of the economic transaction.

In Pathein, the importance of payment methods became clear again in the contrast between small businesses and new large foreign-owned garment factories, a topic I discussed with the young workers who were employed there. These workers received their salaries for a month's work only on the third day of the following month, a practice they disliked. Receiving the salary after the end of the month made it difficult for some to get by during the first month of employment, when they had to work full time without receiving any money as yet. Making workers wait another three days after the end of the month was something the workers suspected to be a strategy to enhance the likelihood that they would stay and work for another month. This might seem like a small detail, but the method of salary payment matters in several regards, and not only for purposes of household budgeting. Giving out salaries at the end of the month, as is typical in many modern employment situations, is a way for employers to ensure that their workers show up at work. This is opposite to the payment model found in small businesses, where the salary is often paid in advance, sometimes even for several months. Although receiving the salary in advance has often been analysed as a form of debt bondage, it can also be viewed from a different angle. Compared to the payment method in factories, the message sent by employers here can be understood as: 'I trust you'.

However, advance payment can also lead to conflicts and problems for both sides. I got to know a twenty-three-year-old ethnic Chinese woman, Khin May Kyaw, who worked in the retail shop that her parents had set up. Selling clothes, handbags, furniture, and toys over four storeys, the store was one of the biggest of its kind in Pathein. The family employed around seventy workers, most of them young women, to stock the shelves, clean the shop, and serve the customers. Khin May Kyaw was responsible for managing the workers. This included considerable emotional labour, as she was regularly approached by workers to help solve conflicts they had with one another. Khin May Kyaw paid the workers three to four months in advance. I asked her if it ever happened that workers stopped coming to work after they had been paid in this way. It happens occasionally, she replied. What did she do in such a situation? 'Usually I try to call her [the worker] or her family a couple of times. I try to pursue her to come back. I also get angry on the phone'. And what if she has no success in bringing the worker back? 'Then, I just regard the payment as a donation to the family', said Khin May Kyaw, laughing briefly. She chose to adjust her attitude, rather than take further action.

Such problems are typically solved informally, but in some cases the police or courts become involved. One elderly Karen woman in Pathein's Baptist community, an activist on behalf of female migrant workers, reported cases of householders suing housemaids for theft when the latter had left prematurely after an advance payment had been made to them. In these cases, this activist would offer assistance, emotionally and financially, and occasionally support workers in court cases. Many young (often underage) girls migrate from the countryside to the cities to work as housemaids. In these settings, they can easily become the victims of physical violence and other mistreatment. The activist said that it was typically after such incidents that housemaids run away. If the employer then sues one for theft, the housemaids have very little power, and their accounts of violence too often remain unheard, especially since householders may offer bribes to the police and lawyers, according to the Karen activist.

Despite elements of patron-client relations, agreements between employers and workers were clearly marked by calculated and often quite formalized financial considerations. This was true even in settings that appeared rather close and informal, for example, when only two people worked together as employer and worker, as the following example will show. I have already mentioned May Wah, the wife of Ko Ko, the water seller. May Wah produced small pottery items, which she sold as toys for children or as candle-holders to be used in pagoda compounds. On some days, May Wah hired a young woman from the neighbourhood to help her with packing and painting. The relationship between them seemed quite close and affectionate. The worker often had her small child with her, and the women talked about their worries and exchanged gossip from the neighbourhood. However, May Wah remained in the role of employer when calculating benefits. Her worker was paid per day and additionally was given lunch, but only in the dry season, when May Wah produced more and thus had more income. During the rainy months her worker could still eat with her, but May Wah would deduct 500 kyat from her salary for it. While fulfilling different responsibilities, employers usually made no attempts to enable their workers achieve any upward mobility. No matter how long a work relation lasted, workers rarely be integrated into the employer's family, despite employers sometimes using the rhetoric of kinship to instil loyalty, as we shall see below. Workers remained workers, a category fundamentally different from employers in both status and wealth.

Hierarchies and Inequalities

Accounts of how hierarchies and control are negotiated exist for many workplaces, from households (on domestic workers, see Constable 2007; Yan 2008) via family firms (Yanagisako 2002) and small businesses (Ram 1991, 1994; Moule 1998) to larger work places, such as factories or plantations (Burawoy 1979; De Neve 2005). They touch upon matters of class, control, patronage, and power, using different theoretical frameworks to analyse them (see, for example, Thompson and Ackroyd 1995, on Foucauldian perspectives in such studies). Ethnographies have shown that workers are not mere passive subjects in these circumstances. Despite structural limitations, they manage to resist in different ways and different work settings (Burawoy 1979; Turner 1995; Moule 1998; De Neve 2005; Ong 2010), both openly and collectively, as well as more subtly, as Scott (1985) has argued for peasants. However, it would be too simplified to understand workplace relations solely in terms of domination and resistance, as people's thoughts and actions are complex and ambivalent. In Pathein's small businesses dominance can be strong, but elements of care and affection come into play as well. However, employers are not concerned about their workers' well-being out of pure benevolence. The difficulties in finding and keeping reliable workers make it necessary to create an attractive work environment. Moreover, mutual obligations between employers and workers ultimately do not transcend hierarchies and the socio-economic gaps between them.

Hierarchies in Pathein's businesses were obvious to the observer. The workers' subordination to their bosses became visible, for instance, in speech and gestures. Workers who complained to me about the work-related aspects of their lives refrained from confronting their superiors openly. When a conversation between a worker and an employer took place, workers would often sit in a lower position than the boss, for example sitting on the floor, while the employer had a chair. This reflects the general pattern that subordinates try to occupy a physically lower position than those who are of higher standing, most usually older people or members of the sangha. When passing a person of higher standing, people usually bow their heads slightly. Certain forms of power are believed to reside in the body (such as *hpoun:*), and they should not be threatened or disrespected by violating the physical order. Similar behaviour also reflects gender hierarchies: for example, women's laundry would be hung out to dry lower than men's laundry, and if possible women should not sit in a higher position than men.

Along with hierarchical differences, economic inequalities too were quite prominent in many settings. Employers could often afford cars and owned comparably large houses, while workers lived in small shacks made from bamboo or leaves. The economic gulf was usually neither criticized nor challenged openly. When one of my informants, the owner of a pottery workshop, upgraded his house from a wooden one-room construction to a large cement building, his workers told me how happy they were for him and his family. They did not show any sign of envy, nor did they regard it as undeserved or demanded anything for themselves, such as a rise in wages. Many workers seemed to take the view that their employer belonged intrinsically to a different group, that is, to those who were better off. In this case the two parties were bound by ties from which both benefited in one way or another. Some people invoked the law of *kamma* in this context to explain that each person has his or her place in society as a result of actions in past lives.

However, while economic differences and social hierarchies may be perceived as stemming from *kamma* to a considerable extent, this does not mean that people passively accept the behaviour of superiors that they regard as rude or humiliating. In the sphere of work, ensuring autonomy whenever possible can be a means of remaining relatively unconcerned and avoiding the strains and demands of these hierarchies, as we have seen with workers who chose self-employment over employment at the beginning of this chapter. Despite the clear hierarchies and socio-economic differences between employers and workers, in some cases workers were in a position to make demands. The problem of labour turnover gave them some bargaining power. After all, employers relied on people being willing to work for them. In the traditional parasol workshop, the employer, Myo Aung, needed workers with specific skills, such as the painting of artistic patterns, and he faced difficulties in hiring new people. At some point, he planned to move his workshop to a different location in Pathein. The workers, however, did not want to spend money and time on transportation. Most had their huts and their families near the current location. In the end, Myo Aung left the workshop where it was, as the workers had continued collectively to oppose the move.

Mutual obligations resulting from employer – worker relations usually do not transcend the power relations and socio-economic gaps between them. However, there can be situations in which the hierarchical pattern stemming from the employer – worker relation conflicts with other hierarchies, such as those resulting from age differences. Twenty-six-year-old Win Zaw had worked abroad for a few years before coming back to Pathein, and he used his savings to start his own bus line and transport people from Pathein to other nearby cities. Only the savings he had earned in Malaysia had enabled him to move from the position of a worker to that of employer at a fairly young age. He bought two buses and hired two drivers and two ticket-sellers, all of whom were much older than him. While his position as the boss gave him authority, it was nevertheless difficult for him to criticize his employees, because in this case the workplace hierarchies did not correspond to the age hierarchies. Win Zaw found himself on particularly difficult terrain when he decided to fire one of his drivers, who was regularly drunk while driving the bus. 'He is a good person. But he cannot drink when he drives. For me, this was very difficult. Because I am very young, and he is old. And we are a small business, so we are very close. So, how could I fire him?'

Win Zaw saw himself caught between his responsibility for his employee and the fact that he could not endanger the company's reputation, nor the lives of his passenger or other people on the roads. He felt he lacked the necessary authority over someone almost twice his age. To overcome this conflict, he went so far as to invent a story of another man having asked him for a job as a driver. He told his employee that this other man needs money urgently, so that he could not decline his request, and the two of them would have to share their working hours between them. Win Zaw knew that reducing work hours was not an option for his driver because it would not pay him enough to feed his family. Even this invented story was not delivered directly by Win Zaw to his driver. Instead, he asked the ticket seller to inform the driver. The latter then called Win Zaw and said: 'I cannot accept this message from the ticket seller. You are the boss. You tell it to me, and I will accept it'. Win Zaw repeated his story and the driver accepted it, resigning in order to find another full-time job. At the peak of this conflict, the driver specifically requested Win Zaw to act in his role as employer. Win Zaw was sure the driver knew the real reason for him being fired, being aware that driving while drunk would not be tolerated. Nevertheless, he felt that including other people in the communication process and making up an alternative reason allowed him to add a moral dimension to his action by pretending to help another work-seeker. Win Zaw held that all of this was needed to solve the problem without offending his much older employee. He had to negotiate carefully to cause as little social damage as possible.

I have shown how, given the preference for the autonomy of self-employment among those who only have access to low-income and low-status, usually manual work, small businesses are forced to implement and combine different strategies to attract workers and bind them to the shop. These strategies include economic aspects (advance payments), social aspects (hiring people from the same family or village; trying to instil loyalty), as well as material and spiritual ones (providing food and shelter, with additional care if needed, and enabling workers to pursue religious progress through occasional meditation retreats and blessing ceremonies). However, there is another strategy employers use, and while it is not new it seems to be becoming increasingly common: hiring particularly vulnerable people who are not in a position to make demands. In many cases, these are migrants from the countryside. Migration to the cities separates workers from their families and leaves them at the mercy of their bosses. Arguably, on the spectrum of the migrating workforce, the most vulnerable are the many children who work in Myanmar's businesses, from small shops to mines and factories. I will devote the following section specifically to this particular category of worker by analysing the case of a tea shop that employs children.

The Least Autonomous: Children as Economic Actors

In November 2015 the US Ambassador to Myanmar, Derek J. Mitchell, posted a photo on Facebook of himself in a Myanmar tea shop. Tea shops (*la'pe'ye hsain*) are plentiful in the country. Open from dawn to dusk, these popular and affordable venues serve sweet tea, coffee, soft drinks, and a

range of classic Myanmar dishes. Ranging from only a few plastic tables on
the side of the road to concrete buildings with several storeys, tea shops are
packed with people at breakfast, lunch, and dinner. Groups of friends,
usually men rather than women, meet to eat and discuss their private affairs
or the latest news. I was told that when the military was still officially
controlling the country, tea shops were also strategically frequented by spies
to catch any whispers of political opposition. While one might speculate that
the ambassador's photo of his presence at a typical Myanmar establishment
was meant to underline his commitment and connection to the country's
ordinary people, it got the embassy into some trouble. The photo was
quickly removed after people had raised concerns online that the tea-shop
staff featured in the photo might be child workers. By frequenting and
promoting such an establishment, so went the criticism, the ambassador
would have accepted or, had he consumed tea there, even financially
supported the employment of underage workers.[95] While the political
concern is understandable, finding typical Myanmar food in street
restaurants can become very difficult if one wants to avoid places that
employ children, since child work, in many different sectors, is a common
phenomenon in Myanmar. In tea shops, almost all the waiters are usually
under age. Tea-shop owners told me that ten years ago they did not hire
children on a regular basis because it was still possible for them to find adult
waiters.

Myanmar is a good example of how changing economic conditions
are bringing about new patterns of work experience, and with it the
emergence of new forms of child labour. Children became part of a workforce that emerged to satisfy the demands of the increasingly liberalized
economy. While it is not as such new for children to take over economic
responsibilities and contribute to their household, child labour has assumed
new forms in recent decades. Children, like adults, are migrating more and
more often to the cities to work in urban industrial settings, far away from
their families. Children work for wages that adults cannot afford to accept if
they are the main breadwinners of their families. Furthermore, children are
not only paid less, they are also easier to control. As their wages are
typically paid directly to their parents, they have no degree of financial independence. They are expected to follow orders without questioning them,
which results from the employer's authority in three intersectional roles: as
an employer, as a caregiver on behalf of the parents, and simply as an adult.
Being less autonomous and cheaper, they constitute an attractive workforce
for many small businesses, especially since these have to compete for labour

---

[95]   https://coconuts.co/yangon/news/us-embassy-removes-myanmar-tea-shop-facebook-snap-
over-child-labor-concerns/. Accessed on 24.10.2017.

with the big new garment factories. These entities, in compliance with international labour regulations, do not hire children, but they absorb a large part of the adult labour force, which increasingly pushes owners of small businesses to resort to hiring underage workers. The children I encountered working in Pathein's small businesses all came from the countryside or from the poorer margins of the town.

What kinds of work do children in urban areas do, and who are the employers? Much children's work can be observed in public. Waiters in restaurants and tea shops are only one example: one can also see children stocking the shelves of grocery stores, carrying bricks or sacks of rice, and selling snacks or bus tickets. Many other children work behind closed doors, for example, as housemaids, in factories, and also in industries that are especially harmful, such as mining or prostitution. Myanmar has also repeatedly been listed among the countries with a high high number of child soldiers (UN 2018). As for adults, the conditions under which children work vary widely, as does their relationship with their employers.

Regulations and Statistics

The Myanmar 'Child Law'[96] of 1993 defines children as persons under sixteen years of age. The legal minimum working age for children in factories, shops, and establishments is fourteen years, and an additional change to the Factory Act and the Shops and Establishment Act states that children of fourteen to fifteen years should work no more than four hours per day (MCRB 2017: 28, 36). New draft laws are inconsistent concerning the legal working age of children (Chau 2017), and moreover, current laws do not cover all the sectors in which children work, so that much of their labour happens in a legal grey zone. The current government, after its election in 2015, announced it would further review and amend laws concerning children's rights. The results of this pledge remain to be seen. The 2014 census offers some numbers which highlight the magnitude of child work in Myanmar and also provide some insights into formal education and school attendance. Only five years of schooling are compulsory in the country (approximately age groups five to nine), and most children attend school during these compulsory first years. According to the recent census, 85 percent of children aged nine were enrolled in school. However, completion rates for the following stages drop dramatically. In the age group from ten to fifteen years, only 25 percent were full-time pupils. Seventeen percent were employees, another 17 percent contributing family workers, and 7 percent

---

[96] The State Law and Order Restoration Council, 'The Child Law' Law No. 9/39, 14th July 1993.

'own account workers'. Fourteen percent did household work, and 6 percent were listed as unemployed (Myanmar Department of Population 2017b: 48).

In summary, the situation in Myanmar clearly does not comply with international laws and guidelines, and in many cases not with national laws either. Many children in Myanmar are too young to work, work under excessively harsh conditions, and work too long hours (MCRB 2017: 19–20). The government has invested very little in education in recent decades, and even though primary school is legally free, parents have to pay for materials, transportation, and additional afternoon classes (tuition, Burmese *kyu shin*, from the English word), which are widely regarded as obligatory (MCRB 2017: 12–13). These additional tuition classes, even though illegal, have become common practice at all educational levels, creating a 'nation-wide educational black market' (Myat Thein 2004: 115). Especially in rural areas secondary schools are rare[97], so that those who want to attend them have to leave home and stay in a boarding house close to the school, creating additional expenses for the family. These economic aspects are crucial when looking at the reasons why children quit school and start working.

Children as Economic Actors

Journalistic and policy-related reports have investigated and addressed the topic of child labour in Myanmar, focusing mostly on contributory socio-economic factors (e.g. MCRB 2017). Media reports claimed that recent economic developments have allowed child labour to thrive, as Myanmar's government has admitted (Pyae Thet Phyo 2018). However, no one has yet studied in detail the social nuances of everyday interactions between children and employers in Myanmar, nor the moral and value-related underpinnings of these processes, or of child labour in general, areas where an anthropological approach can contribute. It is safe to say that children who take over economic tasks are by no means a new phenomenon. Every-

---

[97] Some informants noted that in the past there were more monastic schools that offered education in remote areas as well. In pre-colonial times, monastic schools offered almost universal education for boys. They lost this function under colonialism. During the military period and up until today, monastic schools still had a sort of stopgap function in the failing state-run education system. However, Lorch (2008: 151) reported that in the 1990s and 2000s rising poverty made it harder for people in rural areas to donate to the sangha, and thus many monastic schools, as well as other sangha-run welfare projects, faced increasing difficulties in offering their services in the face of rising demand. The economic problems in society, which threatened the sangha as well, were one of the reasons why a large number of monks took part in the 'Saffron Revolution' protests of 2007. However, in Pathein, workers in monastery-led welfare projects reported to me that support from the laity had increased in recent years (see Chapter 6). Similar data have also been described for Taungoo, another medium-size town (McCarthy 2016).

where in the country in the past children from poorer backgrounds have played an important role in the sustaining of the family, thus being not only consumers, but also providers.[98] In Pathein, I have observed parents teaching work- and household-related processes to their children from a young age. I have seen children as young as three being given money by their parents to buy snacks from a shop in a different part of the neighbourhood. Once, while sitting in a bus waiting to depart from Pathein, I observed a boy of maybe eleven years selling water bottles at the bus station. He was looking after his mother's stall while she was absent for about half an hour. During this period, the boy sold several bottles of water, went to other shopkeepers to change money, and angrily scolded his younger sister when she jumped on a pile of bottles, causing it to collapse. The boy seemed to be fully accepted as the stall's host by other vendors, as well as customers.

Anthropologists, like scholars from neighbouring disciplines, have dealt with childhood more generally (Montgomery 2009; Lancy 2012 for an overview; Lancy 2015a; among early classics is the work of Margaret Mead 1928), as well as with children as economic actors more specifically (Liebel 2004; Spittler and Bourdillon 2012; Lancy 2015b; for a bibliography see Lancy 2017). These contributions have highlighted the cultural flexibility of ideas regarding which tasks and responsibilities are appropriate for children, as well as of concepts of childhood and personhood more generally. For example, Evans-Pritchard noted that a child among the Nuer is only fully acknowledged as a person when it is about six years old, i.e. when it can look after goats and cattle, and fulfil other livelihood-related tasks (Evans-Pritchard 1956: 146). In a similar manner, Lancy, with reference to a range of anthropological works, points to the crucial role of economic activities in defining life stages. In some societies it is perceived that infancy ends, and childhood begins, when a child can be 'useful' to the family or wider community (Lancy 2015b: 546). In many parts of the world children begin to help in the household, take care of younger siblings or engage in farming and herding activities from a very early age.

While, as mentioned above, parents in Myanmar teach basic economic activities to their children early on, the situation for migrant child-workers is fundamentally different from helping one's family in the subsistence economy (Gailey 1999). Global comparisons have shown that, in situations where there is total adult employment, such as fast-growing industrialization, but also war, children function as a kind of reserve labour force (Lancy 2015b). In Myanmar, as elsewhere, child workers primarily come from poor

---

[98] Boys in particular also function as spiritual providers for their parents by becoming novices, which is thought to be beneficial for the *kamma* of their parents, especially their mothers.

families, such as landless labourers in rural areas or the urban poor. Children work in the countryside, herding buffalos or engaging in agriculture, but also in the cities. While in many cases children work alongside grown-ups and fulfil the same tasks as the adults (such as unloading boats), tea shops and restaurants are sectors that employ primarily children (ILO 2015: 9). If children migrate for work, many of them cease to live with their parents. The connection nonetheless often remains intact, and in most cases the children's salaries are given to the parents directly. Children also often work only for a relatively short time in one business and then return home, either for a visit before starting to work somewhere new, or for a longer period. However, there are also cases in which entire families migrate to the cities (mostly Yangon) and often settle in the town's slums, where they might be condemned as squatters and where children then work alongside their parents.

Child Workers in Thin Zar's Tea Shop

One tea shop that I regularly visited was run by a couple in their forties, Thin Zar and Ko Phyo. They had set up the tea shop in 2003. Thin Zar and Ko Phyo combined entrepreneurial activity with wage labour, as Thin Zar also worked as a teacher. As in many similar cases, their business started off very small, with only the two of them preparing and serving food. Bit by bit the tea shop grew, and after a few years they were able to buy a piece of land on which to build a house, in which they were living with their thirteen-year-old son and Thin Zar's mother when I got to know them. I am talking mostly about Thin Zar here, not about Ko Phyo, because the former was my main informant in the tea shop. Besides, it was she who was mainly responsible for looking after the workers.

From my observations in Pathein, I estimate that the average age of the tea-shop waiters was between twelve and fourteen. The youngest boy I saw working full time in a tea shop was nine years old. Thin Zar and Ko Phyo employed eighteen workers (approximately, because the workforce is not stable), fifteen of whom were under sixteen years of age. While the tea shop also had some cooks (mostly young women) and a tea-maker, here I will focus on the twelve waiters aged between eleven and fifteen. Much of what I describe in this case study corresponds to what I identified as typical patterns earlier in the chapter – hiring strategies, employers' attempts to instil workers' loyalty, and responsibilities that exceed the mere payment of wages. However, care obligations, as well as the power and control of the employer, are intensified by the vulnerability of the children. The young waiters in Thin Zar and Ko Phyo's tea shop worked sixteen and a half hours a day, from 05.30 am to 10.00 pm, seven days a week. They took orders, sent them to the kitchen, served the food, and when a customer attempted to leave, counted all the empty dishes and cups on the table, calculated the prices, and collected the money from the customer. Then they carried the bank notes to Thin Zar or her husband, one of whom always sat in a plastic chair at the side of the shop. The employer gave them any change due, which the children returned to the customer. They then cleared the tables. At breakfast time and in the early evening the tea shop was especially busy, with all of the around thirty plastic tables occupied, and the children shouting orders to the kitchen, running around balancing dishes and cups full of tea, while the air was filled with the chatter of customers. In the hot afternoon hours the shop was quieter, the children relaxed and sometimes read comics, slept or played a game on a smartphone.

Plate 6. A tea shop in Pathein.

Salaries in the tea shop differed between categories of workers according to their tasks, ages and education or experience levels. The young boys earned 30,000 kyat (ca. 21.7 EUR) per month. The girls who cooked were usually a bit older, between fifteen and seventeen, and earned 50,000 kyat (ca. 36 EUR) per month. The tea-maker, an adult man, earned around 80,000 kyat (ca. 58 EUR). I found the salaries mentioned here to be consistent among the different tea shops I studied in Pathein. Workers were not all equally valuable to the shopkeeper. The tea-maker, or rather 'tea master', as *la'pe'ye hsaya* translates as, is the heart of the tea shop, said Thin Zar. He skilfully prepared the tea and mixed it according to the order, with specific amounts of sweet milk and sugar, before pouring it into the small cups to be served. The tea-maker was of especial importance to the employers because a good tea-maker can attract many customers, and if he changed his work place, the customers might follow him.[99] As for the waiters, Thin Zar deliberately hired children with a low level of education. If a waiter had completed four or five years in school, she would be expected to pay more. As the job of a waiter demands only a minimum level of education (the boys need to calculate the prices by adding up the single amounts for each dish), it was more profitable for Thin Zar to hire boys who had not even completed primary school. The salaries were paid for several months in advance (between three and six) directly to the children's parents.

The children in Thin Zar's tea shop all came from villages outside Pathein, most of them from Thin Zar's home village, about four hours driving time from Pathein. When Thin Zar went back to her village, every few months, she recruited workers from there. Her own social capital was her preferred employment strategy. Thin Zar tried to avoid agents because of the fees they charge. She also complained that agents often let the children stay for only a short period of time in one shop, mostly around three months. Afterwards, they place them in a different shop to receive another commission. This is inconvenient for both the children, who have to cope with a changing work environment, and for the employers, who have to train new employees. Employing children from the same village means there is a connection between the children, and they can form friendships more easily. Within these relations, children also developed hierarchies among themselves. Older children, or those who have worked longer, would train those who were new, but also tease them often and exert authority over them (in disputes such as 'who gets to use the smartphone longer'). While the boys became acquainted with some regular customers who would joke around with them, these interactions were fleeting, and there was certainly no close contact between the boys and the wider neighbourhood community because they basically never left the tea shop. Thus they did not integrate into the neighbourhood as new 'residents', but remained in the position of temporary workers restricted solely to their workplace, both physically and socially.

---

[99] Thin Zar has already lost one tea-maker. The young man had left in secret, together with Thin Zar's niece, who had come from a village to Pathein and worked in the tea shop's kitchen for a while. The couple stole several hundred thousand kyat from Thin Zar. Even though she knew where they went, she decided not to go after them to get her money back. She does not want to spark conflicts within her family and gave this incident as an example of why it is not good to hire family members. Hiring close family members as full-time workers is uncommon among Burmans (see Chapter 4).

Obviously, child labour results from a mixture of unfortunate circumstances. While most of the children in Thin Zar's tea shop stayed in touch with their parents when they worked in Pathein, there are also particularly severe cases. Thin Zar brought an eleven-year-old boy to her shop after she had been back to her village. His mother had left the family, and his father was in jail, allegedly because of indebtedness and gambling. The boy had an older sister, but he said she 'went to China' to live there with a man. Rumours spread that the girl had become a victim of trafficking, or had been sold by relatives. Staying behind with his grandmother, who was unable to care for him properly, the boy was glad when Thin Zar took him to Pathein to stay in her shop, where other boys from the same village already worked. 'I want to stay here', the boy stated; 'I will never go back home'. While such especially dramatic circumstances were not the rule, it is safe to say that children working in tea shops usually come from the economically most disadvantaged groups.[100] However, sometimes reasons other than just economic ones play a role, too. One of the waiters in Thin Zar's shop said that his parents had divorced and both remarried. He did not want to get caught up in their quarrels and did not feel at home in either of the new households. Going to Pathein for work seemed like a better option for him. Moreover, some boys said that they found it adventurous to go to a city, as instead of herding animals or farming, they wanted a different kind of job.

---

[100] In some severe cases, parents give their children away. I visited a couple of places that are referred to as 'orphanages' (Burmese *mi.ba. me' kalei: gei ha*), often run by religious organizations, where children are cared for by local volunteers and receive a basic education. These places rely on donations from the local community. Abandonment did not always result from the parent's death but sometimes from economic factors (poverty), as well as from social factors (e.g. children resulting from extramarital relationships). Furthermore, many such 'orphanages' (in Yangon and Mandalay, but also in Pathein and thus probably elsewhere, too) host a large number of boys from the country's war-torn areas, mostly Shan State. Apparently, the initiative to bring them from there came from a network of Buddhist monks. The reply to my question why only boys are transferred to the lowlands was that they are in danger of being recruited by armed groups. As this seems to happen on a large scale, the question occurred to me whether this could be not only a way to protect the children, but also a calculated attempt to weaken ethnic armed groups by taking away potential recruits from them.

Like a Family? Kinship Rhetoric as a Strategy

Thin Zar said 'these workers are like my children'[101] several times. Other employers also tried to intensify loyalties by using kinship rhetoric, emphasizing that the workers are part of a family (Burmese *mi. tha: su.*). This kinship rhetoric is a means to call on the workers' loyalty to pressure them to work well and to stay with the 'family' (that is, the shop). This use of kinship terms is ambivalent, as it can create affection, affinity, and reciprocity, but also pressure and hierarchies (De Neve 1999: 122). Referring to the workers as her children mirrored Thin Zar's role as a trust-worthy carer, a responsibility she had towards the children's parents. When Thin Zar said 'these workers are like my children', she continued the sentence by saying: 'Whenever they need something I have to provide it'. Thus, Thin Zar linked the kinship aspect more to her duties than to feelings of affection. The children lived in the shop. They had their meals there, and at night, Thin Zar locked the children into the shop, the girls and boys separated from each other 'to prevent them from becoming lovers', as Thin Zar put it. The children slept on the floor or on the tables. Thin Zar bought clothes for them, washed them, and took them to the hairdresser's. She gave them medicine when they fell sick and generally felt responsible for their nutrition, hygiene, and health. Her role as an employer had elements of maternalism, and these elements contributed to the ways in which she acted. Once, she forgot to lock the tea shop in the evening. At night, the children left the shop and went to a stream to catch fish. In the rural areas where they grew up, catching fish had been part of their everyday activities. They caught some fish in the stream and brought them back to the tea shop, where they lit a fire, grilled the fish, and ate them. Thin Zar was furious when she arrived the next day. Not only had the boys ignored the rules, they had also put themselves and her shop at risk by roaming the streets at night and starting a fire. She said she had to beat one of the older boys, whom she suspected of having instigated the nightly excursion, as a punishment. Thin Zar acted here as both an employer and a carer who was responsible for the children's safety.[102] The children are not allowed to leave the shop, and

---

[101] On the other hand, when Thin Zar talked to me casually about her workers she would refer to them as *kalei:* (child) more generally, not *tha:thami:* (Burmese, literally '*son-daughter*') which would imply a more affectionate relationship. *Tha:/thami:* are terms used in many conversations to address acquaintances or even strangers who are considerably younger than oneself. Thus, by not using these terms and sticking to the more general *kalei:* when talking about her employees, Thin Zar even created a certain distance, perhaps to emphasize the difference in status.

[102] I have heard of more cases of children being beaten in tea shops when they broke the rules. Corporal punishment, according to many friends in Pathein, was also not uncommon within

employers assert their power by controlling much of the children's space, time, tasks, and other factors, such as what they eat (see also Constable 2007: 96–110, on housemaids). Once, after Thin Zar had noticed that some children were keeping some of the change, she searched their clothes and found the money. She scolded them and explained that they have to be honest and reliable, that it is only if her tea shop runs successfully that can she hire waiters like them to support their families.

Not only were hierarchies very clear in tea shops, so were the socio-economic differences between employers and workers. In all the tea shops that I studied in Pathein, the owners had children of their own. These children were in the same age group as the workers, though their economic situations were much better. Thin Zar's thirteen-year-old son never had to help in the shop. He attended school, and since he liked cars, she hoped that he would study engineering later and find a good position in the public sector, or in some big private company. He lived in the parents' house together with them, a few minutes away from the tea shop, where the waiters slept on the floor. They ate different food and were certainly not entitled to any inheritance. The economic contrast between the owners and the workers was obvious. While tea-shop owners definitely felt a responsibility for the children that went beyond the mere payment of wages, it did not get to the point where hired children were ultimately considered, or treated as, family members, despite a rhetoric of kinship that tries to suggest otherwise. No upward mobility was made possible for them.

Agency and Resistance

Unlike their employers, workers rarely used the rhetoric of kinship. This helped them to avoid growing feelings of loyalty or a 'debt of obligation' (Scott 1972: 93), making it easier to leave the workplace. When the children in Thin Zar's tea shop were drawing pictures with me, most of them drew their home villages, a rural setting with rice fields, buffalos, a stream, and small brown houses. From the waiters' perceptions it was clear that they did not regard the tea shop as their home, nor the shopkeepers as their parents. In most cases, children would only work in the tea shop for a few months, not long enough to build a deep and lasting relationship with its owners. Thus, despite the efforts of the employers to instil a kind of kinship-like loyalty, many relations between workers and employers remained rather loose, with

---

families. While I was in the field, people reported to me that there had been new government regulations making beating children in schools 'illegal' for all teachers. However, I am not aware of any official changes to the Child Law from 1993, which does not prohibit corporal punishment at home or in school. Perhaps these new regulations were sent out internally to educational institutions.

workers feeling no obligation to remain in a certain business longer than had been agreed. Reasons for changing a job (for workers in general) include finding a better deal somewhere else, wanting to return to their families, or dislike of their current work, employers, or co-workers.

The children's room for resistance in the tea shop was limited. As I have indicated, due to their vulnerable position they were less able to assert a preference for autonomy than adults. However, they were able, at least, to find spaces for leisure. When the shop was not busy, they talked to each other, joked around with customers, read comics, played on a smartphone, or took a rest. While the authority clearly and strongly lay with the employer, in some instances children asserted agency and took active steps in order to change their circumstances. For example, when they themselves initiated their leaving of a work place. Two brothers working in one of Pathein's biggest tea shops took the initiative to ask the owner of a different restaurant, when he was visiting the tea shop, if he could employ them. They did not like working in the particularly busy tea shop where they were currently employed. The other restaurant owner agreed, and it was arranged that the children would change their work place accordingly.

On the other hand, workers might also decide by themselves to remain in a shop, as another account involving Thin Zar shows. One of her workers was a fifteen-year-old boy with whom she did not get along well. She also did not like his mother back in the village, whom she described as rude. The boy occasionally drank and smoked, and 'teaches this to the younger boys as well', Thin Zar said. Moreover, he had stolen money from her. So Thin Zar took him back to the village with the intention of not letting him work in her shop any longer. However, when she and her family were about to return to Pathein from the village, he simply got into the car with them. 'He just came with us again, so what can I do?' Thin Zar said. She did not want to risk open disputes with his family or the wider village community. Besides, she felt sorry for the boy and decided to give him another chance to change his behaviour. In other cases, however, Thin Zar has fired workers who were particularly unreliable or who misbehaved. Thus, there is no general reluctance on her side to look at the children mainly with regard to their labour power. Nonetheless, in the situation described above the employment continued, and Thin Zar used this incident to present herself as a compassionate employer.

Religion

When talking about the incident of the boys going out fishing at night, Thin Zar got angry again just telling me about what they had done. She explained that she plans to restructure her shop once her son has completed high school so as to employ only female workers. According to her, girls cause less trouble. However, her explanation not only has a managerial dimension, but also a moral one: when the children misbehave, she finds herself shouting, using rude words, and getting angry (Burmese *dawtha. htwe'*). Referring to Buddhism, Thin Zar said that these actions were 'bad' and that she wanted to avoid them. Similar to the Thais, in Myanmar there exists the concept of 'losing face' (Burmese *mye' hna pye'*, literally 'destroyed face', a similar translation to the Thai *sia naa*), associated among other instances with an inability to control one's feelings and a loss of composure, especially in public. Thus, Thin Zar wants to have workers who do not bring her to such a situation. This statement makes two important points. First, employers attribute different behavioural tendencies to different genders, which influences their hiring decisions. Girls and women are often regarded as more reliable and hard-working, and they are preferred employees in certain sectors, such as housework or grocery stores. While I have also seen girls around the age of twelve working in tea shops, this was rather rare. Most of the waiters were boys because parents felt uncomfortable letting girls of that age leave home (for more on gender norms and morality, see Chapter 3). However, it is not uncommon to find girls around the age of fifteen working as housemaids in cities or cooking in restaurants. Secondly, Thin Zar's statement reveals that she sees a danger in her relationship with her workers, namely the danger of conflict and anger being religiously adverse for her.

Based on this observation, I suspect that a reluctance to step into close social relations that come with hierarchies and obligations (as argued by Keeler 2017) might result partly from the fear that these relationships could ignite conflicts and lead to emotions that are perceived negatively in Buddhism, such as anger. In fact, feelings such as anger and greed are not only inappropriate but are also believed to cause demerit. Anger, for instance, is believed to lead to ugliness, greed to poverty, in a future life (Keyes 1983c: 163). The religious labelling of such emotions as 'sinful' or 'negative' was one of the reasons why the Urapmin studied by Robbins (2007) struggled when transitioning from a culture that highly valued manifold close social relations to Christianity. The latter condemned certain emotions such as anger, which tend to appear within close social relations, and I argue that the same is true of Buddhism. Trying to avoid such extremely negatively perceived emotions could be a part of the explanation for what scholars of Buddhist societies in Southeast Asia have termed 'loosely structured social systems' (for an overview of the debate see Keyes 1977: 163–167) and for the general importance of autonomy, as recently discussed by Keeler (2017). Buddhism is not the cause, but it offers a basis for both valuing autonomy and offering a certain room for individual action in social relations on the one hand, and showing one's concern for others on the other hand (see Chapter 6).

Thin Zar was not only concerned with her own, but also with her workers' spiritual paths. Every year during the holiday of Thingyan, the Buddhist New Year, she and her husband arranged for the children to go home to their villages for a few days to spend the holiday with their families. However, sometimes the children chose to stay with the couple. One year, for example, they took a few of the children to the beach. Additionally, every October, during the religious Thadingyut festival, she arranged a trip to a famous Buddhist site. The purpose of these trips was not only one of 'team-building' and giving the children a fun experience, it was also meant to provide them with the opportunity to do something beneficial for their *kamma*, as religious pilgrimages are believed to generate a great deal of merit. In the year of my fieldwork, Thin Zar and her husband rented a bus and took their workers to the famous Kyaikhtiyo Pagoda, also known as the 'Golden Rock', one of the most important pilgrimage sites in Myanmar located about seven hours drive to the east of Pathein. At the pagoda site, which is filled with stalls and shops, each child was given some pocket money to buy souvenirs.

In another tea shop in Pathein, many of the child workers were ethnic Karen and Christians by religion. The Buddhist owners of this shop allowed the children to participate in important church events, and they also permitted a weekly visit by a Christian pastor, who gave the children Bible study. However, when the owner's own son, aged six, attempted to join the Bible study group out of curiosity, his parents prevented it. They emphasized that, while they accept and tolerate the children's different religion, they should also understand more about Buddhism and how important Buddhist values are for them (the owners). Occasionally the employers tried to teach basic Buddhist ideas to the child workers in passing. By taking the children to Buddhist pilgrimages in the one case, and enabling attendance at Bible studies in the other, the employers acknowledged the importance of their workers' respective religions. Moreover, especially in the case of the Christian children, supporting their religious studies was probably also helpful in maintaining a good impression with the children's families back in the Karen village, from which they had been recruiting workers for several years.

While the work of children in tea shops does not conform to current laws, it is practised openly throughout the country, even though I saw tea shops in Pathein being regularly frequented by government staff and police officers. Also, tea shops attached to official institutions, such as educational centres, openly employ child workers. This does not mean, however, that child labour is generally seen as unproblematic. I will now discuss how child labour is judged morally, and which arguments disputing or justifying the use of underage workers are brought up by different parties, including the children themselves.

Whose Fault? Moral Discourses on Child Workers

When talking to people about child workers, quite often my interlocutors felt a need to explain or even justify child labour, indicating that the topic is controversial to some extent even among Patheinians. Sometimes tea-shop customers expressed regret over the fact that children have to work and said they feel sorry for them. The situation of the tea-shop children, however, was not necessarily contrasted with receiving an education (which Western observers often see as the obvious better alternative to working), but more with 'being with one's family'. Thus, the problem was seen less that the children did not study, and more that they were far away from home, which is precisely the aspect of child labour that has increased in recent decades. In contrast, the general perception that children should contribute to the household income if necessary was shared by many.[103]

How do working children themselves perceive their situations? When I talked to a twelve-year old waiter in the tea shop about his life back in the village, he said: 'There is nothing to do. It was so boring there'. 'Is this why you came here?' I asked. 'Yes', he replied; 'I didn't want to go to school. I didn't like it'. While I did not comment on the child's statement, another tea-shop customer, a middle-aged woman, had heard his reasons by chance while passing by. She said to the boy: 'Don't you know that education is important?' The child did not respond for a moment. Then he replied suddenly, and with what appeared to me as a mix of sadness and stubbornness: 'My family is in debt. We have to pay back several *lakh*.[104] If we work in the fields, we will get very little money, and we will only get paid day by day. How can we pay back a loan like this? We need a larger sum of money at once. Here, I can get the salary in advance for three months. My parents

---

[103] Contributing financially to the household can happen in different ways, not only through physical work. I was told of one case where a child born with a disability acquired some regional fame because it was said to be able to cure diseases. Many visitors approached the family, asking the child for its help, and they made financial donations. The child thus contributed to the household budget considerably, and the family allegedly became wealthy. This case has parallels with one of Myanmar's most famous fortune-tellers, 'ET', who passed away in 2017. She too was disabled, unable to walk or speak. But with her sister as a 'translator' she was regularly consulted by highest-level business people and politicians from Myanmar, and Thailand, and her family is known to be very wealthy.

[104] One *lakh* is 100,000 kyat.

need that. It is important to support one's family, isn't it?' While the tea-shop boys often acted cheerfully, joking and playing, this boy had to fight back tears when explaining his family's situation. After he had spoken, he quickly went back to work. Later he returned to my table, now in a happier mood again.

This encounter illustrates two important things. Firstly, the boy considered his situation shameful. This feeling resulted from two aspects, first from his family's dire economic situation, which he initially tried to hide, and secondly from his position as a worker, given that working for someone else is *per se* considered rather degrading, especially in low-income manual jobs. That is why the boy first said he was simply not interested in studying. He tried to present his situation as his free decision, taking the responsibility away from everyone else. Only when a stranger confronted him with the importance of education did he opt to change his narrative, making it clear that he was well aware of this, but that he had no choice. He felt that, instead of being scolded, he deserved some acknowledgement for doing what had to be done, namely supporting his family. The waiter shifted the focus from the rather degrading position of a worker to his respectable role as a provider, emphasizing the latter to justify the former.

Secondly, even at twelve years of age, the boy displayed detailed knowledge of his family's financial situation, including details about debt relations and different payment schemes. I have repeatedly encountered how working children emphasized their own agency, presenting it as their own decision to work resulting from boredom in the village and a desire for new experiences. However, I see these narratives also as offering a way for the children to conceal their family's dire economic situations, which they regarded as shameful, as well as their own dependencies and unfreedom. Insisting on their role as providers, a respectable role in contrast to the degrading status of a worker, is their attempt to give the situations a positive twist.

When it comes to the role of the employer, there is a common perception that shopkeepers help the children and their families by offering them employment and shelter, an opinion which contrasts with common Western attitudes toward employers who hire children. This perception was expressed to me by tea-shop customers, the shopkeepers themselves, and families whose children work in tea shops. One customer said: 'The children have no education, and the families have no money. If they are lucky, some friendly shop-owners take the kids'. Another customer said that he heard the rumours that the children had been beaten once because they had run away without the owner's permission: 'I feel sorry for them. But I also think they should ask the owner's permission first, otherwise he is worried. I want to be open with you, I don't like it that he beat the kid, but he has to control them. And also, *he gave them many opportunities* by letting them work here'. Tea-shop owner Thin Zar employs more boys than she needs to run the shop. This shows that her actions cannot be driven merely by profit. She says that sometimes, when she went back to her village, parents approached her, almost begging her to give their children employment.

Customers and employers, as well as families whose children work, saw the situation of working children as resulting from a number of conditions. The effect of *kamma* was mentioned quite a few times. Thin Zar, while watching the children clearing tables, said 'here, we are all the same [humans, colleagues], but our past lives have not been the same'. By means of this religious explanation, she tried to reconcile her attempt to paint a picture of a good working relationship and equality with the obvious fact that some members of the business were in a better economic position than others. Despite these religion-based accounts, it was socio-economic factors that prevailed as explanations for child labour.

While the government was occasionally criticized for not doing enough to fight poverty and for not expanding educational opportunities, actors tended to blame each other, rather than attributing the situation to overall socio-economic circumstances. The accounts of parents, agents, and employers I collected revealed the strong moral underpinnings of the issue. In this triangle, justifications and explanations often included putting the blame on one of the other parties, while at the same time one's own role in the process was presented in morally positive terms. The tea-shop owners would say that the children have to work because their families are poor, or because their parents cannot deal with money and do not understand the value of education. Some even went so far as to say that adults would rather send their children to work than work themselves. The agents would say that, if the employers were more generous and would pay a higher salary they would find more adults willing to work, but they prefer hiring children because it is cheaper. Parents would say that they tried to persuade their children to continue in school, but the children had no interest in doing so. They said that the children found it boring and wanted to quit.

These somewhat surprising but frequently-declared statements by the parents expressed two things. Firstly, they confirm the relative high degree of autonomy and room for individual choice the Burman kinship system grants within the family. Parents perceived it as a normal process that children, even at a young age, should decide such things themselves. Secondly, these claims also indirectly showed the parents' awareness of the importance of formal education in providing status and prestige, something I have discussed in more detail in Chapter 4. Discontinuing school in order to become a worker was seen as shameful, and parents tried to deny responsibility for their children taking that path somewhat. However, without wanting to deny the children a 'will of their own' (Liebel 2004), it is likely that in many cases the parents, whether openly or passively, agreed to the decision or initiated it because the child's income reduces the family's economic burden or is even necessary for survival.[105] These accounts of mutual accusations show that child labour, in its urban industrial form, was indeed seen as something that is morally questionable and has to be justified. Everyone involved tried to present their own role as being either helpless (the parents), or supportive towards the children and their families (employers and agents): it is others who are seen as responsible for these conditions in the first place. These others are concrete social actors more often than politicians or overall structural conditions.

Conclusion

The owners of small businesses repeatedly complained to me about their difficulties in finding workers, and generally about the high turnover of labour. To explore the value-related reasons for this, I brought in the concept of autonomy in work contexts. For workers, small-scale self-employment usually offers more freedom to pursue individual wants while also managing family obligations. Employment in low-income sectors, in contrast, not only means a loss of flexibility and self-determination, it also comes with subordination to a boss, which is often perceived as degrading. Thus, employers need to offer enough structural and financial benefits to become worth submitting to for workers. Accordingly they deploy a number of strategies to attract workers which go beyond the mere payment of salaries, for instance, hiring workers who have connections with one another, as well as offering food, shelter, support in emergencies, and loans. Many employers pay salaries to workers several months in advance, a form of debt bondage which is, however, often actively asked for by the workers themselves, who also interpret advance payments as a sign of trust from the employer. All of these duties are part of what Carrier (2018) described as a type of 'moral economy' stemming directly from specific interpersonal economic interactions of which all the involved parties have clear expectations. In changing work environments, such relations inevitably change as well. As we have seen, in factories where the compensation for work is solely

---

[105] This does not mean that the children's unwillingness to continue school might not be real. Even some teachers were understanding about the children's view of school being boring. Many interlocutors criticized the fact that the curriculum demands only rote learning and never asks for pupils' own opinions or thoughts.

monetary, disappointment among workers unveiled the expectations that were deeply embedded in their moral consciousness. In these examples, morality relates more to obligations than to values. Employers stress their responsibility and concern for their workers, indicated a wish for 'embedded' work relations and stressing their own role as valuable members of society. Workers too have clear expectations that an employer needs to offer more than just a salary, even though workers usually do not use the rhetoric of kinship and try to keep a certain distance from their employers in order to avoid moral indebtedness to them.

However, such mutual obligations do not ultimately alter social hierarchies or socio-economic differences between workers and employers, which in some ways resemble patron–client ties (Scott 1972), although they are temporally often rather short-lived. Inequalities remain, as employers usually do not make attempts to integrate workers into their families or to allow them any social upward mobility. Among child workers levels of vulnerability are particularly high, while the authority of the employer is intensified. Discussions surrounding child labour among people in Pathein show that, especially in urban industrial settings where children work away from their families, it is morally contested and demands justification. Employers and workers (adults as well as children) negotiate control within workplaces, with employers controlling much of the workers' time, space, and tasks. If an employment situation is perceived as unpleasant, workers often do not hesitate to quit a job if they are not bound for longer periods through having received an advance payment. Unlike those who can gain status through formal education and respected jobs, workers in the manual low-income sector can, if anything, only opt for self-employment to avoid conflict and humiliation in strictly hierarchical work relations.

Chapter 6
The Community

Introduction

Having explored family and workplace relations, I will now expand my focus to the wider social landscape. While still taking business owners and the small-scale self-employed as my main subjects, I am leaving the immediate world of business behind here. The activities described in this chapter are neither specific to self-employment, nor linked directly to business activities.[106] However, when studying people's livelihoods, it is crucial to take them into account. Business owners, just like public- or private-sector employees, are linked to friends, acquaintances, neighbours, and strangers through economic transactions in various ways, including beyond their businesses. This happens, for example, through direct support relations with others, engagement in charitable activities and donations, membership in saving groups or through money-lending. Such economic links constitute a non-state social support system which has the wealthy and the poor occupying different roles. It is crucial in mitigating vulnerability in a country where the state fails to offer social protection and support to a large part of the population.

Overall tax revenues in Myanmar are among the lowest worldwide (The Economist 2017), hence no systematically enforced tax system could be used to redistribute wealth. While business owners pay a range of 'fees' to obtain a business license, commercial taxes are usually low and are negotiated with local officials on a case by case basis. Reports suggested that many business owners understate their incomes in these negotiations (Bissinger 2016: 32). However, a reluctance to pay taxes must be understood as a symptom of the distrust of government institutions rather than an un-

---

[106] It should be kept in mind that, in the large sector of the small-scale self-employed, the category of 'business owner' is a rather fluid one, as many people combine small-scale self-employment with formal employment or start a business only after their retirement, or run business activities only in specific seasons.

willingness to give up some of one's money for redistribution. The state is just not seen as capable or trustworthy enough to arrange this redistribution, and thus many people deem projects initiated by themselves, other private individuals or religious institutions as more appropriate recipients of donations.

In 2015, the World Bank estimated that less than 5 percent of Myanmar's population was covered by the state's social-security schemes (Dutta et al. 2015: 31–32). Actually, private firms with more than five employees should legally register their workers under the contributory Social Security Board, which provides medical care and financial support in cases of sickness, maternity/paternity, death (funeral grant), and work injury. However, in reality many workers remain unregistered, and the Board thus only covers a tiny fraction of private-sector workers. Pensions and additional benefits, such as the provision of free or subsidized housing, only apply to a small number of government or military staff under certain conditions. Despite recent reforms concerning public sector employment, formal support remains small especially for public-sector workers in lower positions (Dutta et al. 2015: 20–21). Furthermore, the vast majority of people in Myanmar do not have access to banks that could provide loans or to private insurance programs.[107] So far, despite some investment in past years, Pathein has not yet seen a significant increase in attractive, stable, and long-term waged employment options. The new jobs are concentrated mostly in a number of large garment factories. At the same time new opportunities to spend money have appeared, as recent years have seen more goods and technology being imported into the country. People also frequently report that prices for some basic necessities like rice, vegetables, and petrol have gone up.

Myanmar has become a place in which wealth is distributed very unequally. While the ongoing transformation has benefited some, many parts of the society have been left behind in a constant struggle to balance income and expenditure. Most available jobs are marked by precarity[108] and only

---

[107] This includes many business owners (see DEval 2014). Estimations said that only between 5 and 10 percent of the country's population have a bank account (Turnell 2017: 125; Förch 2018: 202). Thus, very few people have access to bank loans. Besides, it has been stated that fewer than 3 percent of Myanmar's population have any type of formal insurance (Turnell 2014: 6). If people have extra money, they will either use it for donations, an investment in spiritual and social terms, as I will describe later, or they will try to buy land or gold. Both are seen as a much safer way to save than keeping cash.

[108] Studies of precarity have mostly dealt with situations of retreating welfare states, as in some Eastern European postsocialist countries. In these cases, the experience of 'precarity' was defined by this retreat and its consequences. However, others have argued for the applicability of this concept also in contexts where the welfare state has not retreated but has perhaps even expanded. Guy Standing (2011) defined the 'precariat' more broadly as a new global class, a consequence of 21st century capitalism. For Myanmar's neighbour, Thailand,

provide low and often uncertain and fluctuating incomes. People's demand for money comes from everyday expenditure on food, transportation, education for the children, maintaining the house, and socially important spending on life-cycle events and ceremonies. There might also be demands linked to business activities. Finally, money is often needed unexpectedly in cases of emergency, like illness or the death of a close relative.[109] Social support and protection start with measures at the household level and within the family. However, households and families are no isolated units, and thus, it is necessary to go beyond these levels to understand social support. I will therefore analyse different community arrangements, many of which emerge and are sustained without any involvement of the state.

Conceptualizing Social Support

Throughout the country, Myanmar's communities have developed complex strategies of self-help and charitable arrangements. Such arrangements range from direct economic support for the disadvantaged to different advocacy activities in the interests of specific groups that can be categorized as political activism (South 2008; Prasse-Freeman 2012). After the catastrophe of Cyclone 'Nargis' in 2008, people on the ground demonstrated an impressive and immediate community-based response to help survivors with food, shelter, and health treatments, given the very limited resources they had (Jaquet and Walton 2013). This sheds light on the existence of social support structures outside the sphere of the state.

Relations of economic support beyond the household are often no different from ordinary social and economic relations with neighbours, friends, kin, patrons or clients, and so on (von Benda-Beckmann et al. 1997: 109). Very often they are clustered in a relatively small geographical space. Even in times of growing migration and expanding rural–urban links, which play a role in particular for kinship support, physical proximity remains important for the organization of community-level support networks. Support can come in the form of assistance or insurance, and it always

---

Claudio Sopranzetti argued for the relevance of the concept if precarity, defining it as an experience 'created by a variety of forms of unstable, flexible, unbounded, and individualized employment, one only marginally protected by social benefits, legal provisions, or collective bargaining. These include the informalization of labor, seasonal and temporary employment, homework, flex and temp work, subcontracting, freelancing, and self-employment' (2017: 86). In that sense, the people I refer to here are living precarious lives. They may not have experienced a considerable retreat of a welfare state, but they nevertheless find themselves increasingly struggling to make a living in sectors like those listed by Sopranzetti.

[109] Difficulties can also affect a larger number of people, as in the case of flooding that Pathein experiences during the rainy season. People reported to me that such floods have occurred with increased frequency over the past years.

includes the transfer of goods and services (see von Benda-Beckmann et al. 1988: 13, who speak of non-state 'social security'). Consequently, it often involves some form of interdependence, and thus power differentials (p. 16). Moreover, it must entail social and material resources, because supporting others cannot be done without them. Finally, as with all social relations, support networks also involve the potential for less desirable effects, such as control, coercion, and exclusion (von Benda-Beckmann et al. 1988: 8; Rogaly and Rafique 2004; Bähre 2007a, 2007b). One difference from most forms of state social security is that community-based ways of support require more active participation by the people involved (Lont 2005: 7).

Von Benda-Beckmann et al. (1997: 112) distinguish four concrete pillars of a non-state social-security system in Kenya, a description that makes sense in many other contexts as well, including Myanmar. The first pillar is based on individual provisions derived from individual economic activities. As this chapter deals with the community level, I will not go into detail about it here. The second pillar consists of membership in traditional solidarity networks, including the extended family and neighbourhood units. The third pillar consists of membership in cooperative or social welfare associations such as self-help groups, savings and credit groups, and cultural groups. Concerning this third pillar, I would add that these associations operate in parallel to more commercially oriented institutions such as moneylenders, pawnshops, and microfinance programs.[110] In reality, they cannot be neatly separated. Because of the links between them, I will investigate non-commercial as well as commercially oriented sources of credit together in the second half of this chapter. The last pillar listed by Benda-Beckmann et al. is based on the benefits provided by non-governmental voluntary organizations, churches, and trade unions. Regarding this last pillar, I will concentrate on the role of charitable organizations and Buddhist monasteries in welfare provision in Pathein. These four pillars constitute a network of relatives, friends, neighbours, associations, community-based charity programmes, and religious institutions that people can draw on. Its single components seem to consist of quite different things at first, and they have often been analysed in isolation from each other. However, in reality they are interlinked in many ways, with several of them being simultaneously relevant for one household. The protective network of mutual assistance is 'chameleon-like and kaleidoscopic in nature, catering to every taste, purse and preference' (Bouman 1994a: 116).

---

[110] See Turnell (2017) for a recent analysis of microfinance in Myanmar.

The processes in these support networks are dynamic, and the social structure they are embedded in is not egalitarian. In Theravādin societies, wealthy people have long played a key role as donors to Buddhist institutions, as well as to the disadvantaged. However, they did not donate to the sangha or to the poor merely out of compassion or to enhance their own social standing, but also because there is a clear expectation, even pressure, for them to be generous (Bowie 1998: 476).[111] Among those who are the recipients of charity, the economically vulnerable, the boundaries between receiving and giving, security and indebtedness, can shift quickly and are generally rather blurred. Like all social activities, support is linked to moral ideas (von Benda-Beckmann et al. 2007: 17; see also Nguyen 2015, on the topic of care). This becomes particularly obvious in contexts of adversity and aid. Here, different mechanisms of support, as well as socio-economic inequalities and adversities as such, are also partly explained with reference to Buddhist concepts. For instance, people refer to Buddhist ideas when engaging in charitable activities, as well as when talking about topics such as indebtedness and charging interest on loans.

Various kinds of support arrangements, including those mentioned above, have been analysed as 'community based' or as part of Myanmar's 'civil society' (James 2005; Lorch 2006, 2007, 2008; South 2008; McCarthy 2016). Such terms often emerge in development discourses and are meant as a contrast to state initiatives and projects set up by outside actors.[112] Since I am more concerned with understanding social dynamics on the ground than with a macro-level analysis of political processes, I will not use the category of 'civil society' as an analytical tool. However, my informants themselves sometimes contrasted their social support activities with the state, saying 'the state does not help us, so we have to do it ourselves'. Among Burmans, charity and social work activities are often described within the categories of *luhmu.ye:* (Burmese 'social affairs') or *parahita* (Burmese, but originally Sanskrit, 'welfare of others').

The term 'community' is also relevant in so far as, for many of these support mechanisms, physical and social proximity matters. Arrangements like savings and credit groups are set up by neighbours or by people who share an occupation. Other support arrangements are organized through

---

[111] In Thailand Bowie (1998) found that richer people worried that the poor could steal from them or rebel against the status quo if they show no generosity toward them (p. 476).

[112] A state-centred perspective would also categorize many of them as part of the 'informal sector', meaning that these transactions are not supervised by the state, nor regulated by official state laws.

religious institutions that run health programs or orphanages.[113] Donations
that go through these channels, even though they might benefit complete
strangers, can also be seen as a means to support a wider community – the
'Buddhist community', the 'Christian community', and the like. Some
projects, like paving roads, are organized on the ward level, another, more
formalized type of 'community' defined by administrative boundaries.

Acknowledging systematic support activities, both current ones and
those that have existed for many decades, has helped debunk the idea that
nothing like a 'civil society' outside government-led activities could exist
under a military dictatorship, as had been argued for the Ne Win era
(Steinberg 1999). It also suggests that studies of communities in Thailand
and Burma in the 1950s and 1960s should be revisited, particularly those
adhering to the 'loosely structured' (Embree 1950) hypothesis, which
emphasized the lack of permanent cooperative groups (see Bunnag 1971, for
a discussion of this). Tamura, a bit later, went so far as to say the Burmese
village community 'lacks coherence, solidarity, and any principles which
prescribe social relationships' (1983: 11, as cited in Kumada 2015: 819).
While some scholars have attributed observations of that kind to Buddhism,
with its alleged emphasis on individual responsibility (Phillips 1967: 363–4,
as cited in Bunnag 1971: 11), it was rather the plentiful resources that made
permanent systematic cooperation in groups unnecessary (Bunnag 1971: 10–
12). What Bunnag described for relatively stable village contexts in Thailand
resembles what the economist Mya Maung called a 'lack of economic
anxiety' (1964: 758–759) in rural Burma. According to him this was a consequence of the affluence of basic necessities, as well as cultural values. In
contrast to these examples from Burma and Thailand, in Sri Lanka, where
land and water were scarce, people systematically cooperated in groups
organized around lines of kinship to protect the survival of the next generation and their own individual interests (Bunnag 1971: 11, referring to Leach
1961). This underlines the role of socio-economic conditions in the formation of cooperation, even though religious ideas and institutions may
function as a moral and organizational framework for such cooperation.

I have already suggested in Chapter 4 that after market liberalization
the economic importance of kinship became increasingly visible, for
example, due to the rising importance of intergenerational property transfers
for wealth generation, and also to increasing levels of migration leading to
economic support being provided at a distance. Such changes in practice
have the potential to redefine ideas about kinship as well. Similar processes

---

[113] Walton (2017b) noted that the popularity of groups of monks, such as the MaBaTha,
whose members have spread nationalistic and Islamophobic sentiments, needs also to be
understood in light of their engagement in welfare and community programmes.

happened to community structures. While the wealthy have certainly supported the poor in the past (and linked to that were specific understandings of *dāna* and merit, see also Bowie 1998, on Thai villages), it seems that organized charitable activities have increased in Myanmar in recent decades, especially in urban areas. This is indicated at least by social workers in Patheinian orphanages, who reported that donations have gone up in recent years, making it possible for them to upgrade buildings and accept more children. In other towns in Myanmar, a rising number of formalized social-support groups have been observed as well. Such groups have appeared more often, especially since the economic changes toward a market economy in the early 1990s, when government suppression of local organizations eased while at the same time livelihoods became a more demanding task for many (McCarthy 2016: 315–16). Socio-economic changes, such as increasing demand for support networks, in turn, might then redefine perceptions of *dāna* and ideas of charity, deservingness, and appropriate recipients.

Religious ideas also play a role with regard to social inequalities, as we have seen for the differences between employers and workers in the previous chapter. Inequalities are present also in the wider social landscape. Also here, some people invoked the law of *kamma* (Burmese *kan*) to explain them. The concept seemed to function here as what Terpe (2018: 14), in a recent discussion of Weber's 'spheres of life', called 'quasi-natural life orders' (see Chapter 3 for a more detailed explanation of *kamma*). However, how much importance is attributed to *kamma* in particular individuals' socio-economic situations differs from person to person. Bunnag (1973: 21) reported for Thailand that wealthy businessmen might attribute their wealth to their own hard work rather than to *kamma* to emphasize his achievements in the current life. However, in Pathein I experienced the opposite, for example, the case of Daw Cho Cho, whom I shall describe later in this chapter. Here, business owners would often downplay economic factors in their success, such as a good location for their businesses or their smart investments, and stress instead that it was due to their *kamma* that they had become wealthy. Concrete economic advantages and their ability to use them were also presented as resulting from their *kamma* in the first place. After all, overly stressing one's economic ability carried the risk of being seen as greedy, too concerned with material possessions, or too proud. Referring to good *kamma* instead suggests a high moral standing.

As I mentioned in Chapter 3, *kamma* not only stresses determination but also one's own responsibility to act in one's present life to work towards a better rebirth.[114] In a survey I conducted with forty business owners in the course of my project, one question was: 'Why do some people in this country live in need?' Respondents were asked to select the most important reason and the second most important reason out of a list of possible replies. Most often they chose 'Because of laziness and lack of willpower' as the most important reason (22 people out of 38 who returned valid data sets) or the second most important reason (10 people), thus very much emphasizing this-worldly self-responsibility. Other replies that scored high were 'because of injustice in our society' (5 times as the most important reason, 9 times as the second most important reason). However, other replies included 'Because of their bad *kan*'[115] (9 times in total as the most important or second most important reason), 'because they lack religious faith' (9 times in total as either the most important or second most important reason), as well as 'because they have no moral virtues' (7 times in total as either the most important or second most important reason). Thus, *kamma* as a component is seen to combine with other factors like people's own worldly attitudes and actions as well as wider social conditions, in explaining inequality. Moreover, believing that someone is at least partly responsible for his own circumstances (whether through actions in past lives or current laziness) does not necessarily reduce people's will (and duty) to help those in need (Jaquet and Walton 2013: 59–60).

Dāna and the Collective Dimensions of Buddhist Practice

Myanmar was ranked the 'most generous country in the world' for three years in a row, from 2014 to 2016, decades after anthropologists had attributed to Burmans a lack of solidarity and cooperation (Tamura 1983: 11, as cited in Kumada 2015: 819). The respective ranking, called the World Giving Index, is published annually by the London-based Charities Aid

---

[114] Some people believe that, despite the general inalterability of past *kamma*, a person can influence, through good behaviour in the present, good deeds from the past outweighing bad ones. One monk invoked the metaphor of a lake: 'Imagine a lake. It contains all of your good and bad *kamma* from the past. It is up to you to decide where its water will flow. It depends which side you start digging on'.

[115] The original reply-option my research group phrased in English (also to be asked in other countries) was 'Because they are unlucky'. The Burmese word for 'luck' is *kan* (which is the Burmese word for the Pāli *kamma*). To be lucky is translated as *kan kaun-deh* ('*kan* is good'). This word inherently contains the idea of cause and effect. One is only 'lucky' if enough good *kan* from past lives is available. It is often used in situations when an English speaker would use 'luck' rather than 'fate', e.g. Burmans buying lottery tickets would say *kan san-deh* ('to test one's *kan*'). Thus, their understanding seems different from the coincidence implied by the word 'lucky' in English. With their reply in my survey, people are not saying 'because they are unlucky' but rather 'because of their bad *kan* (*kamma*)'.

Foundation (CAF).[116] The survey behind the CAF ranking did not simply measure documented amounts of donated money in a country's population. Instead, it asked about people's subjective *willingness* to be charitable, as well as their concrete recent acts of charitable behaviour, such as volunteering, helping strangers, and donating (religious donations included). Given these criteria, the result can come as no surprise to those who study Myanmar society, where donating is so directly linked to merit-making. Religious donations can be observed everywhere, on the morning rounds of the monks, in pagoda compounds, at festivals or at the sides of the roads, where people regularly collect donations from cars passing by. Apart from the individual concern with merit-making, donations are also a way to support the *sāsanā*[117] and prevent its decline. Donations also strengthen community ties and bring social prestige to the donor, while some donations are crucial for welfare projects.

Donations constitute acts of *dāna* (see Chapter 3). Many people in Pathein visited pagodas weekly (preferably on the weekday of their birth), others only on full-moon days. Some of my informants claimed to donate half of their incomes to monasteries, and I have seen people giving sums equivalent to hundreds of euros during pagoda festivals. When I asked people what they would do with a lottery win, almost everyone replied that they would donate all or at least a large part of it. Unexpected increases in income often result in higher donations or a religious pilgrimage for the whole family. Monasteries often keep lists to display which family in the neighbourhood is supposed to donate lunch to the monks on which day of the week. Often, regular donors have quite a close relationship to the head monk of a monastery. Monasteries are open institutions that regularly engage with the lay community through events. Besides financial donations, many people also spend time volunteering at monasteries to cook or do other tasks. Donations are often used to organize religious festivals and ceremonies, joyful social events accompanied by worldly pleasures, such as food and music (see also Spiro 1966: 1168). Some people sponsor a meal (usually lunch) at a monastery not only for the monks but for the whole neighbourhood. The food will be served after a sermon reading and after the monks have eaten. Such events are perfect occasions to reaffirm one's social ties by sharing joy and sometimes expenses (Bunnag 1971: 19). Such events may also be linked to honouring kinship ties, as families often sponsor celebrations and feasts at monasteries (Burmese *ahlu*, literally meaning 'offering') on specific occasions, like a wedding anniversary or the an-

---

[116] Ranking results can be downloaded under https://www.cafonline.org/about-us/publications. Accessed on 29.11.2018.

[117] The *sāsanā* is the entirety of Buddhist teachings, practices, and institutions.

niversary of the death of a parent. As the sponsor of such an event, a family will be the centre of attention and gratitude. In popular monasteries, there are long waiting lists for potential donors. Even though people often say that if a donation is made merely to show off it is considered unfruitful when it comes to merit, one monk expressed to me the commonly shared pragmatic attitude that 'it is good anyway, because some people are fed', thus emphasizing the collective and worldly dimension of the event.

However, while almost daily meals are sponsored at Patheinian monasteries, most donations that people make are used to maintain or renovate monasteries or other religious buildings, alongside materially supporting the sangha. Nevertheless, I suggest that the social aspects matter here as well, albeit in a more indirect way. Patrice Ladwig (2017) suggested that Buddhist temples in Laos must be seen as 'sacra' in Gudeman's sense. Gudeman (2001) defined 'sacra' as particularly important, even defining elements of a community, similar to what he called 'commons', but stronger and more indispensable (p. 28). Commons are understood here as material things or knowledge which people share, which are regulated through social obligations, and which have a strong social meaning for the community. Strengthening the commons means strengthening the community, and allowing access to the commons means allowing access to the community. Consequently, to damage the commons is also to damage the community (Gudeman 2001: 27).[118] If we regard a Buddhist temple or a monastery as 'sacra', then supporting even just the material shape of the temple through donations means more than just a promise of individual merit: it strengthens the core of the community. This means both the concrete face-to-face community of the respective neighbourhood, as well as the wider imagined community of Buddhists more generally.

---

[118] Gudeman lists talismans, amulets, and sourdough starters, which are passed between households, as well as St. Peter's in the Vatican, as examples of commons (2001: 27).

Plate 7. Donation box at Soon Oo Pon Nya Shin Pagoda in Sagaing.

A Buddhist monk was the first person I met who criticized the scope of religious donations in Myanmar. I met him in Sagaing, where I spent my initial weeks of research. Filled with clusters of monasteries and temples, Sagaing hosts thousands of Buddhist monks, nuns, and laypeople, who devote their time to meditation and the study of Buddhist teachings. 'Many people misunderstand the point about donations', this senior monk of a monastic school told me. 'They believe that the act of giving helps them to gain merit – which would result in a better situation in their future existence. They think, "the more the better". In the end, they donate too much. Any extra money that people have is immediately given to the monasteries. But the Buddhist teachings say very clearly how you should handle your wealth: divide it into four' (this refers to the *Sigālovāda Sutta*). Slightly different from the original teachings and adapted to the situation of a contemporary business, the monk suggested the use of each fourth as follows: 'One fourth for yourself and your family, one fourth for business investments, one fourth for donations and social welfare, and the last fourth you save'.[119] Hence,

---

[119] The original *sutta* does not mention reserving one part specifically for donations, but instead even suggests investing two fourths in the business. However, donations to the sangha

according to this monk, there was a mismatch between religious teachings and many people's actual behaviour. Criticism of the vast amount of donations from lay people was only mentioned to me by close acquaintances after a quite long time in the field.[120] 'People will think I am a bad person when they hear me saying this... But I think we have enough monasteries', one informant said. Someone else felt that Buddhist donations were not economically efficient, as they are not channelled into business investments, but largely spent on religious buildings. Despite such critical mutterings, religious donations remained a common practice for most people in one form or another.

While the majority of donations go to the sangha, for the purposes of this chapter it is crucial that people have a broader understanding of *dāna* that goes beyond gifts from the laity to the sangha. It includes gifts *between* lay people, including those gifts to lower social standing, like beggars (Bowie 1998), as well as gifts to other beings, such as animals or spirits (*nat*s). Some forms of *dāna* cannot easily be distinguished from activities referred to as *luhmu.ye:* (social affairs or social obligations) or ordinary giving, and the boundaries are often blurred (Kumada 2004: 8). The wish and duty to help is sometimes phrased with reference to concepts like *myitta* (Pāli: *mettā*, loving kindness) and compassion (*karuṇā*). The *Mettā Sutta*, which preaches kindness towards all beings, is among the most popular sermons, regularly chanted by monks and recited by laypeople. Several lay people mentioned it to me as the one teaching that means the most to them personally, and I met parents who proudly demonstrated to me that their three-year old child can already recite parts of the *Mettā Sutta*. *Mettā*, like merit, seems to have an almost substance-like character, as people say they 'share' *mettā* or 'send' *mettā*, for example, to someone who is sick.

A large number of welfare projects in Myanmar have been set up by Buddhist monks and are organized through monasteries: one famous example is the so-called Sitagu Hsayadaw, a monk who has set up various projects throughout the country.[121] The social engagement of such monks seems to have changed perceptions of *dāna*, putting more focus on the needs of recipients instead of on their spiritual power (see also Jaquet and Walton 2013: 65–66). Support through religious institutions takes many forms. For

---

and charitable causes are included in the first part meant for family, friends, personal wants, and enjoyment (DN 31).

[120] For most people it was unthinkable to criticize Buddhism, its institutions and practices. Also, there are sections in the Myanmar Penal Code (295A and 298) that prohibit insulting religion, and people have been charged and jailed for violating it.

[121] However, among the sangha and also among the laity, opinions differ on whether monks should become socially engaged or not. Some people held that monks should remain detached from worldly matters and focus only on *dhamma* studies and meditation.

instance, Buddhist monasteries have a long tradition as educational centres for children from poorer backgrounds (Lorch 2007), but they also run orphanages and care centres for the elderly in Pathein. Moreover, free clinics offer regular basic health-care to people in Pathein on certain days of the week. One monastery in Pathein that I visited regularly financed eye-surgery for several older patients who were suffering from a loss of vision and could not afford the treatment themselves. In some cases, the initiative comes from just one monk, while other projects are run by large Buddhist organizations that have branches in different parts if the country.[122]

Monasteries also offer a refuge for individuals or groups of people. When parts of Pathein were severely flooded in August 2016, many people found shelter in Buddhist monasteries and were supported by small charitable organizations. These organizations, some of which were formed spontaneously, collected money from passers-by on the main roads, and some received crucial support from wealthy community members. While the sangha has always been a refuge and a possible avenue for upward mobility for boys from poor backgrounds, sometimes lay people too find shelter on monastic grounds if they own no house and have no means of paying rent. They might work in the monastic compound and be given a place to stay. A student I knew in Pathein lived in a monastery compound because he found the student dormitory where he had stayed previously too loud for him to be able to concentrate on his studies. In exchange for his room in the monastery, he regularly acted as a driver for the abbot and other monks, driving them to ceremonies in Pathein and the surrounding villages. Monasteries are also a special case in terms of taxation, property, and landownership. Down the decades, the Myanmar government has con-fiscated buildings and land from people. To prevent this, some landowners would rather donate their land for religious purposes. Often they themselves were able to stay on the land, which was now protected from confiscation by the government. Moreover, as sacred property it would also be excluded from taxation.

Sometimes support patterns bridge ethnic and religious boundaries.[123] Many monastic orphanages and schools accept children of non-Buddhist

---

[122] The state is not completely uninvolved here. Some projects, such as religious *dhamma* schools that fulfil certain criteria, receive state support. Also, the government may provide financial assistance to town wards for infrastructural improvements like paving roads. But in many cases this only covers a small percentage of the costs, so that community contributions still make up the largest part.

[123] However, in Taungoo McCarthy observed that people sometimes saw other groups, in particular Muslims, as not possessing the same moral qualities necessary to build such support organizations. Social support activities thus can also serve as a means of group formation and self-identification in contrast to 'others' (McCarthy 2016: 322–323).

faith. Furthermore, events might be co-organized by people of different faiths. Daw Hla Hla Myint, a Catholic woman who ran a restaurant on the margins of Pathein, had a close connection to the head monk of a nearby Buddhist monastery. As her deceased husband's relatives were Buddhists, she regularly invited Buddhist monks from this monastery to her restaurant for blessing ceremonies, followed by a family lunch. Once per year Daw Hla Hla Myint teamed up with the head monk to organize an event to honour the elderly of the neighbourhood. Around forty elderly people would be brought to the monastery, where sermons were read to them and they received packages containing money and presents (containing soap, towels, and some snacks). They were also provided with lunch. Besides these activities, Daw Hla Hla Myint was also engaged in several Catholic charitable projects.

Daw Cho Cho: Supporting the Poor and Strengthening the *Sāsana*

To learn more about charity and redistribution, I regularly visited several orphanages (Burmese *mi.ba. me' kalei: gei ha*) accommodating children who either had no parents, or whose parents were not able to care for them. These orphanages were typically funded through a small amount of government support for rice provision, funds from religious institutions, and donations from local people. One such place, which I call 'Morning Sun', was located in a northern ward of Pathein. Bordering a Buddhist monastery whose abbot is a key supporter, the orphanage hosted forty-two boys between five and eighteen years of age at the time of my research. The place consisted of a simple cement building in which each boy had a wooden cot and a small metal box for his personal belongings. The boys attended a nearby public school. Many of them came from conflict-ridden Shan State in eastern Myanmar. Their transport to Pathein had been organized by a network of Buddhist monks. The orphanage building was in poor condition, with a leaking roof and crumbling walls, offering only very limited space for the children. Thus, the construction of a new and bigger building was underway. When I talked to the only full-time social worker at the orphanage, he mentioned a key donor, a woman called Daw Cho Cho, who had donated a considerable amount of money for the construction, her contributions adding up to amounts equalling more than a thousand euros. Just recently she had given money for the two staircases that will lead up to the building. Each staircase is dedicated to one of her parents, whose names will be displayed on plates attached to the stairs.

I formed a plan to get to know Daw Cho Cho in order to understand the motivation behind her actions more clearly. I first met this fifty-six-year-old woman at the monastery next to the orphanage during a novitation ceremony (Burmese *shin pju.*) for twenty-seven of the orphan boys. Daw

Cho Cho was the sponsor of this event. Usually very modestly dressed, as I would find out later, she was wearing her finest clothes that day, her face beaming with happiness and pride. It had taken her months to prepare the novitation ceremony, as she had made sure that every detail was perfect and in accordance with the traditions as far as possible. In a typical *shin pju.* ceremony, the novices-to-be will start the day dressed as princes. They will then go on a procession through the town, on horse carts or in cars, accompanied by followers, many of whom are also dressed up, as deities or other mythical beings. After paying homage to the Buddha, the guardian spirits, and in some cases the *nats*, the boys will return to the monastery, where they will have their heads shaved in a ritualized manner and receive their robes. They stay in the monastery for some time, usually for at least a few days. This procedure is meant to imitate the life of Prince Siddharta Gautama, who later reached enlightenment and became the founder of Buddhism. It took Daw Cho Cho a lot of money and effort to prepare the festival. She needed two full months just to have all the costumes made and fitted to each boy's body. She needed to write invitations and hire the vehicles for the procession. She also hired a master of ceremonies to make sure all the stages would be carried out correctly. When the boys set out to their parade around town, Daw Cho Cho was first in a long line of followers behind them. Being the principal donor of the event brought her the attention and admiration of more than a hundred other attendees. Daw Cho Cho also sponsored lunch and breakfast for the novices and the monks on the two consecutive days around the ceremony. She had noticed that the boys were struggling with the practice of their not having any food after lunch, which is a rule for members of the sangha. She asked the head monk if he would allow her to bring them candies or snacks in the evening, but he replied that this would make it even more difficult for them to bear the hunger, an explanation which Daw Cho Cho accepted immediately. The most important thing was the spiritual step that she had enabled the boys to make. It is believed that a novitation ceremony brings great merit for the novices' parents, specifically their mothers. This process is understood as a way for the son to pay back part of the debt he owes to his mother for raising him. The *shin pju.* ceremony is one of the clearest examples of how much im-portance is placed on parent–child relations, manifested in an institu-tionalized religious practice.

Shin pju. celebrations are, like life cycle events elsewhere, also a way to display one's social standing. They range from ostentatious events among the wealthy to rather modest versions among those who do not have great financial means. If parents are unable to organize a *shin pju.*, it is not uncommon for others to act as donors for such boys, which enables them to receive merit in their turn. Daw Cho Cho explained that she had no children of her own and that these boys have no parents. She felt sorry for them and wanted to make sure they have a perfect novitation. A *shin pju.* is the precondition for full ordination as a monk later in life. 'Who knows where these boys end up in their lives. Maybe they will become influential, rich or famous. If they are ordained as monks one day, it is because I made it possible for them. They will remember me', Daw Cho Cho said with excitement. She is a devout Buddhist and an experienced donor. Her donations must have added up to amounts equalling several thousand euros in past years. She mentioned to me a roof that she had donated to a different orphanage (for forty *lakh* = ca. 2,900 EUR), donations to an elderly home in Pathein, and regular sponsoring of meals for large groups of people in monasteries. She also donated a special Buddha statue to another monastery. The statue had been ordered from Mandalay, and its consecration was accompanied by a big ceremony which the whole neighbourhood attended. Moreover, Daw Cho Cho had organized and sponsored a *dhamma* talk, an event where monks preach to the laity from a stage. Now, with the novitation ceremony, she had sponsored an opportunity for orphans to become sangha members. She sees these three events as her contribution to the three 'jewels of Buddhism': the Buddha, the *dhamma*, and the sangha. Daw Cho Cho emphasized the aspect of a collective social experience a lot. 'When the Buddha statue arrived, the whole neighbourhood celebrated. Everyone from around here!' And speaking about the novitation ceremony, she said: 'I saw some people who could not help but weep when they saw the little boys in their costumes'.

However, Daw Cho Cho was not only a donor, she was also a business owner. Her two large houses were located close to the orphanage. One was a boarding house for more than one hundred female university students, each of whom paid around 20,000 kyat (ca. 14.5 EUR) per month. The second house, which was attached to the boarding house, accommodated a retail shop for clothes and bags on the ground floor. Daw Cho Cho lived on the two upper floors together with her aunt. Daw Cho Cho's mother had purchased the land here in 1975 for 2000 kyat (now ca. 1.4 EUR) in instalments, when the area consisted of only farmland and swamp. Together with three siblings, Daw Cho Cho grew up on a military compound. Her father was a low-ranking military officer, and her mother was a street vendor who had had only four years of schooling. Daw Cho Cho completed her matriculation exam and graduated from university. She then started working as a teacher and later became a public servant in a state ministry in Pathein, where she stayed for twenty-six years. After her father retired from the military, the family had to leave the army compound. They therefore moved to the piece of land they had purchased in the 1970s, where Daw Cho Cho still lives today.

The location turned out to become very profitable in the 1990s, as new university buildings had been constructed nearby. Since then, the streets had become increasingly filled with students. By renting out space to them, the family could make enough money to upgrade their house step by step. Later, they also started selling clothes and bags. Over the years, Daw Cho Cho was also able to buy and resell other plots of land, which brought her further wealth. Plenty of tea shops, retail shops, copy shops, and dormitories have since opened in the area, and Daw Cho Cho can profit from the prime location that her house now occupies. Having grown up with very limited means, she was now a wealthy woman. Her two brothers and her sister all got married and left Pathein to pursue jobs in the military elsewhere and start families. Some of her nieces and nephews have become doctors. Daw Cho Cho herself never married and remains childless. She lived with her parents until they died a few years ago. Her mother and she had been running the businesses together. Her father had suffered a stroke shortly after his retirement and needed extensive care, being unable to get up, speak, eat, or wash himself. Daw Cho Cho cared for him for nineteen years until his death. Not only did she feed and wash him, she also regularly read Buddhist sermons to him or played them from a cassette. Sometimes she took him to monasteries in a wheelchair, thus being considerate of his spiritual needs.

In 2006, Daw Cho Cho had been offered a promotion in her government job. However, this would have required her to transfer to a different place. She decided to quit her job to care for her parents, and since then she has lived comfortably from the incomes from the boarding house, the clothes shop, and her investments in land. This was the moment when Daw Cho Cho exchanged secure and prestigious employment for autonomy, not only for her own pleasure, but partly because she had to fulfil kinship obligations (see Chapter 5). As I have mentioned already in earlier chapters, every move toward autonomy demands that one makes sure one is valuable to the community in other ways in order to retain its respect. Running a business would not help to achieve that – rather the opposite. Thus, Daw Cho Cho began to stress her role as a carer for her parents and greatly increased her donation activities.

Daw Cho Cho does not seem to take much pride in her businesses. In fact, when we had to pass through the clothes shop to reach the residential part of the house, she rushed through it. Whenever I asked about her shop and her boarding house, Daw Cho Cho replied rather briefly. She very much preferred talking about her parents, Buddhism, or her donation activities. I had to be quite persistent to learn more about her businesses as this was nothing that Daw Cho Cho identified with, or that she presented as a great achievement in itself (I have explored the reasons for this common attitude in Chapter 4). However, her businesses served her as a means to different ends. They enabled her to devote a lot of time and money to donation activities and other forms of religious practice. She liked to take me to the top floor of her house, where she devoted an entire room to her religious activities. The room had a big Buddhist shrine to which Daw Cho Cho made offerings of food and drink twice a day. The walls were filled with photos of her parents and of donation events that she had organized. On many of the photos she was shown standing next to a monk together with other family members who had participated in the donation. Various certificates were also displayed that Daw Cho Cho had received for donating money, each one mentioning the respective occasion and the amount she donated. This was Daw Cho Cho's personal collection of merit-making memories. The room was a private space, only open to those she decided to take there.[124]

Her religious activities combined several functions for Daw Cho Cho, besides making merit. She paid homage to her parents by dedicating many of her donations to them. In fact, when we talked about her donation activities, the conversation would sooner or later always move on to her parents and how she cared for them. Once I asked her whether she also meditates. She said she did not have much time for that and seemed almost embarrassed. However, a moment later she mentioned how she had taken care of her parents when they were old and sick. 'Meditation is about understanding suffering and impermanence. That is what I saw first-hand with my parents. So it was a kind of a meditation'. Once again she had managed to connect Buddhist concepts to caring obligations within the parent–child relationship. Moreover, she also gained prestige and admiration from her public acts of generosity. Dedicating the donations to her parents led to her being recognized as a caring daughter, increasing still further the respect she received. Not having children of her own was never something Daw Cho Cho or anyone in her family or wider social environment mentioned as a problem. Caring for her parents and regularly appearing as a strong supporter of the *sāsanā* had ensured her not only an accepted, but also a highly respected role in society.

Many earlier studies of *dāna* have stressed its worldly implications of social prestige, status, and admiration, rather than compassion toward others (e.g. Spiro 1966; Keyes 1983a: 268; 1990: 175; Lehman 1996: 29). How-

---

[124] Unlike many others, Daw Cho Cho did not broadcast her donation activities on Facebook. Spreading proof of one's donations on social media has become common in recent years, and such posts usually receive a lot of approval in the social media currencies of 'likes' and praising comments.

ever, these aspects need not contradict each other. Daw Cho Cho reluctantly criticized those who only donate to 'famous monks' and who cared more about building new pagodas than helping those in need. Her own activities displayed a diverse pattern. We can see that for her too, the perceived spiritual power of a recipient of donations mattered on some occasions. She took a day off from work a few years ago to make offerings to a particularly well-known monk who was visiting Pathein. On another occasion, when the floor tiles in the central pagoda in Pathein, the Shwe Moke Taw Pagoda, were being renewed, she donated money for a new tile. She emphasized that the floor will probably not be replaced for a long time to come, so 'we got a great opportunity there'. Daw Cho Cho and her family had to be quick, as countless potential donors were competing with each other, and the pagoda trustees had to limit the number of people who could put their names on a list of contributors. On the other hand, Daw Cho Cho regularly donated to orphanages and homes for the elderly, and she also gave food and money to beggars, who are not commonly perceived as the greatest 'fields of merit'. Her concern for merit is here combined with the worldly elements of compassion, pity, and care. When she donates, she said, she never expects anything in return because then the intention would be wrong and the act of *dāna* would be ineffective.

Not all welfare donations are redistributed through religious institutions. Some people donate concrete things for their neighbourhood directly, and donations are also collected within communities for actual infrastructure projects, like the paving of a road. Many improvements are thus the result of a collective effort, with very little to no government support. People often just stand by the side of the road to collect donations from passers-by. On wells or water pumps one often finds a plate with the name of the donor. Furthermore, I remember once hearing an ambulance car from a distance, and my interlocutor mentioned the name of the person who had donated that car to a local health project a year earlier. Often, it was wealthy local people who made crucial contributions to charity projects, both those who were still residing in the town and those who had left and become wealthy elsewhere.

Redistributions that benefit the neighbourhood can happen in various circumstances. For instance, a few weeks before I left Pathein, a person in a nearby neighbourhood was killed in an accident. The driver who had caused the accident paid a sum corresponding to around 1500 EUR to the victim's family. The latter donated more than half of the money, mostly to improve the narrow road in which they lived. While the road was muddy and difficult of access when I first came there, it was wider and had been paved with asphalt by the time I left. The case was solved between the two parties without any official intervention. Using parts of the compensation as a donation seemed to be a normal process for the victim's family and was also somewhat expected by their neighbours and relatives. Such donations will not only benefit the bereaved relatives materially and spiritually, but also, so it is believed, generate merit for the deceased person. This shows that Buddhist doctrines and practices have manifold collective dimensions, not only through acts of *dāna*, but also through merit transfer. Indeed, the mere fact that merit can be shared indicates the social dimension of practiced Buddhism (Gombrich 1971: 219).

Participating in merit-making rituals together is believed to strengthen and maintain social bonds between the participants (potentially even beyond one's present life; see Kumada, 2015). Moreover, there are plenty of rituals for a more general sharing of merit with all sentient beings in religious ceremonies. I experienced the sharing of merit when I attended the annual ceremony of robe donations (Burmese *kahtein*) in a small monastery in Pathein. With around sixty other people I knelt on the monastery floor, my palms pressed together, listening to three monks reciting Buddhist sermons. Earlier, people had donated food, money, and new robes to the monks. When the sermons came to an end, the audience loudly repeated the Pāli word 'sādhu' three times. I had encountered that before. People translated it as 'well done' or 'well said'. While people in Pathein usually left it entirely up to me to participate in any religious ceremony or ritual, in this situation almost the whole audience suddenly turned towards me. The woman sitting right next to me nodded her head vigorously, insisting that I should loudly say 'sādhu, sādhu, sādhu' – so I did, and people seemed pleased. They had insisted on me participating to make sure that I benefited from the merit of the monks who had given the sermon, but I also shared my own merit with others. A teenager used a more unconventional comparison: 'When we do a good deed, we can share the merit we attain from it. It can be transferred. It can travel. It is infinite. It's like... when you share a post on Facebook'. This further exemplifies the interconnectedness of things and the responsibility one has for others, not only materially, but also spiritually.

I have now outlined how donations matter not only for individual merit-making and prestige, but also to the maintenance of a wider social support system, much of which is organized through religious institutions. In the following part of the chapter I will look at reciprocal support among neighbours and more formalized financial arrangements.

The Neighbourhood: Economic Support through Physical Proximity

It is common to see immediate neighbours in Pathein chatting and bringing each other tea or snacks, and the wider community of the area regularly meets for events such as weddings and religious ceremonies. Celebrations at someone's home like weddings and birthday parties are often supported financially by the guests. This happens in a quite formalized way: guests will hand their envelope with money and their name on it to someone sitting at the entrance, who immediately writes down the name of the respective guest plus the amount donated in a list. An exact documentation of people's generosity takes place here, something that contributes to the social pressure to give. It is also common to form working groups, for example, to combine one's voluntary labour to build a road or a well. Sometimes repairing something for a neighbour takes a more directly reciprocal form, for example, when the repair happens in exchange for a meal. Such relations can include people in different economic situations. To illustrate this, I will describe the case of Mary and her neighbours.

Mary was an eighty-year-old woman whose house was slightly bigger than the neighbouring ones. She owned three other places downtown, which she rented out. From having worked at a state-run pharmaceutical company for many years, she received a monthly pension of 28,000 kyat (ca. 20.3 EUR). In addition, one of her daughters worked in Thailand, in jewellery shops and hotels, and regularly sent her money. A second daughter worked as a doctor in Pathein, while a third ran a shop selling items for Buddhist donations. Thus, Mary, while being far from rich, was clearly economically advantaged compared to her immediate neighbours, whose incomes came mainly from trishaw-driving, motorcycle taxi-driving, snack-selling, or fan-making, as in the case of Tin Oo's family, which I shall describe below. Their incomes were far less predictable and much smaller than Mary's, but unlike her neighbours, Mary lived alone. Having enjoyed a good education in a Christian boarding school (from which she got her English name) when she was young, Mary now offered tuition and help with homework for the children in the neighbourhood free of charge or for very little money for those who could afford to give any. When Mary cooked, she often cooked more than she needed and invited neighbours over for a meal. Sometimes she divided the leftover food into small plastic bags, which she hung on her fence outside the house for people to collect when they passed by. This somewhat resembles the act of *pan. dhagu* which is commonly practiced during the annual Tazaungdaing festival: people prepare small bags with food or goods and leave them in public places for whoever needs it. As a decisively religious practice this is yet another example that *dāna* also occurs in transfers to those worse off than oneself.

Mary also donated three water pumps to the community and some-times sponsored festivals at the local monastery. All these instances were stories that Mary enjoyed talking about. As for Daw Cho Cho, for Mary too such donations that served the community are a source of pride and prestige. In emergencies neighbours asked her for money directly, for example, when they needed to buy medicines, though this happened rarely. The usual pattern was that Mary's support came in non-monetary form. The neigh-bours, conversely, regularly checked on the old woman to see if she was alright. As Mary's children were living elsewhere most of the time, these visits provided her with a crucial feeling of security and also a welcome distraction. Women from the neighbourhood often helped her buy groceries, cleaned her house, or gave her leg massages when she felt pain. Emotional labour was involved when they listened to Mary's worries concerning her children, and in return they asked her for advice on their marriage problems. In this case neighbourhood relations consisted of routinized, but not clearly defined or formalized reciprocal support patterns, including material and non-material help. Here, the base for support is the physical proximity with which people lived to each other.

Between Support and Stigma: Financial Arrangements[125]

In addition to such widespread reciprocal and often non-material support patterns, there are many arrangements involving concrete financial trans-actions for the sake of saving money or receiving credit. They are neither a form of *dāna* nor of charity, but nevertheless an important pillar of the non-state social-support system (Benda-Beckmann et al. 1997: 112). In many cases, such financial support arrangements do not involve banks but relatives, friends, neighbourhood groups, microfinance organizations, and private moneylenders. Socially, access to credit cuts both ways. On the one hand, it can be crucial for survival in an emergency, but it can also help to enhance one's standard of living and even one's social standing, for example, when money is used for upgrading a house. On the other hand, it can also lead one into a vicious circle of indebtedness, which can cause social stigma, family conflicts, and personal anxieties. In the following section I will look at different financial arrangements, people' struggles with indebtedness, and the moral judgments involved in these processes.

---

[125] Parts of this section have been published previously in a volume edited by Georg Winterberger and Esther Tenberg (Hornig 2019: 121–140).

Pooling Money: Savings and Credit Groups

Savings and credit groups are a good example of clearly defined financial arrangements embedded within local communities. One such group, with a specific purpose, is funeral groups. Members of such groups regularly pay money into a fund. These payments ensure that when they die their funerals can be arranged and paid for without placing an extra financial burden on their surviving relatives. Other arrangements relevant here are ROSCAs (Rotating Saving and Credit Associations) and ASCAs (Accumulating Saving and Credit Associations). Here, a defined number of people pool their money either to save money (ROSCAs) or to have the option of taking out loans for the group's members (ASCAs). The terms ROSCA and ASCA are not local but were coined by scholars to describe such groups, which occur in many parts of the world. In Myanmar, people usually say *su. ngwei* when referring to such arrangements.

A ROSCA, for instance, can function as follows: each group member contributes a small amount of money each day, and the accumulated amount will be given to each member at some point in the savings cycle. For the sake of illustration, let us imagine an example with savings in euros. Take a group that consists of ten members, each of whom gives one euro per day. Then, every week the whole pot of seventy euros will be given to one member. The saving cycle lasts for ten weeks, until each member receives the pot once. It will usually be decided by lot who gets the pot at which point. One exception here is the organizer of the group, who is usually the first to receive the pot of money. After a savings cycle is complete, the group might dissolve or a new cycle begin, at which point new members can join. This arrangement does not result in any profit for the members, but they will receive a large sum of money at once, which can be invested in house repairs or used for other purposes. Such groups have different functions: protection or insurance (a larger sum of money at once), financial operations (provision and safekeeping of money, pooling for community projects like road-building), and strengthening social ties (Bouman 1994b: 375). Regulations and the management of ROSCAs differ widely between regions, and even within a country. Concerning the wider socio-cultural aspects, anthro-pologists have analysed them as cultural inventions that attempt to reduce uncertainties (Vélez-Ibañez 1983: 1–2). Though Geertz (1962) regarded ROSCAs as a phenomenon that emerges during a shift from a traditional agrarian society to a market-oriented society, later studies have shown that ROSCAs can be found all over the world, in urban and rural areas, among different social strata, and in areas not currently experiencing significant economic transformations. Moreover, they also exist in countries with a highly formalized economic sector, for example, among migrant communities. ROSCAs have been analysed not only by social scientists (Lomnitz 1988; Ardener 1995), but also by economists (Besley et al. 1993; Kedir and Ibrahim 2011).

Anthropological perspectives have analysed ROSCAs as cultural inventions that attempt to reduce uncertainties in people's lives. Moreover, from an anthropological perspective, such financial strategies are especially interesting with regard to the social relations on which they are based. How is access to such groups regulated? Who is considered trustworthy? Who remains excluded? What kinds of conflicts occur, and how are they solved? Having participated in lot-drawing meetings and interviewed ROSCA members and leaders, I soon found that most people I knew in Pathein knew about ROSCAs, and many were or had at some point been members of one. ROSCAs often consist of people with low but relatively stable incomes, such as those running very small businesses and market-traders, but also teachers. There were cases where male business owners would tell me that they do not use saving groups, only for their wives to interrupt them to say that they themselves actually do use them, which their husbands often had no knowledge of. This highlights an important gender aspect. Because women are often responsible for managing household finances, unsurprisingly they are also more usually ROSCA members.[126]

Group sizes are usually small (around ten to twenty members), even though I heard of ROSCAs with more than one hundred members. ROSCAs vary in terms of how personal and close relations between the members are. Some smaller groups meet for every lot-drawing session. These meetings can be cheerful social events, including coffee, snacks, and a lot of talking. Here the ROSCA helps to maintain social relations within the neighbourhood, as well as create new ones. In other groups members do not even know each other, and the group leader collects the money by visiting every member at home or at work. In both cases, however, each member needs to trust that everyone else will pay their respective amount regularly. Generally, ROSCA members emphasized that they only let people join whom they 'trust'. They linked trust to familiarity, which has been identified as an important precondition for trust in other contexts (Luhmann 1988), or to some sort of sameness. The latter aspect made it easier for people to estimate the likelihood with which others will react in certain ways, which is equally important for relations of trust (Dasgupta 1988; see also Gudeman 2009: 20–21 on trust in market relations). Among savings group members, familiarity was often based on location: 'I trust her because she has lived in my street for a long time', 'because we are neighbours', or 'because I know

---

[126] As mentioned in Chapter 3, managing the household finances is not necessarily a sign of power in the Buddhist moral framework.

her well' are common explanations. Sharing the same locality also comes with a high degree of social control. Thus, trust in those cases might come from the assumption that no member would want to put their reputation in jeopardy by not paying their share.

As in every group organization, there is the risk of negative aspects: exclusion, pressure, and conflicts occur, especially if someone is unable to pay their share. As there is usually no official contract, de jure sanctions against someone who breaks the rules would be difficult or even impossible and in the main are not considered an option. People I talked to about ROSCAs had often heard stories of group members disappearing after they had received the full pot of money at an early stage in the cycle. However, even though many people had stories to tell about such incidents, stealing from the group seemed to be rare. Those who did so would be subject to gossip, and after their eventual return they would not easily be accepted again as a group member. People who were known to have lost considerable sums of money in gambling, to drink too much alcohol or were seen as immoral for other reasons were also usually not welcome in ROSCAs. However, also the bigger ROSCAs where members do not know each other are usually successful, even without regular face-to-face interactions.

Generally among my informants in Pathein, ROSCAs were seen as a good arrangement that made livelihood management easier. One member explained: 'We just save together, every day a little, you barely feel it … And suddenly you have three *lakh*' (ca. 218 EUR). The emphasis here is on the fact that saving together is convenient, as smaller sums are not so easily spent when they are not immediately to hand. Group members agreed that solitary saving demands more discipline. The same woman quoted above explained that it is also convenient that other family members do not have access to the money she saves in a ROSCA and therefore cannot spend it on 'useless things'. ROSCAs, by storing money outside the household, are thus also a way of keeping money safe from the claims of friends and relatives. It may be difficult from the outside to understand why people use these saving groups when no financial profit results from it. However, their worldwide popularity proves the advantages of group arrangements when money is scarce and having enough individual discipline to save on one's own might be made additionally difficult by financial demands from family members and relatives. Knowing that a larger sum of money will be available at once within a predictable timeframe also helps immensely in the medium-term planning of larger expenses.

As mentioned above, another group-pooling arrangement is the ASCA, essentially a credit group. People give money every month, and after a certain period of time (often a year), the money is given back to the members. So, unlike in a ROSCA, there is no rotation; instead the money is accumulated. During this period, members, and sometimes non-members, can take out loans against interest. This causes the fund grow, and the members profit. ASCAs can become very large and consequently demand a greater organizational effort than ROSCAs. Typically there is not only a leader but also a treasurer, a secretary, and often a board that decides whether a requested loan is to be granted. The first ASCA I came across in Pathein consisted of thirty members, with each member contributing 20,000 kyat (ca. 14 EUR) per month. At the time of my enquiry the whole pot consisted of 600,000 kyat (ca. 435 EUR). Such amounts of money were often stored in a bank account by the group leader. In this specific ASCA money could only be claimed twice per year by the same person, and the maximum amount a person could receive was around 200,000 kyat (ca. 145 EUR). The ASCA had established a list of reasons for which members could take out loans. These reasons included health costs and severe damage to a house, for example by fire. Loans had to be paid back within six months. I talked to one woman in her sixties, Daw Nu Nu, who had used a loan from the group in 2015, when her husband fell sick. They went to see the doctor in a hospital and had to make multiple follow-up visits to a clinic. In addition, the doctor had come to their house a couple of times. It was the loan that had allowed them to cover these costs. Daw Nu Nu said that the group, which consisted of people from the same quarter, was 'like a family. The aim is to help each other because we couldn't afford loans from rich people. They ask for high interest'.

While ROSCAs and ASCAs contribute to the social support system in many people's lives, their functions are limited. Being in a ROSCA does not guarantee help beyond this clearly defined arrangement (Lont 2005: 151). In emergencies, people would rather receive help from family, close friends and charity groups. It is also common to borrow money from relatives or friends. There is an expectation of some interest also for loans between friends or even relatives, but often the rates are not agreed beforehand. Instead, the borrower just pays back a little extra, and the lender accepts whatever the borrower deems appropriate or can afford.

While larger direct financial support (in forms of gifts, not loans) between people outside the family seemed to be rather uncommon, I met one woman who reported that her health treatment was sponsored by a wealthier family that was unknown to them. The strangers had coincidentally overheard her conversation with a relative about how they cannot afford hospital treatment and offered to help. I also talked to Maung Zin, a man who had helped out friends with money and had not received back anything in return. While he was disappointed, he did not want to risk friendships over it and decided to forget about it. If similar situations arose in the future, he said, he had decided to change his response and his perception. 'From now on', he said, 'I will only give out money to friends in real emergency situations, and then I will regard it as a gift, without expecting to get it back. This is more generous and spares me the disappointment'. Maung Zin would thus switch from giving loans to conducting acts of *dāna*, for which the return would come in the form of merit.

Trapped in Debt

ROSCAs and ASCAs were originally designed partly with the aim of freeing people from private high-interest loans. Moneylenders have presumably been around since money exists, and they have recently been joined by microfinance institutions as potential sources of loans. Since a legal basis for such organizations was created in 2011, several of them have set up projects aiming to improve living conditions through affordable small loans. However, neither locally initiated savings and credit groups nor NGO-initiated microfinance institutions could fully replace local moneylenders. Instead, in many cases all these actors have become part of the same debt cycle, meaning they are approached by the same families, with one loan replacing another. I shall demonstrate this by recounting the case of Tin Oo.

Tin Oo, who lives in the east of Pathein, was trapped in a cycle of debt. Partly thanks to support from kin and charitable organizations he managed to get by, but his situation was fragile, and any instance of illness or other unexpected expenses would constitute a serious financial threat to him. Tin Oo was in his mid-thirties when I met him. He was originally from a village outside of town, where his mother had worked as a seamstress and his father as a labourer on other people's farmland. Both parents died young, and Tin Oo had left the village fifteen years before I met him. He had come to Pathein with empty hands. His family did not own land, and he was now living in a monastic compound, together with his wife, three children, and an aunt. The old lady, now in her nineties, had donated a large sum of money as well as some property to the monastery, which is why she was welcome to stay there. Tin Oo and his family were allowed to stay as well due to his kinship links to this woman, but unlike his aunt they had to pay for all the meals which were prepared in the compound. Around twenty other lay people lived in the monastic compound, many of them distant relatives of the head monk, who had come from the countryside, showing how such kinship links can have very concrete benefits. Tin Oo was not certain whether he and his family would be permitted to go on living in the compound when his aunt passed away.

Tin Oo had worked at many odd jobs in recent years, for instance, as a brick-layer, a road digger, and in construction. He owned a trishaw for a while, but had to sell it not long before I met him for 50,000 kyat (ca. 36.3 EUR), money he used to repay a larger loan. Tin Oo's incomes fluctuated and were unpredictable. Sometimes he was hired for a whole week to repair a road, for which he received 5000 kyat (ca. 3.6 EUR) a day. Sometimes he had work further away and needed to rent a bicycle, which costs 500 kyat (ca. 0.36 EUR) from 6 am to 6 pm, money he had to write off his already low income. Sometimes he worked inside the monastic compound for money, but then the pay would be particularly low because the costs for his family's meals were deducted from it. Sometimes days went by without him having any job at all. On such days, the family's diet would consist of only dried fish and oil. Tin Oo's wife made hand fans from leaves. The leaves were brought to the neighbourhood by merchants, and many women from the area engaged in this work, which allowed them to work from home and look after their children. The merchants would come to collect the finished products every few days, paying around 150 kyat (ca. 0.09 EUR) per fan. On a good day, Tin Oo's wife earned around 2000 kyat (ca. 1.4 EUR). The couple estimated their daily expenses to be around 7000 kyat (ca. 5 EUR). Unsurprisingly, they struggled to make ends meet. Tin Oo's wife had been thinking about finding work elsewhere in town. She had found a kinder-garten where she could bring her children, but it would cost the couple 30,000 kyat (ca. 21.7 EUR) per month, which was unaffordable for the family. Without close relatives in Pathein other than the old aunt, they had no choice but to look after the children themselves, which reduced their ability to be flexible. Tin Oo and his wife were hoping to enable their children to receive an education beyond primary school, but they remained sceptical whether this would be possible. Clearly, they could do with some extra income. Tin Oo was reluctant to take longer forms of employment in restaurants or shops, as he found the pay too low for a main breadwinner. He also complained about labour contractors in the construction sector, claiming that he and his colleagues had been repeatedly cheated by the contractors not paying them their full salaries. Tin Oo preferred to be self-employed; he hoped to be able to buy a trishaw again soon, for the upcoming dry season, when business prospects would be more promising, displaying the tendency toward autonomy I described in the previous chapter. Tin Oo 's family was permanently indebted, usually owing around two *lakh* (ca. 145 EUR), to different sources.

These debts did not result from major emergencies, but rather from everyday expenditure and smaller unexpected amounts for minor health treatments. When they or their children got sick, Tin Oo and his wife went to a public clinic, where they 'could not afford injections and thus only got tablets', as Tin Oo explained, one of the many things that made his family different from those who were better off. There was a free charity clinic nearby as well, but the queue was usually long, making it a rather inconvenient and time-consuming option. Tin Oo's income broke down considerably at some point because he tried to overcome his alcohol addiction and quit drinking. The withdrawal symptoms left him unable to work for three weeks and ultimately he started drinking again, albeit less than before. The abbot of the monastery where Tin Oo lived, who had occasionally tried to organize work for Tin Oo or supported the children with a bit of pocket money, had also at some point ceased his assistance. Tin Oo suspected that this was because of his drinking habits: 'He thinks I'm not reliable'. Tin Oo had many friends who drank. When I asked him if some of his friends had debts too, he answered: 'Not some. All'.

Tin Oo and his wife also borrow larger amounts from a microfinance organization. These are relatively new institutions in the field of credit for low-income households. In Pathein, four such organizations have established themselves in the past six years or so. They target several neighbourhoods within Pathein and in the surrounding villages. Loans schemes differ, but usually loans are given for a period of several months to a group of five people. This procedure functions as a form of social collateral for the microfinance organization, as their clients normally do not have much to offer as material collateral. In an arrangement like this, if one person fails to pay back their share, the others have to provide the missing amount. Such programmes have been implemented in various parts of the world, with mixed results (Lont and Hospes 2004). They can count as commercially oriented because they usually aim to be self-sustaining and thus charge interest from the borrowers. In this sense, these programmes always constitute a trade-off between becoming self-sustainable and poverty reduction (Rahman 2004: 28). They offer different loan types with different interest rates. From what I heard, interest rates were somewhere around 2 or 3 percent per month over a borrowing period of several months, which is much lower than moneylenders charge (up to 30 percent per month). Money has to be paid back either in one go or week by week.

The amount of lending depends on how well the organization knows the borrower and how much they trust him or her to pay back the money. Groups that have been lending for a longer time can receive twenty *lakh* (ca. 1,452 EUR) over the course of nine months, so that each group member receives four *lakh* (ca. 290 EUR). Project workers regularly visit the communities to collect the money. I arranged a group discussion with eight women from Mary's neighbourhood, the community I mentioned earlier.

These people have regularly obtained microloans over the past three years. While the original idea of microfinance institutions was to provide initial capital for revenue-generating activities, this only works in a number of cases. The borrowers reported that people instead used the money for different things, and some were better at handling money than others. 'Some people buy a motorbike, some repair their house or buy a TV. Other people just waste the money'. In some cases, the microloans became integrated into a debt cycle. One person involved in the work of a microfinance organization admitted to me: 'On the day when we hand out the loans, the moneylenders are already waiting around the corner'. This shows that it is not enough to look at one credit source in isolation. If one finds, for example, that people are able to repay their microloans to NGOs, this does not mean that the programme is successful in the sense intended; it could just as well mean that this person had accumulated even more debt from another source in order to repay the microloan. The women who explained their use of microfinance loans to me were essentially never free from debt. They explained: 'Our houses look a bit better now', but 'we are indebted. It goes round and round and round. We can never pay back the whole lot'. At the time of the interviews, they reported current household debts of between one and three *lakh* (ca. 72.62–217.86 EUR). All women had children and estimated their daily expenses to be around 6,000 kyat (ca. 4.3 EUR), a sum that the families often struggled to earn.

Microfinance organizations often emphasize the idea of empowering women. While in Pathein it is indeed mostly women who apply for these loans and take care of the household budget, the household as an economic unit in many cases includes men and children as well. In the community I studied, the men were often the ones earning the largest share of the household income, perhaps as labourers or trishaw drivers. In such jobs, the income is unpredictable and unstable. The women reported that frequent conflicts between spouses occur, as they are never sure how much the husband really earns, and whether he had brought home the full sum, or had wasted some of it on other things, like gambling and drinking in the worst cases. Furthermore, some men expressed discomfort with the fact that they had to ask for 'pocket money' from their wives and justify their spending.[127] The pressure to repay a loan added to such tensions. In other studies of

---

[127] One thirty-year-old man told me that he does not like this system and that he does not want to justify to his wife anymore what he does with the money. Some men use the term *maya: kyau'*, literally 'to fear one's wife' (sometimes shortened to *maya: ka*), in such contexts, often half-jokingly. It also came up, for example, when men received phone calls from their wives. Explaining that they really cannot refuse to answer the phone, even if it means interrupting a face to face conversation, they would apologetically say *maya: ka.*

microfinance programs it has been shown that sometimes violence against women increased among the borrowing families (Rahman 1999; Karim 2001). The strategy of creating social collateral (lending a loan to a group of five people) also led to conflicts between different households (see also Smets and Bähre 2004). The women recalled two such cases in the previous year, when one member was unable to pay back her share. According to their reports, a lot of shouting took place, and one person disappeared for a while to escape the anger of the other group members.

Debt relations create interdependencies of various kinds and come with different, often ambivalent social consequences (see Guérin 2014 on indebtedness in Tamil Nadu). My critical observations are not meant to suggest that microfinance programmes in Myanmar are generally negative or ineffectual. After all, the women I talked to plan to keep borrowing money from them. They reported some material improvements that they could afford thanks to the microloans, such as new roofs or more stable building materials for their houses. In this way, microloans may help one not only to live more comfortably but also to earn social recognition for an upgraded house. However, being indebted was also linked to shame and created pressure, being constantly at the back of people's minds. Some women described it as very burdensome, while others saw it rather as an annoyance, as something they have learnt to put up with. They emphasized that solidarity in their neighbourhood was strong, and 'there is always a way to find money'. This indicates how living on credit can work relatively smoothly for a while, as there are a variety of credit sources and supplementary income opportunities. However, it remains a fragile system that could collapse if expenditures rise unexpectedly.

Tin Oo explained that 'it's good for some. Some people have better houses. But ultimately, the rich remain rich and the poor remain poor. And if we use their loans to pay back the moneylenders, it only makes the lenders richer'. Indeed, if Tin Oo and his wife failed to accumulate the sum they owed to the microfinance organizations, they had to 'look elsewhere', as Tin Oo put it, that is, resort to approaching other sources. The merchants involved with the fan trade gave out loans too, they said. I also heard rumours about government officials in the area who get funding from NGOs or government sources meant for improving conditions in the neighbourhood, which they instead use to upgrade their own houses or lend out with interest. In addition, there was another private moneylender near the monastery, Tin Oo explained, a rich Chinese woman. Tin Oo recalled that her siblings owned some ice-cube factories. She was also known for donating to the monastery occasionally. For her loans, she charged 20 percent interest per month, as well as fees for late payment.

Even though Tin Oo occasionally approached the moneylender he mentioned, the act was far from unproblematic. 'The private moneylenders don't trust us', said Tin Oo; 'They give us only one or two *lakh*. And if we fail to pay back in time, they will make a scene and shout at us in front of everyone'. Private moneylenders provide loans on a daily, weekly or monthly basis or over several months. While indebtedness is a growing problem, it is certainly not a new one. People normally talk about moneylenders as *ngwei chei: thu*, which simply translates to 'a person lending money'. However, another term with a more negative connotation one might come across is *chi' ti:*. It is usually not used in the presence of a moneylender but rather when speaking about one. It indicates greed and perhaps even fraud. For instance, people who ask for a reputable moneylender in a certain neighbourhood will be warned not to go to person *yxz*, 'because he is a real *chi' ti:*'. People would also tease each other with the word, for instance, if someone acts stingily or comes into a sudden increase in wealth. *Chi' ti:* is nowadays used to address someone regardless of this person's ethnicity, but it actually contains a link to the past, referring to the Indian Chettiars, many of whom acted as moneylenders on a large scale in the colonial period (see Chapter 2). Through networks, systematic investments, resources, and skills, they undertook large-scale financial operations in the colonial economy, and farmers became indebted to them in considerable numbers. Nowadays a much smaller number of Chettiar communities live in Myanmar. Pathein has an impressive old Chettiar building in the eastern downtown area that dates back to the days of Chettiar wealth in colonial Burma. It is now crumbling and overgrown by plants, closed for reasons of security, its ownership unresolved. Locals also refrain from entering it because it is said to be haunted. A Chettiar family lives next door and cares for the attached temple.

The days of Chettiar dominance in moneylending are long gone. In today's lowland urban areas, while some lenders are Burmese-Indian, many are Burmans or Chinese. Moneylending has experienced a resurgence since the end of socialism, during which it was reportedly less common. Similarly, new forms of spending money linked to addiction have gained popularity, notably illegal lotteries and informally organized sports bets, which were perceived as new social ills by many informants. Moneylending can either be a person's only income or a lucrative side business. Sometimes people are lenders and borrowers at the same time. For instance, May Wah, who I have briefly mentioned in Chapter 4 as the wife of water seller Ko Ko, makes her income by crafting and selling small clay items like candle holders or children's toys. She also occasionally sells curries to construction workers. She does not make a lot of money but nevertheless gives out small twelve-hour loans occasionally to a neighbour. Debt relations thus not only exist between the professional moneylender and his clients but also between relatives, neighbours, and friends, as well as among people from similar income groups.

Even when moneylenders do not have a license to lend money (which seems to apply to most), they still ask borrowers to sign a contract and give a fingerprint over the sum of money and the time-frame to repay it, thus initiating a formalization of the technically illegal procedure. While there are occasional disputes when people are not able to pay back the money, two moneylenders told me that this happens very rarely. According to their accounts, people make sure to pay back the amount on time. Not only would a delay cause trouble for the borrower and come with a fee, they would also no longer be seen as creditworthy in the future. One moneylender explained that the high interest rates in fact help her to get the money back. If the interest rate were low, people might not take it too seriously. Instead, if the amount is high, the pressure of the need to pay interest would be so intense for the borrower that they would do anything to find a way to repay the money as quickly as possible. Borrowers themselves can have other reasons besides acute hardship for borrowing from a moneylender instead of elsewhere and thus accepting a high interest rate. They might, for example, want to build a good relationship with the moneylender in case of future demand, or hide their financial situation from others. Also, high interest rates do not always mean that a borrower cannot make a profit, as we see with small twelve-hour loans, for example. Such twelve-hour loans (Burmese *nei: pyan to:*) are very common in Pathein. The usual procedure is that borrowers take out 1,000 kyat (ca. 0.72 EUR) at eight in the morning and pay back 1,200 kyat (ca. 0.87 EUR) at eight in the evening. These small loans are given either by professional moneylenders or, on a more occasional basis, by shopkeepers. Among the people who obtain these loans, for instance, are snack sellers who need to buy ingredients in the morning or motorcycle taxi drivers who need to buy petrol. Snack sellers who get these loans for the ingredients often sell the snacks that are produced for considerably more money than they borrowed, thus still being able to make a profit (Bouman 1994a: 111).

Credit Arrangements in Business Relations

Credit arrangements also occurred in business contexts. In the previous chapter I have outlined the common practice of advance payments in many sectors. Receiving one's salary for several months in advance functions as a loan but also results in debt bondage. Apart from such advance payments for one's direct labour, employers or former employers can also be an approachable source of additional credit (see also Pyi Phyo Kyaw 2017: 310). When purchasing goods, it is often possible to make arrangements with shop-keepers or traders to pay for the items later or in instalments. Maung Maung, the rice-trader I portrayed in Chapter 4, said that 'no one can sell anything in Pathein if he is not able or willing to sell on instalments'. Another business owner, who sold motorbikes, could not recall a single case in which he did not sell the motorbike on instalments. 'People from the countryside buy only around the rice-planting period or around the harvest period. That's when they have money. But even then they only buy on instalments'. While in most cases he had no problem getting all his money back, some clients remained indebted to him. He would go after his money by calling the customers, and in severe cases he used the service of formal or informal debt-collectors, some of whom use intimidation to make customers repay their debts.

Pathein also had several pawnshops, often shops that otherwise sold gold and jewellery. Here, people could pawn gold for money. It was also possible to pawn electric goods. One reason, besides a distrust of banks and inflation, why people prefer to save in gold rather than in cash was that they would spend cash more easily, and gold can always be pawned if needed. Maung Maung, the rice-trader I described in Chapter 4, ran a pawnshop for a while before starting his rice business. In the late 1980s, he said, people pawned everything for money. They brought old clothes. Sometimes they brought mosquito nets and cooking equipment in the morning to get money for the expenses of the day. In the evening they would come to get their items back, which they needed to cook dinner and for sleeping. After a while, people stopped coming back and Maung Maung found it difficult to resell the old things, as the opening up of the economy in the early 1990s had brought in new goods and clothes. He stopped his pawnshop a long time ago, but was still giving out small loans besides his rice-trading activities when I met him.

Moral Judgments: Debt, Interest Rates and the Excluded

As I have shown, many people consider it an unavoidable part of their everyday economic reality that money frequently changes hands through lending and repaying. But the situation became particularly severe when people kept borrowing more than they could repay, either because of low and unstable incomes, miscalculations, an unexpected emergency, or other problems such as an addiction. This indicates the thin line between credit as assistance and credit as a further step towards poverty, dependence, and hardship. Constant indebtedness constituted a serious burden and a social stigma for families like that of Tin Oo, which I took as an example. In extreme cases, social marginalization can lead to a complete exclusion from credit sources and neighbourhood support. Participating in social-security networks requires at least a minimum amount of capital. To participate in savings groups, one must have some money to save. To obtain a loan, one needs contacts and a decent reputation. While Tin Oo and his family at least received marginal support from the monastery and his aunt, and managed to juggle money from different credit sources, Ko Naing was an example of what happens when such factors are lacking.

At forty-two years old, Ko Naing earned money by collecting plastic at night, which he then resold. He also washed glasses at a food stall and sold balloons to children at an evening market. While diversifying one's income by having several small jobs was a common economic strategy for many in Pathein, whether at higher or lower income levels, for Ko Naing it was a matter of survival. Abandoned by other relatives, he lived with just his wife in a small wooden shack, for which they had to pay 1,000 kyat (ca. 0.72 EUR) a day to the owner. They had lost their former house after his mother died, and he could not provide any written proof of ownership. As it is not uncommon that such documents are missing, he suspected that the officials simply used this as a pretext to evict him and his wife for other reasons. He explained that his wife was HIV-positive. Since this had become known they had experienced unfriendly treatment from others and had been denied access to savings groups or other financial support by friends or relatives. He refrained from approaching moneylenders, as he knew that paying back a high-interest loan was impossible for him at the moment. Ko Naing and his wife now lived in immense poverty, resulting from a mixture of factors – social exclusion and stigmatization, and finally a lack of even minimal economic capital. Eventually, this created a downward spiral and the couple fell outside of the usual social safety net of family and neighbours. While I have certainly seen several cases where the disabled or sick (including HIV cases) have been taken care of devotedly by their relatives or found help through charity organizations, Ko Naing's case should be taken as a reminder that the social support system is not without its limitations. Ko Naing, without hesitation, explained his misfortune with reference to bad *kamma* from his past lives.

With further reference to the problem of stigmatization, I shall now explain how it was linked to indebtedness more generally. Whether someone borrows from a moneylender, an organization or a friend, having debts was generally considered something to be avoided. Mary, whom I mentioned earlier, linked this to religious ideas, explaining how the loss of autonomy through indebtedness could even surpass one's current life:

I don't buy anything on credit. If I see something that I want to buy I will say 'I get the money first, and then come back'. The shopkeeper would usually say 'No, I know you, just take it and pay when you pass by next time'. But I don't do that. I am eighty years old. I might go any minute. And if I go without paying back the money... In Buddhism, we believe that if we steal something, or take money or other things from someone without giving it back, we have to serve this person in the next life. Some people are angry if you ask for money. But I am angry if you don't ask for money, because I don't want to come and work for you in the next life.

A concern for future rebirths was present in Mary's reasoning. However, among my informants in Pathein, there were important nuances in how indebtedness was viewed and judged. Small amounts of debt were seen as almost unavoidable among the less well-off, but being overly indebted was seen as a sign that an individual lacked self-control and the ability to handle money. Similarly, the reason for taking out a loan mattered for moral judgments. People differentiated, for instance, between borrowing for a health treatment on the one hand and borrowing for gambling or buying unnecessary luxury items and the like on the other hand. I have come across cases of people who got into debt because of gambling activities and left the town for a while to escape repayment claims and their sense of shame. However, if a person was considered honest and hard-working but was nonetheless in need of credit, either for business purposes or because of unexpected expenses, and they had the ability and discipline to repay, there were usually no great consequences for their reputation. In other words, some cases of indebtedness were more socially acceptable than others. Not only was the process of borrowing subject to moral considerations, so was the process of lending. Here, accepting interest payments was not generally considered negative. However, if the amount charged was very high and people made their living from such interest rates, that was regarded as greedy and exploitative by many. Instead, low interest rates were seen as justified, and many even saw the provision of credit itself as a generous act of assistance. Shopkeepers who occasionally gave out loans would often emphasize that they only charge very little interest and were therefore less greedy than professional moneylenders. Thiha, a man whose family runs a grocery store, explained:

I give loans to people for a very low interest rate. I don't want them to go down. I want them to go up. With some lenders, if you take fifty dollars, after one year you have to give back one hundred dollars. I don't want to do this. Why do you borrow money? It means you have no money, right? So I need to help you. But I cannot give it to you for free. I also need money. So I give you fifty dollars, and next year you give sixty dollars back. That's enough.[128]

Even though Thiha saw money-lending as a form of assistance to those in need, the mere fact that he felt the need to justify charging interest and underlined how low his rate was shows how much he wanted to avoid the impression of greed. However, in practice there were also ways to restore one's moral stance for those who charge higher interest rates, namely by making higher donations to monasteries. Moneylenders actually often assured their clients that they would donate a part of the profits earned from the interest. In that way, the high interest would benefit the lender as well as the borrower spiritually because the donation was believed to create merit for both. This shows how money acquired through a morally dubious practice (the charging of high interest) can be transferred into something meritorious by turning it into a donation, which in a way is a process of moral money-laundering. Thus, not only does the moneylender neutralize the act of charging interest, but the borrower too, who is likely to be in financial difficulties anyway, does not have to worry about sparing extra money for the monastery for merit-making. This brings us back to the beginning of this chapter in which I outlined the role of donations. While it remains unclear to what extent moneylenders really donated their profits, the promise alone brings these two very common economic activities together: money-lending and donations are linked not only in terms of livelihood management, but also in a spiritual logic.

Conclusion

This chapter has left the immediate world of business to explore wider social connections between individuals, including the urban poor. I have shown how people are interconnected through a non-state social support network, also across class lines. The single components of the social support system come with their own logics, risks, and benefits. However, in practice they are interlinked, as people in Pathein may draw pragmatically on several, often simultaneously. For this reason, it is important to understand financial activities in their wider context. It is not enough to look, for example, at one household in isolation because households are interconnected through support arrangements, financial flows, and social bonds. In that context I have looked at underlying moral considerations concerning economic in-equality, redistribution, and deservingness, showing how religious ideas are deployed to rationalize and sometimes justify certain overall conditions and

---

[128] Thiha used dollars in his example only for purposes of illustration. People usually borrowed money in kyats.

specific activities. Most people in Pathein are not covered by any state social-security scheme. Since the economic transformation after 1988, economic disparities have grown among Myanmar's population. There are not enough opportunities for secure and well-paid employment in many areas as yet, and people struggle to make ends meet, with low, fluctuating, and unpredictable incomes.

To meet financial needs and mitigate vulnerability, we have seen that people rely on charity projects, formalized and informal neighbourhood mutual aid, access to informal financial arrangements like ROSCAs and ASCAs, and other sources of assistance and credit. In this social support system, a great deal is organized through religious institutions. Buddhist monasteries run schools, orphanages, and old-age care and health projects. Here, moral values and religious ideas are strategically deployed in manifold ways. They influence understandings about the origins of economic hardship, aid and gift-giving (e.g. through concepts like *kamma*, *mettā*, and *dāna*). Through my ethnography in the first part of the chapter, I have underlined the manifold collective dimensions of Buddhist teachings and practice. Charity projects are financed largely through donations by lay people (acts of *dāna*). Larger public donations, whether those used for temple buildings only or those used for social causes, also lead to social admiration and community strengthening. Prasse-Freeman and Phyo Win Latt (2018) expressed concern that increasing wealth stratification, potentially a moment of 'explicit class consolidation' (p. 405), could lead to the erosion of horizontal as well as vertical social bonds. The latter mainly because the new elites might orient themselves toward an exclusionary upper-class culture, circling around consumption, instead of acting as patrons for the poor, as was common before (p. 412).

While people in Pathein experienced a certain degree of such developments within families and work relations, ethnographic evidence here has shown that members of different economic strata still remained linked through manifold ties at the point of my research. Local support for charitable causes came from Patheinians who accumulated some wealth, and even some of those who have left the area still occasionally provided support. Reports from on the ground even indicated that donations to charitable projects have increased (see also McCarthy 2016). However, this does not mean that such patterns of redistribution are not becoming endangered by intensifying neoliberal processes and the growing inequalities in the country. Furthermore, while support based on donations helps to mitigate vulnerability, it was never meant to alter overall socio-economic structures. Rather, it helps to reproduce it: 'Merit making bound the haves with the have-nots, the givers with the receivers, in a relationship in which gifts were "sacrificed" for the maintenance of social inequality' (Bowie 1998: 476, on Thailand). While social and financial networks provide some degree of assistance and security, they are not without limits, nor free from negative effects, like exclusion and pressure, as we have seen especially with regard to credit, which entails a thin line between receiving crucial assistance and becoming trapped in heavy debt.

Chapter 7
Conclusion

For most people, constructing a 'good life' consists of both ensuring material subsistence down the generations and the production and reproduction of certain moral aspects, such as values and norms. Economy and morality are connected in the processes in which people organize their livelihoods, both as individuals and as members of collective groups. This book has explored economic processes in the medium-sized town of Pathein, based on a total of fourteen months of ethnographic field research from August 2015 to August 2016, and again in February and March 2018. I have studied the social 'embeddedness' (Polanyi 2001 [1944]) of economic ideas and actions, as well as their 'ethical context' (Hann 2018: 247). The book was divided into seven chapters, including the introduction and conclusion. It was based on the argument that Theravāda Buddhism constitutes a major framework for moral considerations (which for the purpose of this book is understood to consist of both values and norms) among Burmese Buddhists. The ethnographic part of the book, which consisted of three chapters, explored economic activities in three social domains of interaction – relations within the family (Chapter 4), relations between employers and non-kin workers (Chapter 5), and relations within the wider neighbourhood community (Chapter 6).

Within these domains, a range of different activities were addressed – within the businesses and beyond. The business owners portrayed in Chapter 4, like other business owners I refer to elsewhere, made use of the rather short-lived opportunities in the early 1990s to set up successful small businesses. Today, these business owners belong to the wealthier part of Pathein's population, and in some cases their children were the first members of their families to receive a university education. I specifically traced the histories of two businesses, which enabled me to outline perceptions of intergenerational social mobility over three generations and address the role of the family in making business decisions. Important points in intra-family negotiations included status considerations, gender roles, and questions of self-identification. Attitudes concerning these points contrasted between ethnic Burman and ethnic Chinese business owners. I analysed these aspects in the context of historically different socio-economic conditions for both portrayed families, which entailed differences in opportunities and constraints. In the first case it became clear that the Burman couple did not plan to pass on their parasol business to their daughter. This was a typical pattern among Burman business owners: children who engaged in business themselves would start their own firms, rather than becoming involved in those of their parents (see also Berta 2019 on Denmark). The family system here encouraged children to set up their own households and their own means of livelihood after marriage, instead of combining intergenerational labour and capital systematically. An even more favourable option was that children pursue formal higher education and find prestigious employment, even if this would mean a loss of autonomy and a lower income compared to what their parents' business generated. 'Doing business' is not highly regarded by many Burmans, as it does not bring any great prestige in itself, even if the income it generated was high. While this may change in light of new structural developments, it was still very much true for my informants.

In contrast, in the second ethnographic case, an ethnic Chinese family had built up a two-generation rice-trading firm by systematically utilizing relatives' labour and capital. This case constituted a 'family business' more closely resembling those described in other studies (e.g. Yanagisako 2002 on Italy). The business was regarded as a family legacy worth maintaining, and it functioned as a source of pride. Comparing these cases underlined the importance not only of the role values play in economic processes, but also of historically different opportunities and constraints. Many Chinese had been excluded from jobs in the public sector and even from certain tertiary educational institutions, so that they came to rely on trade and entrepreneurship. Outlining these two business histories has shown how the business landscape of Pathein is not a result of 'natural' economic processes alone but also of inner-family negotiations since these contribute to the growth of some businesses and to the disappearance of others.

Beyond the family, relations between employers and non-kin workers were addressed, starting out from the frequently mentioned problem that of employers have difficulties in finding and retaining workers. Value aspects come into play here since there is a clear preference for self-employment among those who had no access to prestigious and well-paid jobs. Small-scale self-employment such as trishaw-driving or snack-selling offered more autonomy, the advantages of which can be grouped under the categories of flexibility and dignity. Working for someone else, on the other hand, was something that many people saw as degrading, and additionally, available employment in the low-income sectors usually did not offer many structural benefits (such as insurance or long-term stability). For employers, this meant that they had to deploy a range of strategies to attract and bind workers to their shops. In addition to wages (often paid several months in advance), employers offered food and shelter, tried to establish some sort of relationship with the workers' families, and included workers in religious rituals, for example, at Buddhist New Year. Employer–worker relations resembled patron–client ties, although they were strictly limited to work periods and were thus often of rather short duration. Nevertheless, these patterns have shaped the more general idea of how a 'good' employer should act. In some cases such ideas clashed with the new work environments, for example, in the big garment factories, which resulted in disappointment and complaints from workers.

The responsibilities of an employer are especially far reaching when the workers are children, as is the workers' vulnerability. Children have become an increasingly common workforce in urban areas. While there is nothing new in children working, they are more and more often part of the migrating population that is leaving the countryside in order to find work in the cities, where many children end up working far away from their homes under strangers. A case study presented in Chapter 5 revealed how power and resistance are negotiated in the tea shop. Moreover, discussions with several of those involved – actor–employers, the parents of working children, agents, and the children themselves – have shown that urban child labour was a contested issue that produced feelings of shame and stimulated accusations directed at other parties rather than seeking explanations in structural factors. Instead of openly addressing economic reasons and their own dependencies, children themselves would emphasize their roles as providers for their families, a role that deserves acknowledgement and respect.

Outside of the immediate sphere of the businesses, intra-household links and community based networks provide a crucial social support system, in a context where the state fails to provide even minimal welfare to most people. This system includes non-monetary neighbourhood support, charity projects, and access to savings groups and credit. I have argued that, if we only look at one of these arrangements, we miss their interconnectedness. Take, for example, different sources of credit, such as microfinance organizations, several of which have set up projects in Pathein in recent years, and informal moneylenders, who often charge strikingly high amounts of interest (up to 30 percent per month). If we only consider microfinance institutions and check whether people are successful in repaying their loans, we might miss the fact that they sometimes borrow from moneylenders to repay these loan. Thus the repayment by no means indicated any freedom from debt.

In the realm of charity, many activities are linked to concepts such as *dāna, mettā* (loving kindness) and *karuṇā* (compassion), indicating the collective dimension of Buddhism. Acts of charity connect people of very different socio-economic strata, such as wealthy business people with destitute orphans, as in my ethnographic example. However, while such arrangements entail elements of wealth distribution, they do not funda-mentally alter socio-economic differences. Arguably, they are in fact repro-ducing certain hierarchies, as the act of giving ensures the donor social prestige, while the recipient remains in a subordinate position. With regard to credit, cases of landless poor families that struggle to make ends meet and constantly have to juggle incomes and expenditure have shown that credit cuts both ways: on the one hand it can provide crucial, even life-saving assistance in emergencies; on the other hand it easily leads to stigmatization and even social exclusion. Indebtedness and moneylending are both evalu-ated morally by people in Pathein.

Throughout these chapters, the book has presented ethnographic evidence for the importance of autonomy and individualism within a highly hierarchical society, as well as the importance of life's collective dimen-sions, binding ties, and responsibility for others in both the family and the wider community. This exemplifies how lived realities always constitute a negotiation of all such factors. The value of autonomy is a good example of a specific aspect that must be constantly negotiated within society's stark hierarchies, and yet as a value it is so strong that its importance prevails and has direct effects in economic terms, contributing, for instance, to a relative scarcity of Burman-owned inter-generational firms, a prevalence of small-scale self-employment, and a high turnover of labour. In many of the moral aspects discussed in this book the Buddhist religious tradition shone through as a framework for inspiration on moral conduct, as well as for rationalizing and reasoning in how people mediated between individual autonomy and collective ties. Sometimes its importance was directly observable, while in other contexts it played itself out in more hidden ways. Buddhist ideas influence economic behaviour, from specific acts such as downplaying one's wealth earned through business activities or publicly donating to monasteries or charity causes to more general ideas of inner-family support, societal inequality, and redistribution. Where do we go from here? The ethnographic data has offered indications of both: change of economic circumstances and the resilience of certain religious concepts with implications for ordinary action. Ongoing economic change will lead to further adaptations of values and vice versa, maintaining a tension between 'community and market' (Gudeman 2008).

Whither Myanmar?

On the evening of November 8, 2015, the streets of Pathein were oddly quiet. Most shops were closed, there was little traffic, and the majority of people had already gone home. I met with a group of acquaintances. We were sitting in a tea shop by the river where customers were chatting, keeping their voices down; everyone seemed a little tense, but also excited. Only men occupied the small tables, because it was unusual for women to be outside late in the evening. It required a close look at the men's hands to see a trace of the significance of the day. They all had one fingertip tainted blue from ink – a sign that they had voted in Myanmar's first open general elections in twenty-five years. It was an event that, unlike in 1990, would lead to a new democratically elected government. The excitement was great in Pathein, as elsewhere in the country, when the results were broadcast a few days later. However, the hope for a quick and clean shift to democracy has, not surprisingly, dimmed. The new government faced a whole range of challenges. It not only had to deal with its own lack of leadership experience, but also with the persistent political influence of the military, which had reserved 25 percent of the seats in parliament for itself prior to the elections. At the same time, the shift came with intense economic changes, many of which posed challenges for the population, some entirely new, others intensifying.

The Emergence of New Social Classes or a 'Double Movement'?

Already the introduction of a market-led economy since the 1990s led to increasing exploitation of what Polanyi (2001 [1944]: 71–80) saw as 'fictitious commodities', namely land, money, and labour, despite state restrictions in key sectors. Processes like those which Harvey termed the accumulation of wealth 'by dispossession' (Harvey 2003, 2004), have occurred as well (Prasse-Freeman and Phyo Win Latt 2018). In these developments, earlier 'Fordist' working classes did not disappear in the same way as in those cases that Kalb (2011) refers to for other regions, nor were welfare and public institutions dismantled to the same extent as happened in other contexts of transformation (but had rather been largely inexistent to begin with). Nevertheless, rural dispossession has increasingly propelled people towards the cities, first and foremost to Yangon and Mandalay, where not enough opportunities are available to allow a decent standard of living for most (Prasse-Freeman and Phyo Win Latt 2018).

A widening social divide or class cleavage could be the consequence. Especially since land prices have exploded, inequalities along lines of land ownership have become more pronounced. While inequalities of wealth have definitely increased, it remains a different question whether this will also be accompanied by a stronger class consciousness. After the 'plural society' (Furnivall 1957) of colonial Burma, in which differences were defined along ethnic rather than class lines, had ceased to exist, post-independence class divisions were described as running between a small wealthy elite, higher civil servants who constituted a very small middle class, and the urban proletariat, small-scale traders, and the peasantry (Lissak 1970). Socialism has hampered private wealth accumulation and kept income differences relatively minor apart from a small wealthy elite. In all periods, the sangha retained a special position as the most respected group in society, regardless of the economic backgrounds of its individual members.

Myanmar has not seen the emergence of masses of factory or mine-workers creating a working-class identity over several generations to the same extent as has been described for other socialist contexts (see, for instance, Kesküla 2018, on Kazakhstan). While a few areas, like the gem-stone mines in the north or the salt farms in the delta, have employed industrial workforces for decades or even centuries, and in some cases perhaps members of the same families over generations, the overall economy under socialism was defined by agriculture, and state-owned enterprises employed only a small fraction of the working population. Even today, industrial work is marked by a high turnover of labour, and many people take part in labour circulation rather than permanent migration, meaning they return to their villages temporarily after a period working in urban industrial settings or in the mines. However, Yangon has certainly seen the emergence of more permanent slum-like settlements of factory workers and the first signs of a new and growing, or at least more publicly expressed, working-class awareness. This is indicated, for instance, by labour protests and the formation of unions since they were officially permitted in 2012. Public administrators, especially the higher ranks, also continue to constitute a distinct group, and the public sector still appears like an attractive employment option to many, mostly for its prestige, the possibility of upward mobility, and the additional benefits such as housing that sometimes come with the otherwise relatively low income. Furthermore, a modernized business elite is becoming more visible through the media, and the wealthy at the top now certainly constitute a distinct if small upper class, one that seems increasingly detached from the rest of society and yet is a group that more and more people aspire to join.

Concerning the general population, however, we should remember that Myanmar is a country of great diversity that offers people plenty of other markers of self-identity, apart from economic class or occupation: religion, ethnicity, and origin would be the most obvious ones. The workforce in small businesses, for example, often consists of migrants from the countryside. These could be described as proletarians, but this does not often translate into pronounced class consciousness as such. At the same time, older patron–client ties are eroding, and employment situations are becoming increasingly defined by monetary aspects, not social ones, a development that provokes regret and confusion for both employers and workers as I have mentioned in Chapter 5. However, at least in small businesses, traces of traditional patterns of patronage are to some extent still observable. Among people from different economic backgrounds, the rural/urban distinction, educational levels, and suspected religious merit are the usual factors defining a person's standing. Only observations over a longer period of time will allow us to see whether the ongoing developments alter these factors considerably and lead to new class consolidations and a pronounced class consciousness. On an intellectual level, class discourses and the socialist vocabulary that comes with it are now largely associated with the Ne Win period and thus with an ideology that many people do not want to go back to. Instead, public discourse on economic matters circles largely around a rhetoric of 'development', often presented as a sort of catch-all for all occurring processes and an alleged solution for various problems, as the only way forward (Prasse-Freeman and Phyo Win Latt 2018: 408–409).

However, continuing dispossession and wealth generation that does often not need (or not considerably benefit) labourers is likely to evoke further feelings of injustice. We have already seen an increase in protests around land-grabbing, certain laws, and industrial plans. Public anger, expressed in such protests but also in media discourse, is directed towards the investors who buy the land, as well as the Burmese politicians who sell it to them (ibid.: 413). Whether articulated with regard to class or not, some responses to intensifying livelihood struggles have the explicit or implicit aim of taming some of capitalism's consequences and may be seen as constituting a 'double movement' in Polanyi's (2001 [1944]) sense. On the ground, measures taken by people include a rising number of ad-hoc grassroots charitable projects, as a way to mitigate hardship by offering health care, education, and other forms of support. Amid the increasing economic challenges, what could be labelled 'civil society' in Myanmar is multifaceted and strong, often infused with religious ideas and organized through religious institutions.

This does not mean, however, that the state is not generally seen as in charge. Demands are there, and the NLD government is taking steps to fulfil them. It has increased workers' minimum wages, raised pay rates for civil servants, announced it would work hard to settle land conflicts, and undertaken the first efforts to reform the education sector as well as to expand coverage of the social security and insurance system. Also these reactions to a situation in which the market principle 'threatened social peace' (Hann 2016: 4) are steps which Polanyi would see as a 're-embedding' of the economy (Polanyi 2001 [1944]). My impressions from Pathein suggest that many people in Myanmar welcome and demand such forms of state intervention. Not all felt comfortable in the new economic environment, as we saw, for instance, when employer-worker relations stopped resembling earlier patron–client ties, like in large-scale garment factories. Initial negative reactions of people in the low-income groups to the new capitalist realities express attitudes countering purely liberal-individualist ideas which can translate into a demand for a degree of state-organized social security countering purely liberal-individualist ideas.

Populism and Islamophobia on the Rise

Intensifying economic insecurity can also be linked to the emergence of new religious movements and political attitudes in the form of populism. The latter often thrive when political figures exploit fears and systematically nurture them. We have seen such processes in many places, including Europe (Kalb 2011: 14). Especially outside observers of Myanmar have expressed deep disappointment over developments within the first two years of the new government, in which a mass exodus of Muslim Rohingya to neighbouring Bangladesh constituted the peak of the crisis. It would not be right to end this book without taking a look at these terrifying events, asking whether and if so how economic developments may have played a part in them.

Several attempts have been made to explain the phenomena of rising nationalism in Myanmar, and linked to that the widespread hostility toward Muslims more generally and the Rohingya in particular. Many Burmese regard the Rohingya as illegal migrants from Bangladesh, thus excluding them from their imagined moral community of the nation. Fuelled by the nationalist and anti-Islamic rhetoric of some Buddhist groups and by news reports of terrorist attacks elsewhere in world, a considerable number of people started to see themselves, their country, and their religion as coming under threat from Islam. The prevalence of such sentiments is striking. They are by no means confined to the areas where the Rohingya live but can be found across the country as a whole, permeating a range of social groups, up to the highest political levels.

Analyses have rightly pointed to the role of political leaders and their failure to oppose the hatred convincingly in this context. Some observers have explicitly sought to explain such surging sentiments with reference to Myanmar's 'transition'. They voiced the argument that the 'opening up' of the country took the lid off previously existing hatred and conflicts that had formerly been suppressed by party rule (e.g. International Crisis Group 2013), an argument that has been used in exactly the same way to explain the rise of nationalism in some other 'transition' contexts in Eastern Europe. However, research has shown that such explanations are incorrect or at least much too simplistic (Verdery 1996: 84). Can the analyses of these other contexts nevertheless help to shed light on the situation in Myanmar?

Scholars of the former socialist countries of Eastern Europe have indeed identified certain specifically 'postsocialist' factors that contributed to the rise of populism and nationalism, arguing that the organization of socialism had enhanced national consciousness and that socialism's dismantling had aggravated it further. Katherine Verdery (1996) mentioned a few possible parts of the puzzle of explanation, including the loss of privileges among the former elites, newly erupting conflicts through privatization (e.g. about land), and, in cases of distinctively multi-ethnic settings, the fact that the socialist shortage economy might have fuelled ethno-nationalisms in so far as shared ethnicity was in some cases a basis of mutual support among people. She also suggested that the end of the socialist states meant the loss of former 'others' to inform people's private and public self-identifications, for instance, foreign capitalists or one's own political rulers. After the transition, new unacceptable 'others' were now increasingly defined by ethnicity (pp. 83–103).

However, ethnic 'othering' in nationalist discourses is not unique to these specific transformation contexts. A more class-centred perspective suggests that 'Western and Eastern European nationalist populisms have broadly similar social roots and not incomparable constituencies' (Kalb 2011: 17). These roots lie partly in certain consequences of neoliberal realities, namely material and cultural experiences of dispossession and disenfranchisement that are displaced on to the 'imagined nation as a community of fate' (ibid.: 1). Such experiences have happened to some extent all over Europe and elsewhere in the world. The era of globalization has also seen the emergence of a new cosmopolitan class, which includes ruling elites and their allies, that has become morally estranged from the idea of the nation as a 'community of fate', contributing to dissatisfaction on the ground (ibid.: 7).

Myanmar is a special case and in many regards it differs from other postsocialist examples. Nevertheless, the role of economic factors in providing a fertile ground for populist sentiments is important. Islamophobia is certainly not a new phenomenon in the country, and violence against the Rohingya has been going on for decades (see Jones 2017, on the role of the colonial economy and its aftermath). The argument that a recent surge in nationalist-populist sentiments is a phenomenon that accompanies the 'transition' is not necessarily wrong: the question is, which transition? Anti-Muslim riots occurred in different parts of the country in the 1990s and 2000s, and the notorious Buddhist monk Ashin Wirathu, who has repeatedly spread hatred against Muslims, was jailed for incitement in 2003. This was long before the attempts at democratization that started around 2011, but it was after the country embarked on its course toward a market-led economy in the early 1990s. Perhaps analysts have often placed too much focus on the 'wrong' transition, namely the political one, and too little on the economic one. For the livelihoods of my informants in Pathein, urban residents outside the big metropolitan areas of Yangon and Mandalay, the changes of the early 1990s have had a more striking impact than the political changes that began in 2011. This is as true for those who benefited from opportunities to make money three decades ago as it is for those who have been forced into more challenging economic environments. Recent developments were intensifying the economic course introduced earlier, but in the country as a whole, very few have benefited (the main exception being those profiting from certain extractive industries). The recent period of change thus differs from the early 1990s, when, as I have shown through case studies in this book, opportunities to accumulate wealth through small businesses and to purchase land were more readily available, even to those lacking capital.

The current intensification of the economic course has resulted in more dislocation. Farmers have lost their land or sold it for short-term advantage, before being forced to work at extraction sites or to join the increasingly precarious urban labour force. The economic conjuncture combines with historically deeply-rooted xenophobic sentiments (Jones 2017), the government's shortcomings in addressing economic and political problems, and the propaganda of Buddhist nationalist groups that exploit tensions and discontent. Those excluded from the economy seek a new identity by focusing on the nation. They portray themselves as subjects who deserve a share of the resources, in contrast to 'others' who they aim to exclude (Prasse-Freeman 2017). This switch is facilitated by a number of additional factors, including the workings of the state media, social media, and the agenda of the military.

Possibilities for Future Research

I would like to use this section to provide a few thoughts on possible further research. Of the people I met in Pathein prior to the elections, almost all were hoping for a change in government. They desired democratic rights such as the freedom to develop, discuss, and openly share their political opinions. Concerning economic realities, however, there was some nostalgia for the time when 'a father could feed the whole family with his income', as people put it, which adults remembered had been the case in the 1970s. One intriguing topic for future research therefore concerns livelihoods in the socialist past. The public image of socialist Myanmar is dominated by its dire economic circumstances and harsh military oppression. There is a lot of truth to these depictions, but nevertheless it would be worthwhile to nuance them with actual memories of people from within Myanmar. For a long time no outside researchers could conduct on-the-ground studies in the country. And, even more extreme than in most of the postsocialist contexts of Eastern Europe and Central Asia, this continued to be the case for roughly another fifteen years after the country's turn to a market economy after 1989.

As a consequence, most works on socialist Myanmar are macro-analyses which (rightly) emphasize the collapse of the overall economy, but have not included the voices of actual citizens and their lived experiences throughout changing economic currents. The more personal accounts from the past often deal with political life, many of them being voiced by dissidents and political prisoners (see, for example, Fink 2009). Additionally, many such accounts stem from the time around the 1988 protests or later. Such reports are invaluable testimonies of the manifold human rights violations that have taken place. Complementing them with even older, more livelihood-focused perspectives would help us understand even more about the lived realities of socialist Burma. The glimpses of memories I have encountered in Pathein suggest that systematic in-vestigation of life histories and people's accounts of the past, especially those concerning livelihoods, are a worthwhile subject for further studies with a historical focus. Just like revelations about the complex and vast landscape of civil-society organizations that have emerged in Myanmar despite (or arguably because) of an oppressive political system surprised many outside observers, one might find more accounts of livelihood security and relative comfort than one would perhaps expect from a crumbling and generally ineffective socialist system. The political changes introduced from 2011 onwards made systematic long-term research easier. Naturally, such studies must be carried out in the near future with living individuals who have spent a good deal of their adult lives under socialism. This period is already a rather distant past now, and for a large part of the population it is nothing but a topic they hear about from relatives or in distorted history lessons. In that context it is important to note that regional differences matter a great deal when exploring lived realities of the past (as well as currently, since conflicts are continuing): Throughout military rule, armed conflicts have led to systematic forced labour, land-grabbing, extensive relocations and flights, as well as the destruction of fields, infrastructure, and institutions like schools or clinics, thus they have greatly impacted livelihoods in these areas.

To understand Myanmar's economic realities, it is further advisable to look beyond the country's borders. I noticed in Pathein that the bigger businesses which had been established only recently by private people (for instance, large restaurants that target more middle-class customers) have usually been financed through money earned abroad. Locally available income-earning opportunities do not generate enough money to purchase land, let alone land in prime locations, nor to build up a business of such a size. Several owners of the bigger businesses in Pathein turned out to be returnees who had managed to work their way up abroad. One such individual started from stocking shelves at a supermarket in Malaysia and later became the manager of several branches of the same supermarket. In another case, a woman started by cleaning in a hostel in Thailand, later worked at its reception desk, and finally took over managerial responsibility for the entire place. While without a doubt many Burmese migrants work abroad under critical circumstances and are highly vulnerable to exploitation, these examples show that other countries also provide avenues of upward mobility. Studying the role of such returnees in building up local economic entities would not only shed more light on these biographies. Such 'success stories' would also contribute to a more balanced analysis of migration in Southeast Asia, as well as reveal the persisting inability of Myanmar's economy to provide similar opportunities. There are still millions of Burmese people working abroad, and they are not yet returning in great numbers. My observations suggest that those who return seem to do so mostly for personal reasons, such as when they have a child or when their parents are in need of support. I suggest that future studies systematically explore these people's views and experiences and the social and economic contexts of their lives, as well as compare their role as migrants with their role as returnees. Also here, the Myanmar case would integrate well into a large existing body of scholarship.

Furthermore, it remains important to shed light on economic challenges facing more disadvantaged groups such as landless labourers in rural areas, of which Myanmar has many. Many people portrayed in this book, while far from belonging to the richest in the country, are not among the economically most vulnerable groups. The economic challenges and political responses to livelihood struggles of people from different backgrounds should be investigated more closely. Observing Myanmar's further development can enable us to put the country into other contexts, comparing it, for example, with its Asian neighbours or with 'transition' countries elsewhere. Hopefully, future analyses will not overlook the importance of moral aspects for people's reasoning, decisions, and actions, and the locally specific frameworks that inform such moral aspects. While I have focused mostly on Burman Buddhists, it would be important to also study economic processes among other ethnic and religious groups in the Myanmar context, some of which have played an important role as traders or entrepreneurs in Southeast Asia for centuries.

Pathein has not been affected by the new wave of economic developments to the same extent as Yangon and Mandalay. Nevertheless, traces of change can be found here as well. I want to end this book with some thoughts on what might happen to the region and a sampling of questions that only time can answer. A few weeks before my first fieldwork period ended in 2016, a branch of the 'Ocean Supercenter' opened in Pathein's Strand Road, in a prominent location next to city hall. Since shortly after its opening the whole area had been completely flooded by heavy monsoon rain, people joked that they now had to go by boat to the Center – 'that's why it is called "Ocean"'. The Center contains various shops for clothes, musical instruments, and smartphones, as well as a huge two-storey supermarket offering all sorts of household items and foods, including imports like cheese and Nutella. Myo Khine, an egg trader I had become friends with, was excited about the new venture. Almost every day he would come to the coffee shop on the ground floor to enjoy the air conditioning, to meet up with friends, and to have a coffee or two.

When Myo Khine spent time in the coffee shop (which he jokingly started calling his 'office' due to his almost daily hour-long visits) either his wife or an employee sold eggs from his stand, which was located just a few metres away from the Center. Was he not afraid that now, with the shiny new supermarket next door, people would stop buying eggs from him? Myo Khine laughed: 'Why would they. The eggs here in the Center are more expensive than what I sell'. Indeed, when I came back to Pathein in 2018, there were rumours that the mall is not frequented very much. Upper-class families would do their household shopping here, but they were rather few. The restaurant on the top floor was often empty. Some people only came for the fun of going up and down the escalator.

A low spending capacity is linked to a lack of attractive income opportunities, and Pathein is a prime example of this. However, the fact that the existing garment factories already struggle with a high turnover of labour does not seem to stop investors from looking at Pathein and its surroundings, so that new employment opportunities may arise. There is no shortage of ambitious plans displayed online, and a number of new projects are already being set up. Condominiums are being built in several areas of the town, a living concept that was previously unknown to many residents here. Furthermore, there are concrete plans for two new large industrial zones as part of a project named 'Pathein Industrial City'. The project promises new job opportunities in food-processing, garment, and forestry-based industries. According to newspaper reports, one Chinese company alone is planning to establish fifty new garment factories (Kyaw Ya Lynn and Su Myat Mon 2019). Plans also exist for the construction of a deep sea port in the Ayeyarwady Region, together with power plants and an express highway to link the new industrial undertakings to Yangon. The area around Pathein and further west on the coasts would then be integrated into the East-West Economic Corridor, a road link that leads over Thailand and Laos all the way to Vietnam. Meanwhile, locals in the affected areas are looking forward to better road conditions, but at the same time fear to lose their land (Kyaw Ye Lynn 2018).

Myanmar is becoming more and more integrated into a global capitalist order. As elsewhere, it will be the task of anthropological research to account for people's agency on the ground to adapt to, resist, and capitalize on the consequences of this integration, while not losing sight of the structural impositions enforced by the neoliberalist process of 'historically specific, spatially uneven and hegemonic project of capitalist social transformation' (Mikuš 2016: 214). Will the new initiatives in Pathein, should they become reality, help to alleviate poverty? Will they provide jobs that enable people to escape the debt trap? Will they prevent locals of the region from moving all the way to Yangon or even abroad for work, where many end up in slum-like settlements? Will they create wealth for the lower classes, providing a larger customer base for the 'Ocean Supercenter'? The experiences of other regions suggest one should remain sceptical. What will happen to the many small and micro-businesses? Possibly new factories will make it even more difficult for small businesses to find workers. As the chapters of this book have hopefully affirmed, the economy is shaped not only by market laws but by social considerations and value-related factors as well. These factors are often overlooked in economic analyses and plans. If the new industries want to attract and retain workers, they must provide conditions attractive enough for people to outweigh the autonomy that otherwise still available self-employment options would entail. They must provide conditions attractive enough to retain all those who would otherwise leave the region. They have to offer not only wages high enough to sustain a family, but also stability, security, and an environment in which work is perceived as dignifying. It remains to be seen whether the new capitalist endeavours can fulfil these requirements and how political developments, including the general elections expected to be held 2020, play out in this regard. The hope persists that future developments will yield a more equal distribution of the wealth in Pathein and everywhere else in the country.

Bibliography

Abe, M., and M. Molnar. 2014. *Myanmar Business Survey 2014: Survey Results,* OECD, UNESCAP, UMFCCI. Available online, https://www.unescap.org/sites/default/files/MBS_Survey_Results.pdf, accessed 20 October 2018.

Adas, M. 2011 [1974]. *The Burma Delta: Economic Development and Social Change on an Asian Rice Frontier, 1852–1941.* Madison: University of Wisconsin Press.

Alexander, J. 1998. Women Traders in Javanese Marketplaces: Ethnicity, Gender, and the Entrepreneurial Spirit. In R. W. Hefner (ed.), *Market Cultures: Society and Morality in the New Asian Capitalisms,* pp. 203–223. Boulder: Westview Press.

Ardener, S. 1995. Women Making Money Go Round: Roscas Revisited. In S. Ardener, and S. Burman (eds.), *Money-Go-Rounds: The Importance of Rotating Savings and Credit Associations for Women*, pp. 1–19. Oxford and Washington: Berg Publishers.

Arraiza, J. M., and O. Vonk. 2017. *Report on Citizenship Law: Myanmar. Country Report.* GLOBALCIT, RSCAS and European University Institute.

Asian Development Bank, United Nations Development Programme, United Nations Population Fund, and United Nations Entity for Gender Equality and the Empowerment of Women. 2016. *Gender Equality and Women's Rights in Myanmar. A Situational Analysis.* Available online, https://www.adb.org/documents/gender-equality-and-womens-rights-myanmar-situation-analysis, accessed 3 August 2018.

Aung-Thwin, M. 1985. *Pagan: The Origins of Modern Burma.* Honolulu: University of Hawai'i Press.

------. 2002. Lower Burma and Bago in the History of Burma. In J. Gommans, and J. Leider (eds.), *The Maritime Frontier of Burma: Exploring Political, Cultural and Commercial Interaction in the Indian Ocean World, 1200–1800,* pp. 25–57. Amsterdam: KITLV Press.

------. 2005. *The Mists of Rāmañña: The Legend That Was Lower Burma.* Honolulu: University of Hawai'i Press.

Bähre, E. 2007a. *Money and Violence: Financial Self-Help Groups in a South African Township.* Leiden: Brill.

------. 2007b. Reluctant Solidarity. Death, Urban Poverty and Neighbourly Assistance in South Africa. *Ethnography* 8 (1): 33–59.

Benda-Beckmann, F. von, H. Gsanger, and J. Midgley. 1997. Indigenous Support and Social Security: Lessons From Kenya. In J. Midgley, and M. Sherraden (eds.), *Alternatives to Social Security: An International Inquiry,* pp. 105–120. Westport: Auburn House.

Benda-Beckmann, F. v., K. von Benda-Beckmann, B. O. Bryde, and F. Hirtz. 1988. Introduction: Between Kinship and the State. In F. von Benda-Beckmann, K. von Benda-Beckmann, E. Casino, F. Hirtz, G. R. Woodman, and H. F. Zacher (eds.), *Between Kinship and the State: Social Security and Law in Developing Countries,* pp. 7–20. Dordrecht: Floris Publications.

Benda-Beckmann, F. von, and K. von Benda-Beckmann. 2007. *Social Security Between Past and Future: Ambonese Networks of Care and Support.* Münster: LIT Verlag.

Bernhardt, T., S. K. De, and Mi Win Thida. 2017. *Myanmar Labor Issues From the Perspective of Enterprises: Findings From a Survey of Food Processing and Garment Manufacturing Enterprises.* Yangon: International Labour Organization, Myanmar Center for Economic and Social Development, Deutsche Gesellschaft für Internationale Zusammenarbeit (GIZ) GmbH, International Development Research Center. Available online, https://www.ilo.org/yangon/publications/WCMS_546641/lang--en/index.htm, accessed 20 January 2019.

Berta, A.-E. 2019. *Entrepreneurs Against the Market: Morality, Hard Work, and Capitalism in Aarhusian Independent Businesses* (unpublished doctoral dissertation). Seminar für Ethnologie, Martin Luther University Halle-Wittenberg/Max Planck Institute for Social Anthropology, Halle (Saale).

Besley, T., S. Coate, and G. Loury. 1993. The Economics of Rotating Savings and Credit Associations. *The American Economic Review* 38 (4): 792–810.

Bissinger, J. 2016. *Local Economic Governance in Myanmar.* Yangon: The Asia Foundation.

Bloch, M. 1973. The Long Term and the Short Term: The Economic and Political Significance of the Morality of Kinship. In J. Goody (ed.), *The Character of Kinship,* pp. 75–88. Cambridge: Cambridge University Press.

Bouman, F. 1994a. Informal Rural Finance: An Aladdin's Lamp of Information. In F. Bouman, and O. Hospes (eds.), *Financial Landscapes Reconstructed. The Fine Art of Mapping Development,* pp. 105–122. Boulder: Westview Press.

——. 1994b. ROSCA and ASCRA: Beyond the Financial Landscape. In F. Bouman, and O. Hospes (eds.), *Financial Landscapes*

Reconstructed. The Fine Art of Mapping Development, pp. 375–394. Boulder: Westview Press.

Bourdieu, P. 1977. *Outline of a Theory of Practice.* Cambridge: Cambridge University Press.

Bowie, K. A. 1998. The Alchemy of Charity: Of Class and Buddhism in Northern Thailand. *American Anthropologist* 100 (2): 469–481.

Brac de La Perrière, B. 2009. An Overview of the Field of Religion in Burmese Studies. *Asian Ethnology* 68 (2): 185–210.

——. 2015. Possession and Rebirth in Burma (Myanmar). *Contemporary Buddhism* 16 (1): 61–74.

Brac de la Perrière, B., G. Rozenberg, and A. Turner (eds.). 2014. *Champions of Buddhism: Weikza Cults in Contemporary Burma.* Singapore: NUS Press.

Breman, J. 2010. Neo-Bondage: A Fieldwork-Based Account. *International Labor and Working-Class History* 78 (1): 48–62.

Brown, I. 2011. Tracing Burma's Economic Failure to Its Colonial Inheritance. *Business History Review* 85 (4): 725–747.

——. 2013. *Burma's Economy in the Twentieth Century.* Cambridge: Cambridge University Press.

Bunnag, J. 1971. Loose Structure: Fact or Fancy? Thai Society Re-examined. *Journal of the American Academy of Religion* 95 (1): 1–23.

——. 1973. *Buddhist Monk, Buddhist Layman: A Study of Urban Monastic Organization in Central Thailand.* Cambridge: Cambridge University Press.

Burawoy, M. 1979. *Manufacturing Consent: Changes in the Labor Process Under Monopoly Capitalism.* Chicago: University of Chicago Press.

Carrier, J. G. 2018. Moral Economy: What's in a Name. *Anthropological Theory* 18 (1): 18–35.

Cassaniti, J. 2015. *Living Buddhism: Mind, Self, and Emotion in a Thai Community.* Ithaca, NY: Cornell University Press.

Chachavalpongpun, P., E. Prasse-Freeman, and P. Strefford (eds.). Forthcoming. *Unravelling Myanmar's Transition. Progress, Retrenchment and Ambiguity amidst Liberalisation.* Kyoto: Kyoto CSEAS Series on Asian Studies.

Chau, T. 2017. Children's Rights Bill Inconsistent over Child Labour Regulations. *The Myanmar Times*, August 23. Available online, https://www.mmtimes.com/news/childrens-rights-bill-inconsistent-over-child-labour-regulations.html, accessed 20 September 2018.

Chin, K.-L. 2009. *The Golden Triangle: Inside Southeast Asia's Drug Trade.* Ithaca: Cornell University Press.

Christensen, P., and A. James (eds.). 2008. *Research with Children: Perspectives and Practices*. London: Routledge.

Comaroff, J., and J. L. Comaroff. 1999. Occult Economies and the Violence of Abstraction: Notes from the South African Postcolony. *American Ethnologist* 26 (2): 279–303.

———. 2002. Alien-nation: Zombies, Immigrants, and Millennial Capitalism. *The South Atlantic Quarterly* 101 (4): 779–805.

Constable, N. 2007. *Maid to Order in Hong Kong: Stories of Migrant Workers*. Ithaca: Cornell University Press.

Crawfurd, J. 1829. *Journal of an Embassy from the Governor General of India to the Court of Ava in the Year 1827*. London: Colburn

Crouch, M. 2015. Constructing Religion by Law in Myanmar. *The Review of Faith and International Affairs* 13 (4): 1–11.

———. (ed.). 2017a. *The Business of Transition. Law Reform, Development and Economics in Myanmar*. Cambridge: Cambridge University Press.

———. 2017b. Understanding the Business of Transition in Myanmar. In M. Crouch (ed.), *The Business of Transition. Law reform, Development and Economics in Myanmar,* pp. 1–31. Cambridge: Cambridge University Press.

Dapice, D. O., T. J. Vallely, B. Wilkinson, M. McPherson, and M. J. Montesano. 2011. *Myanmar Agriculture in 2011: Old Problems and New Challenges*. Proximity Designs. Cambridge: Ash Center for Democratic Governance and Innovation. Harvard Kennedy School.

Dasgupta, P. 1988. Trust as a Commodity. In D. Gambetta (ed.), *Trust: Making and Breaking Cooperative Relations,* pp. 49–72. Oxford: Blackwell Publishers.

Davidsen, S., J. Orac, Z. Mills, Nandar Linn, Daw Soe, and A. Ragatz. 2018. *Myanmar: Pay, Compensation, and Human Resource Management Review (English)*. Washington, DC: World Bank Group. Available online, http://documents.worldbank.org/curated/en/ 167501522309579124/pdf/124697-WP-P162323-PUBLIC-Pay-review.pdf, accessed 11 January 2019.

De Neve, G. 1999. Asking for and Giving Baki: Neo-Bondage, or the Interplay of Bondage and Resistance in the Tamilnadu Power-Loom Industry. *Contributions to Indian Sociology* 33 (1–2): 379–406.

———. 2005. *The Everyday Politics of Labour: Working Lives in India's Informal Economy*. London and Oxford: Berghahn Books.

DEval (German Institute for Development Evaluation). 2015. *Small and Medium Enterprise Survey. Myanmar 2015.* Available online, http://www.deval.org/files/content/Dateien/Evaluierung/Berichte/ 2015_DEval_SME%20Report.pdf, accessed 20 January 2018.

Durkheim, E. 2010 [1953]. *Sociology and Philosophy.* Routledge Revivals. Abingdon: Routledge.

Dutta, P. V., P. B. O'Keefe, and R. J. Palacios. 2015. *Building Resilience, Equity and Opportunity in Myanmar: The Role of Social Protection. Strengthening Social Security Provision in Myanmar.* Working Paper. Washington, DC: World Bank Group. Available online, http://documents.worldbank.org/curated/en/729301467991961477/B uilding-resilience-equity-and-opportunity-in-Myanmar-The-role-of-social-protection-overview, accessed 12 April 2018.

Dyring, R., C. Mattingly, and M. Louw. 2017. The Question of 'Moral Engines': Introducing a Philosophical Anthropological Dialogue. In C. Mattingly, R. Dyring, M. Louw, and T. S. Wentzer (eds.), *Moral Engines: Exploring the Ethical Drives in Human Life,* pp. 9-36. New York and Oxford: Berghahn Books.

Egreteau, R. 2011. Burmese Indians in Contemporary Burma. Heritage, Influence, and Perceptions since 1988. *Asian Ethnicity* 12 (1): 33–54.

Embree, J. F. 1950. Thailand – A Loosely Structured Social System. *American Anthropologist* 52 (2): 181–193.

Endres, K. W., and A. Lauser. (eds.). 2011. *Engaging the Spirit World: Popular Beliefs and Practices in Modern Southeast Asia.* New York and Oxford: Berghahn Books.

European Commission. 2013. *Ethics for Researchers. Facilitating Research Excellence in FP7.* Available online, https://ec.europa.eu/research/ participants/data/ref/fp7/89888/ethics-for-researchers_en.pdf, accessed 10 June 2018.

Evans-Pritchard, E. E. 1956. *Nuer Religion.* Oxford: Clarendon Press.

Evers, H.-D. (ed.). 1969. *Loosely structured Social Systems: Thailand in Comparative Perspective.* New Haven: Yale University Southeast Asia Studies.

Falk, M. L. 2008. *Making Fields of Merit: Buddhist Female Ascetics and Gendered Orders in Thailand.* Seattle: University of Washington Press.

Farrelly, N., and S. Olinga-Shannon. 2015. *Establishing Contemporary Chinese Life in Myanmar.* Sinpapore: ISEAS Yusof Ishak Institute.

Fassin, D. (ed.). 2012. *A companion to moral anthropology.* Chichester: John Wiley and Sons.

Ferguson, J. M. 2015. Who's Counting? Ethnicity, Belonging, and the National Census in Burma/Myanmar. *Bijdragen tot de Taal-, Land- en Volkenkunde* 171 (1): 1–28.

Fink, C. 2009. *Living Silence in Burma: Surviving under Military Rule.* London: Zed Books.

Fischer, E. F. 2014. *The Good Life: Aspiration, Dignity, and the Anthropology of Wellbeing.* Stanford: Stanford University Press.

Foxeus, N. 2013. Esoteric Theravada Buddhism in Burma/Myanmar. *Scripta Instituti Donneriani Aboensis* 25: 55–79.

─────. 2017a. Contemporary Burmese Buddhism. In M. Jerryson (ed.), *The Oxford Handbook of Contemporary Buddhism,* pp. 212–235. Oxford: Oxford University Press.

─────. 2017b. Possessed for Success: Prosperity Buddhism and the Cult of the Guardians of the Treasure Trove in Upper Burma. *Contemporary Buddhism* 18 (1): 108–139.

Förch, T. 2018. Banking and Finance. In A. Simpson, N. Farrelly, and I. Holliday (eds.), *Routledge Handbook of Contemporary Myanmar,* pp. 227–236. London: Routledge.

Franco, J., H. Twomey, Khu Khu Ju, P. Vervest, and T. Kramer. 2015. *The Meaning of Land in Myanmar. a Primer.* Amsterdam: Transnational Institute.

Frasch, T. 2002. Coastal Peripheries During the Pagan Period. In J. Gommans, and J. Leider (eds.), *The Maritime Frontier of Burma: Exploring Political, Cultural and Commercial Interaction in the Indian Ocean World, 1200–1800,* pp. 59–78. Amsterdam: KITLV Press.

Fujita, K., F. Mieno, and I. Okamoto. 2009. Introduction. In K. Fujita, F. Mieno, and I. Okamoto (eds.), *The Economic Transition in Myanmar after 1988: Market Economy versus State Control,* pp. 1–22. Singapore: NUS Press.

Furnivall, J. S. 1957. *An Introduction to the Political Economy of Burma.* Rangoon: People's Literature Committee and House.

Gailey, C. W. 1999. Introduction. Rethinking Child Labor in an Age of Capitalist Restructuring. *Critique of Anthropology* 19 (2): 115–119.

Geertz, C. 1962. The Rotating Credit Association: A 'Middle Rung' in Development. *Economic Development and Cultural Change* 10 (3): 241–263.

─────. 1963. *Peddlers and Princes. Social Change and Economic Modernization in Two Indonesian Towns.* Chicago and London: University of Chicago Press.

Gellner, D. N. 1982. Max Weber, Capitalism, and the Religion of India. *Sociology* 16 (4): 526–543.

–––––. 2009. The Uses of Max Weber: Legitimation and Amnesia in Buddhology, South Asian History, and Anthropological Practice Theory. In P. B. Clarke (ed.), *The Oxford Handbook of the Sociology of Religion,* pp. 48–62. Oxford: Oxford University Press.

Gombrich, R. 1971. 'Merit Transference' in Sinhalese Buddhism: A Case Study of the Interaction between Doctrine and Practice. *History of Religions* 11 (2): 203–219.

–––––. 1991 [1971]. *Buddhist Precept and Practice. Traditional Buddhism in the Rural Highlands of Ceylon.* Delhi: Motilal Banarsidass Publishers.

Gombrich, R., and G. Obeyesekere. 1988. *Buddhism Transformed: Religious Change in Sri Lanka.* Princeton: Princeton University Press.

Graeber, D. 2001. *Toward an Anthropological Theory of Value: The False Coin of Our Own Dreams.* New York: Palgrave.

Gray, J. 2000 [1886]. *Ancient Proverbs and Maxims from Burmese Sources. or the Niti Literature of Burma.* Abingdon: Routledge.

Greenhalgh, S. 1994. De-Orientalizing the Chinese Family Firm. *American Ethnologist* 21 (4): 746–775

Gudeman, S. 2001. *The Anthropology of Economy: Community, Market, and Culture.* Malden: Blackwell.

–––––. 2008. *Economy's Tension: The Dialectics of Community and Market.* New York and Oxford: Berghahn Books.

–––––. 2009. Necessity or Contingency: Mutuality and Market. In C. Hann and K. Hart (eds.), *Market and Society: The Great Transformation Today,* pp. 17–37. Cambridge: Cambridge University Press.

Guérin, I. 2014. Juggling with Debt, Social Ties, and Values: The Everyday Use of Microcredit in Rural South India. *Current Anthropology* 55 (S9): S40–S50.

Hann, C., and E. Dunn (eds.). 1996. *Civil Society: Challenging Western Models.* London: Routledge.

Hann, C. (ed.). 2002. *Postsocialism: Ideals, Ideologies and Practices in Eurasia.* London: Routledge.

Hann, C. 2012. Transition, Tradition, and Nostalgia. Postsocialist Transformations in a Comparative Framework. *Collegium Antropologicum* 36 (4): 1119–1128.

–––––. 2016. A Concept of Eurasia. *Current Anthropology* 57 (1): 1–10.

–––––. 2018. Moral(ity and) Economy. Work, Workfare, and Fariness in Provincial Hungary. *European Journal of Sociology* 59 (2): 225–254.

Harriden, J. 2012. *The Authority of Influence: Women and Power in Burmese History.* Copenhagen: NIAS Press.

Hart, K. 1973. Informal Income Opportunities and Urban Employment in Ghana. *The Journal of Modern African Studies* 11 (1): 61–89.

—. 1985. The Informal Economy. *Cambridge Anthropology* 10 (2): 54–58.

—. 2005. Formal Bureaucracy and the Emergent Forms of the Informal Economy. *Research Paper* 2005/ 011. Helsinki: UNU-WIDER.

Harvey, D. 2003. *The New Imperialism.* Oxford: Oxford University Press.

—. 2004. The 'New' Imperialism: Accumulation by Dispossession. *Socialist Register 40: The New Imperial Challenge:* 63–87.

Harvey, P. 2013. *An Introduction to Buddhism: Teachings, History and Practices.* Cambridge: Cambridge University Press.

Hefner, R. W. 2010. Religious Resurgence in Contemporary Asia: Southeast Asian Perspectives on Capitalism, the State, and the New Piety. *The Journal of Asian Studies* 69 (04): 1031–1047.

Heijmans, P. 2015. Myanmar Criticised for Excluding Rohingyas from Census. *Al Jazeera,* May 29. Available online, https://www.aljazeera.com/news/2015/05/myanmar-criticised-excluding-rohingyas-census-150529045829329.html, accessed 9 December 2018.

Henig, D., and N Makovicky (eds.). 2016. *Economies of Favour after Socialism.* Oxford: Oxford University Press.

Hornig, L. 2019. Between Support and Stigma: On Credit Arrangements in Pathein. In. G. Winterberger, and E. Tenberg (eds.), *Current Myanmar Studies. Aung San Suu Kyi, Muslims in Arakan, and Economic Insecurity,* pp. 121–140. Newcastle upon Tyne: Cambridge Scholars Publishing.

Houtman, G. 1999. *Mental Culture in Burmese Crisis Politics: Aung San Suu Kyi and the National League for Democracy.* Tokyo: Tokyo University of Foreign Studies, Institute for the Studies of Languages and Cultures of Asia and Africa.

Humphrey, C. 1997. Exemplars and Rules. Aspects of the Discourse of Morality in Mongolia. In S. Howell (ed.), *The Ethnography of Moralities,* pp. 25–47. London: Routledge

—. 2002. *The Unmaking of Soviet Life: Everyday Economies after Socialism.* Ithaca: Cornell University Press.

Ikeya, C. 2011. *Refiguring Women, Colonialism, and Modernity in Burma.* Honolulu: University of Hawai'i Press.

ILO (International Labor Organization). 2015. *Rapid Assessment on Child Labor in Hlaing Thar Yar Industrial Zone in Yangon, Myanmar.*

Available online, https://www.ilo.org/ipec/Informationresources/WCMS_IPEC_PUB_27439/lang--en/index.htm, accessed 11 May 2018.

International Crisis Group. 2013. *The Dark Side of Transition: Violence against Muslims in Myanmar.* Available online, https://www.crisisgroup.org/asia/south-east-asia/myanmar/dark-side-transition-violence-against-muslims-myanmar, accessed 14 July 2018.

James, H. 2005. *Governance and Civil Society in Myanmar: Education, Health and Environment.* London and New York: Routledge Curzon.

Jaquet, C., and M. J. Walton. 2013. Buddhism and Relief in Myanmar: Reflections on Relief as a Practice of *Dāna.* In H. Kawanami, and G. Samuel (eds.), *Buddhism, International Relief Work, and Civil Society,* pp. 51–73. London: Palgrave Macmillan.

Joas, H. 2000. *The Genesis of Values.* Chicago: University of Chicago Press.

Jones, L. 2017, September 26. *A Better Political Economy of the Rohingya Crisis.* Available online, https://www.newmandala.org/better-political-economy-rohingya-crisis/, accessed 20 October 2018.

———. 2018. Political Economy. In A. Simpson, N. Farrelly, and I. Holliday (eds.), *Routledge Handbook of Contemporary Myanmar,* pp. 181–191. London: Routledge.

Jordt, I. 2003. From Relations of Power to Relations of Authority: Epistemic Claims, Practices, and Ideology in the Production of Burma's political order. *Social Analysis* 47 (1): 65–76.

———. 2005. Women's Practices of Renunciation in the Age of Sasana Revival. In M. Skidmore (ed.), *Burma at the Turn of the Twenty-First Century,* pp. 41–64. Honolulu: University of Hawai'i Press.

———. 2006. Defining a True Buddhist: Meditation and Knowledge Formation in Burma. *Ethnology* 45 (3): 193–207.

———. 2007. *Burma's Mass Lay Meditation Movement: Buddhism and the Cultural Construction of Power.* Athens: Ohio University Press.

Kalb, D. 2011. Introduction. In D. Kalb, and G. Halmai (eds.), *Headlines of Nation, Subtexts of Class. Working Class Populism and the Return of the Repressed in Neoliberal Europe,* pp. 1–36. New York and Oxford: Berghahn Books.

Karim, L. 2001. Politics of the Poor? NGOs and Grass-Roots Political Mobilization in Bangladesh. *PoLAR: Political and Legal Anthropology Review* 24 (1): 92–107.

Kawanami, H. 2001. Can Women be Celibate? Sexuality and Abstinence in Theravada Buddhism. In E. J. Sobo, and S. Bell (eds.), *Celibacy,*

Culture and Society: The Anthropology of Sexual Abstinence, pp. 137–156. Madison: University of Wisconsin Press.

——. 2007. Monastic Economy and Interactions with Society: The Case of Burmese Buddhist Nuns. Working Paper. Lancaster: Lancaster University.

——. 2009. Charisma, Power(s), and the Arahant Ideal in Burmese-Myanmar Buddhism. *Asian Ethnology* 68 (2): 211–237.

——. 2013. *Renunciation and Empowerment of Buddhist Nuns in Myanmar-Burma: Building a Community of Female Faithful.* Leiden: Brill.

Kedir, A. M., and G. Ibrahim. 2011. ROSCAs in Urban Ethiopia: Are the Characteristics of the Institutions More Important Than Those of Members? *Journal of Development Studies* 47 (7): 998–1016.

Keeler, W. 2017. *The Traffic in Hierarchy: Masculinity and Its Others in Buddhist Burma.* Honolulu: University of Hawai'i Press.

Keskülä, E. 2018. Miners and Their Children. the Remaking of Soviet Working Class in Kazakhstan. In C. Hann, and J. Parry (eds.), *Industrial Labor on the Margins of Capitalism. Precarity, Class and the Neoliberal Subject,* pp. 61–84. London and New York: Berghahn.

Keyes, C. F. 1983a. Economic Action and Buddhist Morality in a Thai Village. *The Journal of Asian Studies* 42 (4): 851–868.

——. 1983b. Introduction: The Study of Popular Ideas of Karma. In C. F. Keyes, and E. Valentine Daniel (eds.), *Karma: An Anthropological Inquiry,* pp. 1–26. Berkeley: University of California Press.

——. 1983c. Merit-Transference in the Kammic Theory of Popular Theravāda Buddhism. In C. F. Keyes, and E. Valentine Daniel (eds.), *Karma: An Anthropological Inquiry,* pp. 261–286. Berkeley: University of California Press.

——. 1990. Buddhist Practical Morality in a Changing Agrarian World: A Case from Northeastern Thailand. In D. K. Swearer, and R. Sizemore (eds.), *Attitudes Toward Wealth and Poverty in Theravada Buddhism,* pp. 170–189. Columbia: University of South Carolina Press.

Kim, E. C. 2012. 'Call Me Mama': An Ethnographic Portrait of an Employer of Undocumented Workers. *The Annals of the American Academy of Political and Social Science* 642 (1): 170–185.

Kluckhohn, C. 1962 [1951]. Values and Value-Orientations in the Theory of Action: An Exploration in Definition and Classification. In T. Parsons, and E. A. Shils (eds.), *Toward a General Theory of Action: Theoretical Foundations for the Social Sciences,* pp. 388–433. New York: Harper and Row.

Kraas, F., R. Spohner, and Aye Aye Myint. 2017. *Socio-Economic Atlas of Myanmar*. Stuttgart: Franz Steiner Verlag.

Kudo, T. 2009. Industrial Policies and the Development of Myanmar's Industrial Sector in the Transition to a Market Economy. In K. Fujita, F. Mieno, and I. Okamoto (eds.), *The Economic Transition in Myanmar after 1988: Market Economy versus State Control,* pp. 66–102. Singapore: NUS Press.

Kumada, N. 2001. *In the World of Rebirth: Politics, Economy, and Society of Burmese Buddhists* (unpublished doctoral dissertation), Wolfson College, Cambridge University.

———. 2004. *Rethinking Daná in Burma: The Art of Giving.* Paper presented at the 'Buddhism and the spirit cult revisited' conference at Stanford University.

———. 2015. Burmese Kinship Revisited: Substance and 'Biology' in the World of Rebirth. *Contemporary Buddhism* 16 (1): 75–108.

Kyaw Ye Lynn. 2018, February 7. Pristine Ayeyarwady Coastline Flagged for New $10bn Industrial Zone. *Frontier Myanmar*. Available online, https://frontiermyanmar.net/en/pristine-ayeyarwady-coastline-flagged-for-new-10bn-industrial-zone, accessed 10 December 2018.

Kyaw Ye Lynn, and Su Myat Mon. 2019, January 2. Garment Sector Poised to Boom in Pathein. *Frontier Myanmar.* Available online, https://frontiermyanmar.net/en/garments-sector-poised-to-boom-in-pathein, accessed 10 January 2019.

Ladwig, P. 2011. Can Things Reach the Dead? the Ontological Status of Objects and the Study of Lao Buddhist Rituals for the Spirits of the Deceased. In K. W. Endres, and A. Lauser (eds.), *Engaging the Spirit World: Popular Beliefs and Practices in Modern Southeast Asia.* New York and Oxford: Berghahn Books.

———. 2017. *The Lao Buddhist Temple and the Intrusion of Statehood. the Emergence of (Dis)Embedded Ritual Economies in the Vientiane Area during the 1950s and 60s.* Paper presented at 'Buddhism and economics: Conceptual and Theoretical Approaches to a Burgeoning Field' Conference at Copenhagen, Center of Contemporary Buddhist Studies.

Laidlaw, J. 2002. For an Anthropology of Ethics and Freedom. *Journal of the Royal Anthropological Institute* 8 (2): 311–332.

———. 2017. Fault Lines in the Anthropology of Ethics. In C. Mattingly, R. Dyring, M. Louw, and T. S. Wentzer (eds.), *Moral Engines: Exploring the Ethical Drives in Human Life,* pp. 174–193. New York and Oxford: Berghahn Books.

Lainez, N. 2014. Informal Credit in Vietnam: A Necessity Rather Than an Evil. *Journal of Southeast Asian Economies (JSEAE)* 31 (1): 147–154.

Lambek, M. 2017. On the Immanence of Ethics. In C. Mattingly, R. Dyring, M. Louw, and T. S. Wentzer (eds.), *Moral Engines: Exploring the Ethical Drives in Human Life,* pp. 137–154. New York and Oxford: Berghahn Books.

Lancy, D. F. 2012. Why Anthropology of Childhood? A Short History of an Emerging Discipline. *AnthropoChildren* 1 (1). Utah State University digital commons. Available online, http://popups.ulg.ac.be/AnthropoChildren/document.php?id=918, accessed 3 June 2018.

——. 2015a. *The Anthropology of Childhood: Cherubs, Chattel, Changelings.* Cambridge: Cambridge University Press.

——. 2015b. Children as a Reserve Labor Force. *Current Anthropology* 56 (4): 545–568.

——. 2017. *Children's Work and Apprenticeship.* Oxford Bibliographies online. Available online, https://www.oxfordbibliographies.com/view/document/obo-9780199791231/obo-9780199791231-0007.xml, accessed 20 July 2018.

Leach, E. R. 1961. *Pul Eliya: A Village in Ceylon.* Cambridge: Cambridge University Press.

Leach, E. (ed.). 1968. *Dialectic in Practical Religion.* Cambridge: Cambridge University Press.

Leehey, J. 2016. *Informal Social Protection in Myanmar's Central Dry Zone.* HelpAge International Briefing Paper. Available online, http://ageingasia.org/eaprdc0038/, accessed 15 July 2018.

Lehman, F. K. 1996. Can God Be Coerced? Structural Correlates of Merit and Blessing in Some Southeast Asian Religions. In C. A. Kammerer, and N. Tannenbaum (eds.), *Merit and Blessing in Mainland Southeast Asia in Comparative Perspective,* pp. 20–51. New Haven: Yale Southeast Asian Studies.

Liebel, M. 2004. *A Will of Their Own: Cross-Cultural Perspectives on Working Children.* London: Zed Books.

Lintner, B. 2000. *The Golden Triangle Opium Trade: An Overview.* Asia Pacific Media Services. Available online, http://www.asiapacificms.com/papers/pdf/gt_opium_trade.pdf, accessed 14 May 2018.

Lissak, M. 1970. The Class Structure of Burma: Continuity and Change. *Journal of Southeast Asian Studies* 1 (1): 60–73.

Lomnitz, L. A. 1988. Informal Exchange Networks in Formal Systems: A Theoretical Model. *American Anthropologist* 90 (1): 42–55.

Lont, H. B. 2005. *Juggling Money in Yogyakarta. Financial Self-Help Organizations and the Quest for Security*. Leiden: KITLV Press.

Lorch, J. 2006. Civil Society Under Authoritarian Rule: The Case of Myanmar. *Journal of Current Southeast Asian Affairs* 25 (2): 3–38.

––––. 2007. Myanmar's civil Society–a Patch for the National Education System? The Emergence of Civil Society in Areas of State Weakness. *Südostasien Aktuell* 26 (3): 54–88.

––––. 2008. The (Re)-Emergence of Civil Society in Areas of State Weakness: The Case of Education in Burma/Myanmar. In M. Skidmore, W. Trevor (eds.), *Dictatorship, Disorder and Decline in Myanmar,* pp. 151–176. Canberra: ANU E Press.

Luhmann, N. 1988. Familiarity, Confidence, Trust: Problems and Alternatives, In D. Gambetta (ed.), *Trust: Making and Breaking Cooperative Relations,* pp. 94–107. Oxford: Blackwell Publishers.

Luong, H. V. (ed.). 2003. *Postwar Vietnam: Dynamics of a Transforming Society*. Oxford: Rowman and Littlefield.

Magha, U. 1967. *Pathein yazawin. (History of Bassein)*. Yangon: Zwe Sapay Press.

Mandel, R., and C. Humphrey (eds.). 2002. *Markets and Moralities: Ethnographies of Postsocialism.* New York: Berg Publishers.

Matsui, M. 2016. Mobile Revolution Lifts Myanmar out of Telecom Time Warp. *Nikkei Asian Review*, July 26. Available online, https://asia.nikkei.com/Business/Mobile-revolution-lifts-Myanmar-out-of-telecom-time-warp, accessed 11 April 2018.

Mattingly, C., R. Dyring, M. Louw, and T. S. Wentzer (eds.). 2017. *Moral Engines: Exploring the Ethical Drives in Human Life*. New York and Oxford: Berghahn Books.

McCarthy, G. 2016. Buddhist Welfare and the Limits of Big 'P' Politics in Provincial Myanmar. In N. Cheesman, and N. Farrelly (eds.), *Conflict in Myanmar: War, Politics, Religion,* pp. 313–332. Singapore: ISEAS – Yusof Ishak Institute.

MCRB (Myanmar Centre for Responsible Business). 2017. *Children's Rights and Business in Myanmar*. Briefing Paper. Available online, https://www.humanrights.dk/publications/briefing-paper-childrens-rights-myanmar, accessed 4 May 2018.

Mead, M. 1971 [1928]. *Coming of Age in Samoa*. New York: Harper Perennial.

Mikuš, M. 2016. The Justice of Neoliberalism: Moral Ideology and Rredistributive Politics of Public-Sector Retrenchment in Serbia. *Social Anthropology* 24 (2): 211–227.

Millar, K. 2008. The Informal Economy: Condition and Critique of Advanced Capitalism. In A. B. Joshi (ed.), *Underground Economy: Issues and Approaches,* pp. 55–74. Hyderabad: ICFAI University Press.

——. 2014. The Precarious Present: Wageless Labor and Disrupted Life in Rio de Janeiro, Brazil. *Cultural Anthropology* 29 (1): 32–53.

Montgomery, H. 2008. *An Introduction to Childhood: Anthropological Perspectives on Children's Lives.* Oxford: John Wiley and Sons.

Moore, B. 1978. *Injustice: The Social Basis of Obedience and Revolt.* London: Macmillan Press.

Morris, J., and A. Polese (eds.). 2014. *The Informal Post-Socialist Economy: Embedded Practices and Livelihoods.* New York: Routledge.

Moule, C. 1998. Regulation of Work in Small Firms: A View from the Inside. *Work, Employment and Society* 12 (4): 635–653.

Murdoch, L. 2015. Myanmar Elections: Astrologers' Influential Role in National Decisions. *The Sydney Morning Herald*, November 12. Available online, https://www.smh.com.au/world/myanmar-elections-astrologers-influential-role-in-national-decisions-20151112-gkxc3j.html, accessed 11 June 2018.

Mya Maung. 1964. Cultural Value and Economic Change in Burma. *Asian Survey* 4 (3): 757–764.

Mya Than. 1997. The Ethnic Chinese in Myanmar and Their Identity. In L. Suriyadinata (ed.), *Ethnic Chinese as Southeast Asians*, pp. 115–146. New York: St. Martin's Press.

Myanmar Department of Population. 2015. *The 2014 Myanmar Population and Housing Census. Ayeyawady Region Report. Census Report Volume 3–N.* Nay Pyi Taw: Ministry of Labour, Immigration and Population.

——. 2016. *The 2014 Myanmar Population and Housing Census. Thematic Report on Migration and Urbanization. Census Report Volume 4–D.* Nay Pyi Taw: Ministry of Labour, Immigration and Population.

——. 2017a. *The 2014 Myanmar Population and Housing Census. Thematic Report on Labour Force. Census Report Volume 4–G.* Nay Pyi Taw: Ministry of Labour, Immigration and Population.

——. 2017b. *The 2014 Myanmar Population and Housing Census. Thematic Report on Education. Census Report Volume 4–H.* Nay Pyi Taw: Ministry of Labour, Immigration and Population.

Myat Thein. 2004. *Economic Development of Myanmar.* Singapore: Institute of Southeast Asian Studies.

Narotzky, S. 2017. Making Difference. Concluding Comments on Work and Livelihood. In S. Narotzky, and V. Goddard (eds.), *Work and livelihoods. History, ethnography and models in times of crisis*, pp. 205-216. New York and London: Routledge.

Narotzky, S., and N. Besnier. 2014. Crisis, Value, and Hope: Rethinking the Economy. An Introduction to Supplement 9. *Current Anthropology* 55 (S9): S4–S16.

Nash, M. 1965. *The Golden Road to Modernity: Village Life in Contemporary Burma.* Chicago: University of Chicago Press.

Nguyen, M. T. N. 2015. Migration and Care Institutions in Market Socialist Vietnam: Conditionality, Commodification and Moral Authority. *The Journal of Development Studies* 51 (10): 1326–1340.

Odaka, K. (ed.). 2016. *The Myanmar Economy: Its Past, Present and Prospects.* Tokyo: Springer.

Okamoto, I. 2009. Transformation of the Rice Marketing System after Market Liberalization in Myanmar. In K. Fujita, F. Mieno, and I. Okamoto (eds.), *The Economic Transition in Myanmar after 1988: Market Economy versus State Control,* pp. 216–245. Singapore: NUS Press.

------. 2018. Agriculture. In A. Simpson, N. Farrelly, and I. Holliday (eds.), *Routledge Handbook of Contemporary Myanmar*, pp. 192–201. London: Routledge.

Okell, J. 1972. *A Guide to the Romanization of Burmese.* London: Royal Asiatic Society.

Ong, A. 2006. *Neoliberalism as Exception. Mutations in Sovereignty and Citizenship.* Durham: Duke University Press.

------. 2010 [1987]. *Spirits of Resistance and Capitalist Discipline: Factory Women in Malaysia.* Albany: State University of New York Press.

Parker, E. 2016. Myanmar's Opening: Doing Business in Asia's Final Frontier. *The Diplomat*, November 18. Available online, https://thediplomat.com/2016/11/myanmars-opening-doing-business-in-asias-final-frontier, accessed 23 June 2018.

Parry, J., and M. Bloch. 1989. Introduction. In J. Parry, and M. Bloch (eds.), *Money and the Morality of Exchange*, pp. 1–32. Cambridge: Cambridge University Press.

Patton, T. N. 2018. *The Buddha's Wizards: Magic, Protection, and Healing in Burmese Buddhism.* New York: Columbia University Press

Pfanner, D. E., and J. Ingersoll. 1962. Theravada Buddhism and Village Economic Behavior: A Burmese and Thai Comparison. *The Journal of Asian Studies* 21 (03): 341–361.

Phillips, H. P. 1967. Social Contact vs. Social Promise in a Siamese Village. In J. M. Potter, M. N. Diaz, and G. M. Foster (eds.), *Peasant Society. A Reader*, pp. 346–367. Boston: Little Brown and Co.

Polanyi, K. 2001 [1944]. *The Great Transformation: The Political and Economic Origins of our Time*. Boston: Beacon Press.

Prasse-Freeman, E. 2012. Power, Civil Society, and an Inchoate Politics of the Daily in Burma/Myanmar. *The Journal of Asian Studies* 71 (02): 371–397.

——. 2017. The Rohingya and the World. *Jacobin*, December 28. Available online, https://www.jacobinmag.com/2017/12/myanmar-rohingya-ethnic-cleansing-aung-san-suu-kyi, accessed 24 July 2018.

Prasse-Freeman, E., and Phyo Win Latt. 2018. Class and Inequality. In A. Simpson, N. Farrelly, and I. Holliday (eds.), *Routledge Handbook of Contemporary Myanmar*, pp. 429–441. London: Routledge.

Pyi Phyo Kyaw. 2017. In the Midst of Imperfections: Burmese Buddhists and Business Ethics. *Journal of Buddhist Ethics* 24: 287–339.

Rahman, A. 1999. *Women and Microcredit in Rural Bangladesh: An Anthropological Study of the Rhetoric and Realities of Grameen Bank Lending.* Boulder: Westview Press.

——. 2004. Microcredit and Poverty Reduction: Trade-Off between Building Institutions and Reaching the Poor. In H. Lont and O. Hospes (eds.), *Livelihood and Microfinance. Anthropological and Sociological Perspectives on Savings and Debt*, pp. 25–42. Delft: Eburon.

Rahula, Bhikkhu Basnagoda. 2008. *Buddha's Teachings on Prosperity: At Home, at Work, in the World.* Boston: Wisdom Publications.

Ram, M. 1991. Control and Autonomy in Small Firms: The Case of the West Midlands Clothing Industry. *Work, Employment and Society* 5 (4): 601–619.

——. 1994. *Managing to Survive: Working Lives in Small Firms*. Oxford: Blackwell Business.

Robbins, J. 2007. Between Reproduction and Freedom: Morality, Value, and Radical Cultural Change. *Ethnos* 72 (3): 293–314.

——. 2012. Cultural Values. In D. Fassin (ed.), *A Companion to Moral Anthropology*, pp. 117–132. Chichester: Wiley-Blackwell.

——. 2013. Monism, Pluralism, and the Structure of Value Relations: A Dumontian Contribution to the Contemporary Study of Value. *HAU: Journal of Ethnographic Theory* 3 (1): 99–115.

——. 2016. What is the Matter with Transcendence? On the Place of Religion in the New Anthropology of Ethics. *Journal of the Royal Anthropological Institute, N.S.* 22: 767–808.

——. 2017. Where in the World are Values? Exemplarity and Moral Motivation. In C. Mattingly, R. Dyring, M. Louw, and T. S. Wentzer (eds.), *Moral Engines: Exploring the Ethical Drives in Human Life*, pp. 155–173. New York and Oxford: Berghahn Books.

Roberts, J. L. 2016. *Mapping Chinese Rangoon: Place and Nation among the Sino-Burmese*. Seattle: University of Washington Press.

Rogaly, B., and A. Rafique. 2003. Struggling to Save Cash: Seasonal Migration and Vulnerability in West Bengal, India. *Development and Change* 34 (4): 659–681.

Rozenberg, G. 2005. The Cheaters. Journey to the Land of the Lottery. In M. Skidmore (ed.), *Burma at the Turn of the Twenty-First Century*, pp. 19–40. Honolulu: University of Hawai'i Press.

Rozenberg, G. 2015. *The Immortals: Faces of the Incredible in Buddhist Burma.* (Trans. by W. Keeler). Honolulu: University of Hawai'i Press.

Sakata, S. (ed.). 2013. *Vietnam's Economic Entities in Transition*. London: Palgrave Macmillan.

Schober, J. 2011. *Modern Buddhist Conjunctures in Myanmar. Cultural Narratives, Colonial Legacies, and Civil Society.* Honolulu: University of Hawai'i Press.

Schumpeter, J. A. 1934. *The Theory of Economic Development: An Inquiry into Profits, Capital, Credit, Interest, and the Business Cycle.* Cambridge: Harvard University Press.

Scott, J. C. 1972. Patron-Client Politics and Political Change in Southeast Asia. *American Political Science Review* 66 (01): 91–113.

——. 1976. *The Moral Economy of the Peasant: Rebellion and Subsistence in Southeast Asia.* New Haven: Yale University Press.

——. 1985. Weapons of the Weak: Everyday Forms of Peasant Resistance. New Haven: Yale University Press.

Shwe Aung. 2016. Rising Number of Unmarried Women Lowering Burma's Birthrate. *Democratic Voice of Burma*, September 28. Available online, http://english.dvb.no/news/rising-number-unmarried-women-lowering-burmas-birthrate/71154, accessed 22 April 2018.

Sihlé, N., and B. Brac de la Perrière (eds.). 2015. Comparative Anthropology of Buddhist Transactions: Moving Beyond the Maussian Terminology of the 'Gift'. *Religion Compass* 9 (11): Special Issue.

Smart, A., and J. Smart. 2005. Introduction. In A. Smart, and J. Smart (eds.), *Petty Capitalists and Globalization: Flexibility, Entrepreneurship, and Economic Development*, pp. 1–22. New York: State University of New York Press.

Smets, P., and E. Bähre. 2004. When Coercion Takes Over: The Limits of Social Capital in Microfinance Schemes. In H. Lont, and O. Hospes (eds.), *Livelihood and Microfinance: Anthropological and*

Sociological Perspectives on Savings and Debt, pp. 215–236. Delft: Eburon.

Smith, M. 2007. *State of Strife: The Dynamics of Ethnic Conflict in Burma.* Washington, DC: East-West Center.

Sopranzetti, C. 2017. Framed by Freedom: Emancipation and Oppression in Post-Fordist Thailand. *Cultural Anthropology* 32 (1): 68–92.

South, A. 2008. *Civil Society in Burma: The Development of Democracy Amidst Conflict.* Washington, DC: East-West-Center.

Spiro, M. E. 1966. Buddhism and Economic Action in Burma. *American Anthropologist* 68 (5): 1163–1173.

——. 1967. *Burmese Supernaturalism: A Study in the Explanation and Reduction of Suffering.* New Jersey: Prentice-Hall.

——. 1982 [1970]. *Buddhism and Society: A Great Tradition and Its Burmese Vicissitudes.* Berkeley: University of California Press.

——. 1986 [1977]. *Kinship and Marriage in Burma: A Cultural and Psychodynamic Analysis.* Berkeley: University of California Press.

Spittler, G., and M. Bourdillon (eds.). 2012. *African Children at Work: Working and Learning in Growing up for Life.* Zürich: LIT Verlag.

Standing, G. 2011. *The Precariat. The New Dangerous Class.* London and New York: Bloomsbury.

Steinberg, D. I. 1997. *A Void in Myanmar: Civil Society in Burma.* Paper Presented at Conference 'Strengthening Civil Society in Burma. Possibilities and Dilemmas for International NGOs' (organised by Transnational Institute and the Burma Centrum Nederland). Available online, https://www.burmalibrary.org/en/a-void-in-myanmar-civil-society-in-burma, accessed 10 January 2018.

Szanton, D. L. 1998. Contingent Moralities: Social and Economic Investment in a Philippine Fishing Town. In R. W. Hefner (ed.), *Market Cultures: Society and Morality in the New Asian Capitalisms*, pp. 251–267. Boulder: Westview Press.

Tambiah, S. J. 1968. The Ideology of Merit and the Social Correlates of Buddhism in a Thai Village. In E. R. Leach (ed.), *Dialectic in Practical Religion*, pp. 41–121. Cambridge: Cambridge University Press.

——. 1970. *Buddhism and the Spirit Cults in North-East Thailand.* Cambridge: Cambridge University Press.

——. 1973. Buddhism and This-Worldly Activity. *Modern Asian Studies* 7 (1): 1–20.

——. 1976. *World Conqueror and World Renouncer: A Study of Buddhism and Polity in Thailand against a Historical Background.* Cambridge: Cambridge University Press.

Tannenbaum, N., and E. P. Durrenberger. 1990. Hidden Dimensions of the Burmese Way to Socialism. In M. E. Smith (ed.), *Perspectives on the Informal Economy*, pp. 281–299. Lanham: University Press of America.

Taylor, R. H. 1995. Disaster or Release? J. S. Furnivall and the Bankruptcy of Burma. *Modern Asian Studies* 29 (1): 45–63.

–––––. 2007. British Policy Towards Myanmar and the Creation of the 'Burma Problem'. In N. Ganesan, and Kyaw Yin Hlaing (eds.), *Myanmar: State, Society and Ethnicity*, pp. 70–95. Singapore: Institute for Southeast Asian Studies.

–––––. 2009. *The State in Myanmar*. London: Hurst Publishers.

Terpe, S. 2018. Working with Max Weber's 'Spheres of Life': An Actor-Centred Approach. *Journal of Classical Sociology.* Available online, https://journals.sagepub.com/doi/10.1177/1468795X18789328, accessed 20 October 2018.

Thant Myint-U. Forthcoming. *The Hidden History of Burma. Race, Capitalism, and the Crisis of Democracy in the 21st Century*. New York: W.W. Norton & Company.

Tharaphi Than. 2014. *Women in Modern Burma*. London: Routledge.

The Economist. 2017. Myanmar Has One of the Lowest Tax Takes in the World. *The Economist*, November 16. Available online, https://www.economist.com/asia/2017/11/16/myanmar-has-one-of-the-lowest-tax-takes-in-the-world, accessed 5 June 2018.

The World Bank. 2016. *Enterprise Surveys. What Businesses Experience. Myanmar 2016 Country Profile.* Washington, DC: International Bank for Reconstruction and Development, The World Bank Group. Available online, https://www.enterprisesurveys.org/en/data/exploreeconomies/2016/, accessed 23 May 2018.

The World Bank, The World Bank Group Macroeconomics, Trade and Investment. 2018. *Myanmar Economic Monitor 2018. Navigating Risks.* Available online, http://documents.worldbank.org/curated/en/986461544542633353/pdf/132847-REVISED-MEM-Final.pdf, accessed 20 March 2019.

Thompson, E. P. 1971. The Moral Economy of the English Crowd in the Eighteenth Century. *Past and present* (50): 76–136.

Thompson, P., and S. Ackroyd. 1995. All Quiet on the Workplace Front? A Critique of Recent Trends in British Industrial Sociology. *Sociology* 29 (4): 615–633.

Tin Maung Maung Than. 2007. *State Dominance in Myanmar: The Political Economy of Industrialization*. Singapore: Institute of Southeast Asian Studies.

Tin Yadanar Htun. 2016. Interfaith Book Highlights 'Metta'. *Myanmar Times*, March 30. Available online, https://www.mmtimes.com/national-news/19728-interfaith-book-highlights-metta.html, accessed 20 July 2018.

Tong, C. K. 2010. *Identity and Ethnic Relations in Southeast Asia: Racializing Chineseness*. New York: Springer.

Turnell, S., A. Vicary, and W. Bradford. 2008. Migrant-Worker Remittances and Burma: An Economic Analysis of Survey Results. In M. Skidmore, and T. Wilson (eds.), *Dictatorship, Disorder and Decline in Myanmar*, pp. 63–86. Canberra: ANU E Press.

Turnell, S. 2009. *Fiery Dragons: Banks, Moneylenders and Microfinance in Burma.* Copenhagen: NIAS Press.

–––––. 2014. *Banking and Finance in Myanmar: Present Realities, Future Possibilities*. Yangon: United States Agency for International Development (USAID).

–––––. 2017. Microfinance in Myanmar. Unleashing the Potential. In M. Crouch (ed.), *The Business of Transition. Law Reform, Development and Economics in Myanmar*, pp. 122–147. Cambridge: Cambridge University Press.

Turner, A. 2014. Saving Buddhism: *The Impermanence of Religion in Colonial Burma*. Honolulu: University of Hawai'i Press.

Turner, C. L. 1995. *Japanese Workers in Protest: An Ethnography of Consciousness and Experience*. Berkeley: University of California Press.

UN (United Nations). 2018. *Children and Armed Conflict.* General Assembly Security Council. Report of the Secretary-General. Available online, http://undocs.org/en/s/2018/465, accessed 2 November 2018.

UNDP (United Nations Development Programme) and CSO (Myanmar Central Statistical Organization). 2015. *Myanmar Business Survey 2015. Data Report*. Available online, http://www.mm.undp.org/content/myanmar/en/home/library/democratic_governance/MyanmarBusinessSurvey.html, accessed 10 January 2018.

UNESCO (United Nations Educational, Scientific and Cultural Organization). 2018. *Women in Science.* UNESCO Institute for Statistic, Fact Sheet No. 51. Available online, http://uis.unesco.org/sites/default/files/documents/fs51-women-in-science-2018-en.pdf, accessed 17 October 2018.

USAID (United States Agency for International Development). 2017. *Success Story. Usaid Supports Government of Burma to Officially Recognize and Adopt National Land Use Policy.* Available online,

http://land-links.org/document/tgcc-success-story-usaid-supports-
government-burma-officially-recognize-adopt-national-land-use-
policy, accessed 7 August 2018.

Veblen, T. 2007 [1899]. *Theory of the Leisure Class*. (Oxford World's
Classics). Oxford: Oxford University Press.

Verdery, K. 1996. *What Was Socialism, and What Comes Next?* Princeton:
Princeton University Press.

Walton, M. J., and S. Hayward. 2014. *Contesting Buddhist Narratives:
Democratization, Nationalism, and Communal Violence in
Myanmar*. Honolulu: East-West Center.

Walton, M. J. 2017a. *Buddhism, Politics and Political Thought in Myanmar*.
Cambridge: Cambridge University Press.

-----. 2017b. Misunderstanding Myanmar's Ma Ba Tha. *Asia Times*, June
09. Available online, https://asiatimes.com/2017/06/
misunderstanding-myanmars-ma-ba-tha/, accessed 2 May 2018.

Weber, M. 1946. *From Max Weber: Essays in Sociology*. (Transl. and ed. by
H. H. Gerth and C. Wright Mills). New York: Oxford University
Press.

-----. 1958 [1916]. *The Religion of India: The Sociology of Hinduism and
Buddhism*. (Transl. and ed. by H. H. Gerth, and D. Martindale).
Glencoe, Ill.: Free Press.

-----. 1992 [1905]. *The Protestant Ethic and the Spirit of Capitalism*
(Transl. by T. Parsons). London: Routledge.

-----. 2004 [1920]. Intermediate Reflection on the Economic Ethics of the
World Religions. In S. Whimster (ed.), *The Essential Weber: A
Reader,* pp. 215–244. London: Routledge.

White, J. B. 2004. *Money Makes Us Relatives: Women's Labor in Urban
Turkey*. Austin: University of Texas Press.

Woods, K. 2014. *A Political Anatomy of Land Grabs.* Transnational
Institute. Available online, https://www.tni.org/en/article/political-
anatomy-land-grabs, accessed 14 October 2018.

-----. 2018. The Conflict Resource Economy and Pathways to Peace in
Burma. *Peaceworks* 144, November 2018. Washington, DC: United
States Institute of Peace.

Yan, H. 2008. *New Masters, New Servants: Migration, Development, and
Women Workers in China.* Durham: Duke University Press.

Yanagisako, S. J. 2002. *Producing Culture and Capital: Family Firms in
Italy.* Princeton: Princeton University Press.

-----. 2015. Kinship: Still at the Core. *HAU: Journal of Ethnographic
Theory* 5 (1): 489–494.

Yegar, M. 1972. *The Muslims of Burma: A Study of a Minority Group.* Wiesbaden: Otto Harrassowitz.

Zaw Zaw Htwe 2018, September 27. Workers March, Call on Govt to Help end Disputes at 5 Factories. *The Myanmar Times.* Available online, https://www.mmtimes.com/news/workers-march-call-govt-help-end-disputes-5-factories.html, accessed 7 January 2019.

Zigon, J. 2007. Moral Breakdown and the Ethical Demand: A Theoretical Framework for an Anthropology of Moralities. *Anthropological Theory* 7 (2): 131–150.

Zin, M. 2012. Burmese Attitude Toward Chinese: Portrayal of the Chinese in Contemporary Cultural and Media Works. *Journal of Current Southeast Asian Affairs* 31 (1): 115–131.

Index

Halle Studies in the Anthropology of Eurasia

1 Hann, Chris, and the "Property Relations" Group, 2003: *The Postsocialist Agrarian Question. Property Relations and the Rural Condition.*

2 Grandits, Hannes, and Patrick Heady (eds.), 2004: *Distinct Inheritances. Property, Family and Community in a Changing Europe.*

3 Torsello, David, 2004: *Trust, Property and Social Change in a Southern Slovakian Village.*

4 Pine, Frances, Deema Kaneff, and Haldis Haukanes (eds.), 2004: *Memory, Politics and Religion. The Past Meets the Present in Europe.*

5 Habeck, Joachim Otto, 2005: *What it Means to be a Herdsman. The Practice and Image of Reindeer Husbandry among the Komi of Northern Russia.*

6 Stammler, Florian, 2009: *Reindeer Nomads Meet the Market. Culture, Property and Globalisation at the 'End of the Land'* (2 editions).

7 Ventsel, Aimar, 2006: *Reindeer,* Rodina *and Reciprocity. Kinship and Property Relations in a Siberian Village.*

8 Hann, Chris, Mihály Sárkány, and Peter Skalník (eds.), 2005: *Studying Peoples in the People's Democracies. Socialist Era Anthropology in East-Central Europe.*

9 Leutloff-Grandits, Caroline, 2006: *Claiming Ownership in Postwar Croatia. The Dynamics of Property Relations and Ethnic Conflict in the Knin Region.*

10 Hann, Chris, 2006: *"Not the Horse We Wanted!" Postsocialism, Neoliberalism, and Eurasia.*

11 Hann, Chris, and the "Civil Religion" Group, 2006: *The Postsocialist Religious Question. Faith and Power in Central Asia and East-Central Europe.*

12 Heintz, Monica, 2006: *"Be European, Recycle Yourself!" The Changing Work Ethic in Romania.*

13 Grant, Bruce, and Lale Yalçın-Heckmann (eds.), 2007: *Caucasus Paradigms. Anthropologies, Histories and the Making of a World Area.*

14 Buzalka, Juraj, 2007: *Nation and Religion. The Politics of Commemoration in South-East Poland.*

15 Naumescu, Vlad, 2007: *Modes of Religiosity in Eastern Christianity. Religious Processes and Social Change in Ukraine.*

16 Mahieu, Stéphanie, and Vlad Naumescu (eds.), 2008: *Churches Inbetween. Greek Catholic Churches in Postsocialist Europe.*

17 Mihăilescu, Vintilă, Ilia Iliev, and Slobodan Naumović (eds.), 2008: *Studying Peoples in the People's Democracies II. Socialist Era Anthropology in South-East Europe.*

18 Kehl-Bodrogi, Krisztina, 2008: *"Religion is not so strong here". Muslim Religious Life in Khorezm after Socialism.*

19 Light, Nathan, 2008: *Intimate Heritage. Creating Uyghur Muqam Song in Xinjiang.*

20 Schröder, Ingo W., and Asta Vonderau (eds.), 2008: *Changing Economies and Changing Identities in Postsocialist Eastern Europe.*

21 Fosztó, László, 2009: *Ritual Revitalisation after Socialism. Community, Personhood, and Conversion among Roma in a Transylvanian Village.*

22 Hilgers, Irene, 2009: *Why Do Uzbeks have to be Muslims? Exploring religiosity in the Ferghana Valley.*

23 Trevisani, Tommaso, 2010: *Land and Power in Khorezm. Farmers, Communities, and the State in Uzbekistan's Decollectivisation.*

24 Yalçın-Heckmann, Lale, 2010: *The Return of Private Property. Rural Life after the Agrarian Reform in the Republic of Azerbaijan.*

25 Mühlfried, Florian, and Sergey Sokolovskiy (eds.), 2011. *Exploring the Edge of Empire. Soviet Era Anthropology in the Caucasus and Central Asia.*

26 Cash, Jennifer R., 2011: *Villages on Stage. Folklore and Nationalism in the Republic of Moldova.*

27 Köllner, Tobias, 2012: *Practising Without Belonging? Entrepreneurship, Morality, and Religion in Contemporary Russia.*

28 Bethmann, Carla, 2013: *"Clean, Friendly, Profitable?" Tourism and the Tourism Industry in Varna, Bulgaria.*

29 Bošković, Aleksandar, and Chris Hann (eds.), 2013: *The Anthropological Field on the Margins of Europe, 1945-1991.*

30 Holzlehner, Tobias, 2014: *Shadow Networks. Border Economies, Informal Markets and Organised Crime in the Russian Far East.*

31 Bellér-Hann, Ildikó, 2015: *Negotiating Identities. Work, Religion, Gender, and the Mobilisation of Tradition among the Uyghur in the 1990s.*

32 Oelschlaegel, Anett C., 2016: *Plural World Interpretations. The Case of the South-Siberian Tyvans.*

33 Obendiek, Helena, 2016: *"Changing Fate". Education, Poverty and Family Support in Contemporary Chinese Society.*

34 Sha, Heila, 2017: *Care and Ageing in North-West China.*

35 Tocheva, Detelina, 2017: *Intimate Divisions. Street-Level Orthodoxy in Post-Soviet Russia.*

36 Sárközi, Ildikó Gyöngyvér, 2018: *From the Mists of Martyrdom. Sibe Ancestors and Heroes on the Altar of Chinese Nation Building.*

37 Cheung Ah Li, Leah, 2019: *Where the Past meets the Future. The Politics of Heritage in Xi'an.*

38 Wang, Ruijing, 2019: *Kinship, Cosmology and Support. Toward a Holistic Approach of Childcare in the Akha Community of South-Western China.*